Directionality in English morphological conversion

Linguistic Insights

Studies in Language and Communication

Edited by Maurizio Gotti,
Emeritus Professor,
University of Bergamo (Italy).

Volume 317

Alba E. Ruz

Directionality in English morphological conversion

PETER LANG
Lausanne · Berlin · Bruxelles · Chennai · New York · Oxford

Bibliographic information published by the Deutsche Nationalbibliothek
The Deutsche Nationalbibliothek lists this publication in the Deutsche Nationalbibliografie; detailed bibliographic data is available online at http://dnb.d-nb.de.

Library of Congress Control Number: 2025016784

This publication has been funded by the Spanish Ministry for Science and Innovation and is supported by the research project PID2020-119851GB-I00, funded by MICIU/AEI/10.13039/501100011033.

MINISTERIO
DE CIENCIA, INNOVACIÓN
Y UNIVERSIDADES

AGENCIA
ESTATAL DE
INVESTIGACIÓN

ISSN 1424-8689
ISBN 978-3-0343-5788-3 (Print)
E-ISBN 978-3-0343-5840-8 (E-PDF)
E-ISBN 978-3-0343-5841-5 (E-PUB)
DOI 10.3726/b22914

Published by Peter Lang Group AG, Lausanne (Switzerland)

info@peterlang.com

www.peterlang.com

Contents

List of Figures

List of Tables

List of Abbreviations

AD	Attestation date
ADJ	Adjective
BNC	*British National Corpus*
D1	First-order derivation
D2	Second-order derivation
Der	Derivatives
DP	Derivational paradigm
EXT	Extended
FIG	Figurative
PHR	Phrasal expression
FO	Frequency of occurrence
N	Noun
nReg	Number of registers
OED	*Oxford English Dictionary*
RR	Range of registers
RU	Restrictions of usage
SD	Semantic dependence
SP	Semantic pattern
SR	Semantic range
V	Verb

CHAPTER 1

Introduction

1.1 Focus of study

The concept of *conversion*, also known as *zero-derivation*,[1] has raised questions since its first attestation in the eighteenth-century English grammars (cf. Sundby 1995: 36–37, 104, 107–108). Under the premise that conversion involves a derivational relationship between the pairs, this book examines one of its central unresolved questions, namely *directionality*, or the identification of which lexeme[2] is the base and which is derived in a pair of paronymous lexemes. Both the unresolved status of this question (cf. Bauer & Valera 2005: 11) and the renewed scholarly attention that it has received over the past years (see, among others, Umbreit 2010; Bram 2011; Kopecka 2013; Lohmann 2017; Kisselew et al. 2016; Valera 2017, 2023; Tribout 2020; Iordăchioaia et al. 2020; Ševčíková 2021; Don 2023; also Ruz & Cetnarowska 2023, on directionality in English affixation) bring to the fore the relevance of conversion as a subject of research.

The focus of this book is specifically on directionality in canonical conversion between nouns and verbs in English, exemplified by pairs such as *jump*^{N} and *jump*^{V}. Cases which have typically been described under the term *conversion* but which do not involve a morphological operation, that is, there is no change of word class, are outside the scope of this study. Some of these cases are, for example, the change in nominal features such as that of mass/count nouns, for example, 'some *coffee*' vs 'two *coffees*', or verb valency alternations of the type causative-inchoative,

1 This book uses the term *conversion* as a widespread descriptive term, without any theoretical implications, or opposition to the use of the term *zero-derivation* as a conceptual device.

2 The term lexeme is used in its traditional sense to refer to lexical items that belong to a single word class (cf. Lyons 1977: 423–424).

for example, '*John* broke *the window*' vs '*The window* broke'. These are sometimes referred to as *partial conversion* (cf. Zandvoort 1975: 266–276; or Valera 1999, for reviews on complete and partial conversion), *secondary conversion* or *secondary word-class change* (cf. Quirk et al. 1985: 1563–1567), or *type coercion* (cf. Bauer et al. 2013: 557–559). Cases involving other major and minor word classes, prepositions, compounds, phrases, participles, or where there are minor formal changes of the type *belief/believe* are not considered here either (cf. the description in Bauer et al. 2013: Section 25.3.1). The conditions for canonical conversion are listed in Section 2.3.2.

1.2 Justification and hypothesis

This study researches Marchand's (1964) criteria for the identification of directionality (cf. also Marchand 1963a for directionality in back-formation) in a sample of English noun/verb conversion. Specifically, Marchand's criteria of content (e.g. semantic dependence, restriction of usage, semantic range, and semantic pattern, cf. Section 2.5.6), and the qualitative-distributional criteria of frequency of occurrence and range of register are examined in this book (cf. Section 2.5.7 for their description). These criteria have often been transmitted uncritically, and their application, as in Bram's (2011) thesis, as the largest study on directionality in English conversion, reveals a degree of indeterminacy that remains unresolved to this day.

A key aspect in this study is its focus on the role of senses, rather than lexemes, as comparable units for identifying conversion, in line with Plank's observations (2010: 87). As a result, the directionality of the conversion process is analysed by examining the various senses associated with the lexeme pairs involved.

The underlying hypothesis is that the controversy surrounding directionality in conversion stems partly from:

i. the inherent complexity of the conversion process,
ii. the criteria used to identify directionality, and
iii. the level (lexeme vs. sense) at which these criteria have been applied.

Although in the literature it is often noted that previous studies have not given semantics the attention it deserves, no reference has yet systematically applied Plank's proposal to study directionality by word senses rather than by lexemes. It remains thus unknown how directionality may vary in conversion according to the selected criteria and their application to the specific senses attested for each lexeme in conversion pairs.

1.3 Aims and methods

This is an experimental study that relies on database evidence for the identification of the relevance of various criteria for directionality described in the specialized literature, and their applicability at the level of sense. Specifically, this study tests several semantic and quantitative-distributional criteria for directionality in a sample of present-day English noun/verb conversion, with the aims to:

i. Study the feasibility of applying the directionality criteria selected at the level of sense, rather than at the lexeme level (in line with Plank 2010).
ii. Determine the reliability of Marchand's (1964) criteria for directionality when applied by senses.

For this, a stratified sample of noun/verb lexeme pairs– which are formally identical, morphologically and semantically related, but categorially different– is extracted from the *British National Corpus* (hereafter BNC), a widely used corpus of contemporary British English.

While etymological criteria are not considered here (that is, the method based on earliest attestations is not followed, cf. Bauer & Valera forthcoming), semantic criteria are an essential part of the study, and, in this regard, the study relies on the *Oxford English Dictionary* (hereafter OED) for an objective classification of the senses that the lexemes can take. The data is subsequently analysed using statistical procedures, where applicable.

CHAPTER 2

Directionality in conversion

2.1 Conversion or zero-derivation

Conversion[3] is typically defined as the word-formation process whereby a word changes its word-class category without undertaking any change on its form (cf. Biese 1941; Zandvoort 1975: 265; Marchand 1969: 359; Leech 1981: 214; Lieber 1980: 187 et passim; 2005: 418; Bauer 1983: 32; Quirk et al. 1985: 1520, 1558; Kastovsky 1989; Lipka 1990: 75; Cetnarowska 1993; Don 1993; Štekauer 1996; Vogel 1996; Bauer & Huddleston 2002: 1640; Bauer & Valera 2005: 8; Manova 2011; Valera 2014, 2015, among others). Examples (1) and (2), synchronically described as canonical cases of noun/verb conversion in English, are the focus of this book:

(1) *love*^{N} / *love*^{V}
(2) *deal*^{V} / *deal*^{N}

Since the early works by Sweet (1891–1898), Kruisinga (1927, 1931/1932), Koziol (1937, in Grzega 2004: 117), Biese (1941), Nida (1949), Zandvoort (1975), Marchand (1969), Lipka (1971), and Kastovsky (1969), among others, various issues surrounding these cases have been a source of disagreement among authors. Even though more than a century has passed since the first works on these cases, many issues surrounding conversion remain unanswered in present-day English description.

One of the issues that aroused interest in the literature, and still does, has been that of which term is more adequate to refer to conversion, as proven by various publications (among others, Bauer & Valera 2005; Iordăchioaia & Melloni 2023) and conference workshops on the issue (Iordăchioaia & Melloni 2020;

[3] Several authors point out that the term *conversion* is probably to be attributed to Sweet (1891–1898; cf. Cetnarowska 1993: 14; Bauer & Valera 2005: 7).

Fernández-Alcaina & Valera 2022; Vasile, Moroianu & Valera 2022; Fernández-Alcaina & Valera 2024). Various terms are available in the literature,[4] but the debate often focuses on the contrast between *conversion* (Bauer 1983: 32; Bauer & Huddleston 2002: 1640) and *zero-derivation* (Marchand 1969: 359; Kastovsky 1989; Lipka 1990: 75).

Although both *conversion* and *zero-derivation* have often been used to refer to the same cases in the literature, it is important to note their different implications. While the term *zero-derivation* highlights the fact that these cases belong to word formation by implying that there is a process whereby a new lexeme is created by means of a *zero morph*, the term *conversion* does not necessarily imply a derivational process. Admittedly, both terms have been used interchangeably in the literature to refer to the word-formation process whereby new lexemes are formed without any formal mark signalling the process. Whenever this is not the case, *conversion* has typically been used to describe a purely syntactic phenomenon (cf. Trnka 1954: 54, cited in Cetnarowska 1993: 14), or in complementation with the term *zero-affixation* to refer to syntactic transposition, for example, the interpretation of the noun *government* as an adjective in *government job* (cf. Marchand 1969: 360).

The adequacy of these terms emerges from a difference in the conceptualization of the process and, consequently, none of the terms is without criticism. In turn, the conceptualization of the process is a major issue, as conversion has been described as "slightly mysterious", and remains unclear (if accepted as a process) whether it is a subtype of derivation or a separate process of word formation (Bauer & Valera 2005: 12). Also, because the base lexeme does not stop to exist as the term would seem to imply, but base and derivative coexist (Bauer & Huddleston 2002: 1641). Zero-derivation has been criticized with the argument that zeros in linguistics have meaning but no substance, which is just opposite to mathematical zeros (McGregor 2003: 111–114, in Segel 2008: 7), or, as Bauer (2019: 18) puts it, because "[...] since a morph is defined as a form, a form with no form is an embarrassment". Arguments against the term *zero-derivation* have also been raised for the difficulty of proving the existence of zero morphemes and for the proliferation of zeros or how to differentiate between possible contrasting zero affixes (cf. Bauer & Huddleston 2002: 1641; Bauer et al. 2013: 563; cf. also Valera 2014: 155, and references therein). However, as pointed out in Valera (2014: 155):

[4] For a more detailed account of the various terms used for conversion, see Lieber (1980, 2004), Don (1993, 2005), Štekauer (1996), Plag (1999), Fábregas (2005), Bram (2011: 36–60), Bauer et al. (2013: 562–567) or Valera (2014, 2015).

> [l]ater discussions of the concept of zero-derivation lay stress on the fact that the contrast between conversion and zero-derivation is less important than the fact that the process in question is a derivational process, and so whichever term is used becomes "[…] basically a metatheoretical-formal question" (Kastovsky 1997: 85–86).

Which term is more adequate to describe these cases lies outside the scope of this study, even if the analysis of directionality might cast light on the differences or similarities of the two terms. The approach to conversion adopted in this book is described in Section 2.3.

2.2 Approaches to conversion

More generally, controversy has arisen on the description of conversion or where to include it in language description. This is a complex issue that has been approached from several perspectives. Since the approach followed for the description has implications in the discussion of directionality, this section reviews the most relevant approaches in the literature and points out whether an analysis in terms of directionality makes sense within each approach or not. Thus, this section is organized as follows:

i. Section 2.2.1 focuses on the approaches to conversion as a word-formation process.
ii. Section 2.2.2 is on approaches to conversion as outside word formation.
iii. Section 2.2.3 describes the approach to conversion in this study.

2.2.1 Conversion as a word-formation process

One of the most widespread approaches in the literature treats the phenomenon as *conversion*,[5] a word-formation process parallel to others such as derivation or compounding (cf. Kruisinga 1927, 1931/1932; Koziol 1937; Bauer 1983; Quirk et al. 1985; Plag 1999, among others). This view, represented in Figure 1, assumes that it entails transposition in the category of the word (Marchand 1969: 360), the new inflectional, syntactic and semantic properties justifying the interpretation that the same form is a different lexeme (Valera 2014: 154–155, 2015: 322).

[5] As mentioned in Section 2.2, the term does not necessarily imply word-class change, and thus, it has been used variously in the literature, to refer to syntactic transposition of a word.

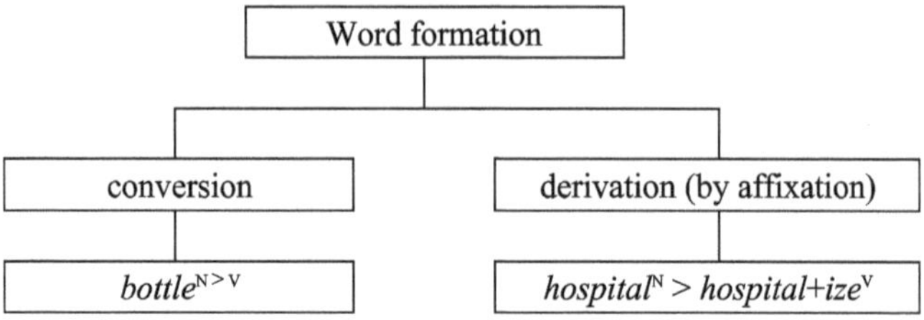

Figure 1: Conversion as parallel to derivation and other word-formation processes.

Another view considers it a process inside derivation and thus calls it *zero-derivation* or *zero-affixation*, by analogy to affixation (cf. Strang 1968: 230, 231; Marchand 1969: 359; Adams 1973: 37; Kiparsky 1982; Kastovsky 1989; Lipka 1990: 85, 86, among others). This approach, represented in Figure 2, postulates a zero suffix or zero morpheme (Ø), on the grounds that zero-derivation has the same function as affixation, namely producing new lexemes in a language (cf. Sanders 1988: 155; Ungerer 2003: 563; Payne 1997: 8, cited in Valera 2014: 155). The difference between word-class changing affixation and zero-affixation is that the latter uses no overt realization.

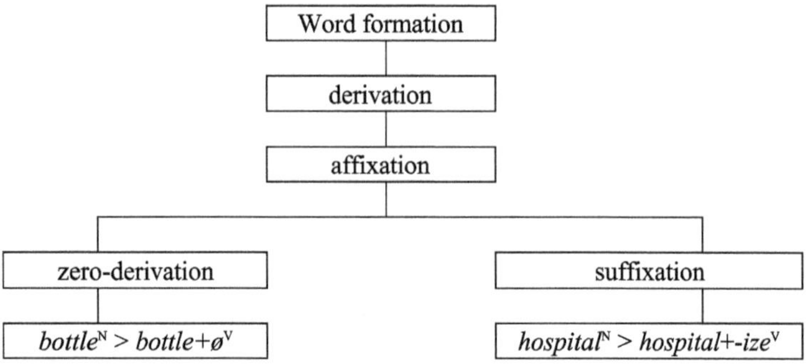

Figure 2: Zero-derivation as affixation.

A third group claims that derivation (including conversion) and affixation are separate processes (cf. Beard 1995, 1998). According to this view, represented in Figure 3, rules of lexical derivation apply before rules of affixation.[6] Thus, in

6 Note that Beard and Volpe (2005: 198) say that LMBM (Lexeme-Morpheme Base Morphology) "denies the existence of a separate morphological process such as *conversion*", arguing that conversion is a case when a given L-rule applies but it is not linked to any affixation rule, that is, it is "marked for no phonological realization at the morphological level" (Beard and Volpe 2005: 199).

both conversion and affixation semantic derivation occurs first, except that only affixation is given overt realization: an affix.

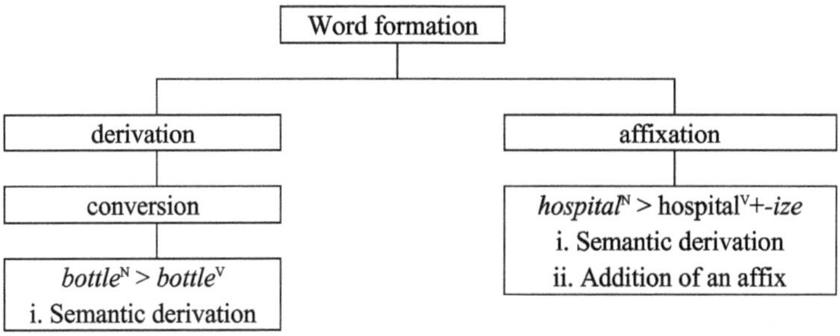

Figure 3: Conversion within derivation and different from affixation.

Even if these views conceptualize the process differently within word formation and the terms carry different implications (see Section 2.2.3), an analysis in terms of directionality is supported under any of the approaches considering conversion or zero-derivation a word-formation process.

2.2.2 Conversion outside word formation

Unlike the views in Section 2.2.1, one can also find several approaches to conversion as a phenomenon outside word formation.

Some authors refer to it as *lexical relisting*, *reduplication*, or *coinage*, among others. They view it as a phenomenon outside morphology, arguing that a word of a certain category may be listed again in the lexicon of a language, as a new word class, just as new words enter a language every day (cf. Lieber 1980: 198–203, 1992, 2004: 95). Thus, Clark & Clark (1979) consider these innovations based on pragmatic principles of interpretation, and Strauss (1982, in Bauer et al. 2013: 564), conceives it as "rebracketing" of a lexical item, for example, [[*empty*]$_{ADJ}$]^{V}. Similarly, Štekauer (1996: 45–46) proposes to analyse conversion as a "conceptual recategorization" of words, as the result of the conceptual reanalysis of words as belonging to different categories following the addition or deletion of nuances of meaning, as in Figure 4.

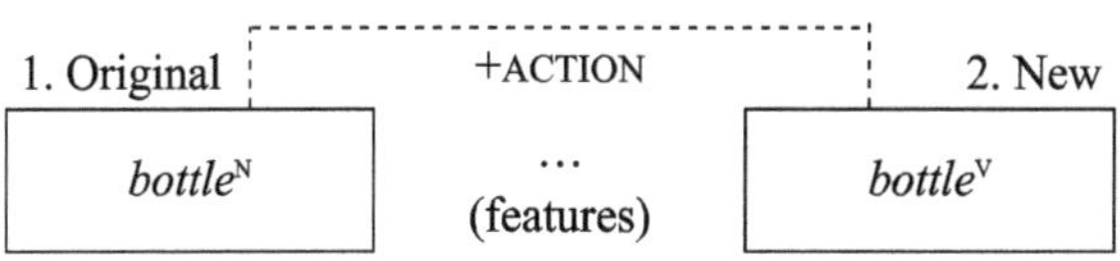

Figure 4: Conversion as conceptual recategorization.

Note that Štekauer mentions directionality as secondary in his approach to conversion. However, even if the phenomenon is seen as outside word formation, it can be argued that there is always a pair of two lexemes belonging to different classes and, consequently, semantic relation(s) between lexical items. Thus, even if not in terms of word formation, a directional analysis is plausible, or as Lieber (1980: 187–188) puts it, "[...] whereas the "syntax" of conversion is non-directional, the semantics of conversion may be governed by directional rules".

Similarly, a directional analysis is also possible under approaches which treat metaphor or metonymy as lexical processes resulting in semantic derivation (Crocco Galèas 1990; Lipka 1990: 140; Dirven 1999; Schönefeld 2005; Kopecka 2013, among others) and, thus, in the production of new lexical items (which involves figurative extension of meaning as well as word-class change, cf. Valera 2017). Valera (2017) also points to various possibilities in the semantic change of conversion pairs in English, from mere change of categorial meaning to change of lexical meaning by figurative extension of meaning, by metaphor and metonymy, without intermediate process, for example, *coffee-house*^{N} 'A house of entertainment where coffee and other refreshments are supplied' > *coffee-house*^{V} 'to gossip'. The interpretation in this case is that the figurative meaning of the verb has been derived directly from the literal meaning of the noun by figurative extension.

Some authors view conversion as *multifunctionality* or *underspecification* (originally in Whorf 1945, cited also as 1937/1956 in Valera 2014; later recalled in Lipka 1971: 213–215; Nida 1975: 99; Robins 1987: 58 as *grammatical neutrals*; or Farrell 2001: 109, 116, 128, among others). They argue that roots in English are unspecified for word class and, thus, that the same neutral lexical element can surface as various linguistic functions depending on the context in which it is found, as in Figure 5. Accordingly, there is only one lexeme, as it does not involve word-class change. Thus, an analysis in terms of directionality between word classes would initially have no relevance.

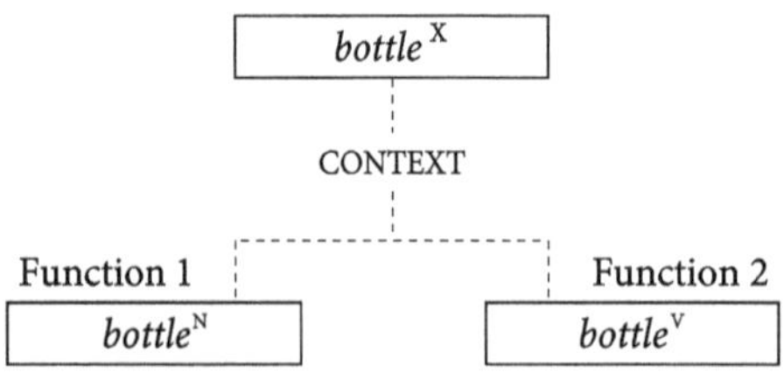

Figure 5: Conversion as multifunctionality or underspecification.

A similar case can be made of the interpretation of these examples as mere inflection (Myers 1984; Josefsson 1997; Giegerich 1999, all cited in Bauer & Valera 2005: 9; Riese 2015), or as *transflexion*, described as "[...] a word-formation procedure common in Slavic languages in which a new word is coined by a change of grammatical morpheme" (Ivanová 2016: 22; also Ivanová & Ološtiak 2015, cited in Valera 2015: 330; cf. similarly *dérivation immédiate*, *transfert grammatical* and *unmittelbare Ableitung* in Pennanen 1984 and Kastovsky 1994, or *paradigmatic derivation* in Nagórko 2016).

Thus, a synchronic analysis of directionality, at least when the study of the semantics is the focus, seems compatible with most approaches to conversion (unless it is said that there is only one lexeme) and may prove relevant independently of whether conversion is a word-formation process or a semantic one. Section 2.5 provides a more detailed discussion of directionality and of the approaches to the issue in the literature.

2.3 The approach in this study

This study considers conversion a directional process, resulting in the creation of new lexemes from already-existing ones in a language. This is in line with Bauer & Valera's (2005: 12) claim that "[...] directionality implies a process and thus in any system which sees conversion as directional it is automatically assumed that conversion is more than just a relationship between static lexemes". This section is organized as follows:

i. Our view of conversion is further described in Section 2.3.1.
ii. The conditions for canonical conversion, which is the focus of this study, are outlined in Section 2.3.2.

2.3.1 Conversion as a lexeme-creation process

Conversion in English is approached in this book as a dynamic or asymmetrical word-formation process whereby a base lexeme is used for the formation of a derivative under the conditions of formal identity and word-class contrast (Leech 1981: 214; Lieber 1980: 187 et passim; Bauer 1983: 32; Quirk et al. 1985: 1520, 1558; Don 1993; Štekauer 1996: 15 et passim; Vogel 1996: 258 et passim; Bauer & Huddleston 2002: 1640; Manova 2011: 55 et passim; Bauer et al. 2013: 562–3; Valera 2014, 2015, among others). It is thus considered that in conversion there are two lexemes, not one, as, for example, in the view of conversion as underspecification (cf. Section 2.2.2). A relation is assumed between the lexemes too and thus also directionality.

As for the lexical relation between pairs of lexemes in canonical conversion, it is here considered to be best covered by the term *paronymy*, just as the relation in pairs formed by affixation (in line with Cruse 1986 and Valera & Ruz 2021).[7] A different position is presented in Bauer et al. (2013: 546), such that conversion lies "[s]omewhere in the range between homonymy and polysemy".

This study takes a synchronic approach, so no distinction is made between conversion and other processes that have resulted in a similar output synchronically "[...] but that may not qualify as conversion diachronically" (Valera 2015: 324). This is because "[...] the synchronic analysis of word-derivation does not always parallel the diachronic formation of a word" (Dearmond 1969: 355, cited in Pennanen 1984: 80), for example, *lúfu* 'love' > *lúfian* 'to love' (OE) corresponding to the pair *love*^{N}/*love*^{V} in present-day English.

2.3.2 The conditions for canonical conversion

The various attempts to identify conversion in the literature have highlighted several aspects of the process such as the fact that it is *non-iconic*, as expressed in terms of Natural Morphology (cf. Manova 2011; Cetnarowska 2011: Section 5.3, 2017; or Valera 2015: 332), *non-concatenative* (cf. Plag 2003: 107; Plag et al. 2009: 104), or *non-compositional* (Crocco Galèas 1990), or the productivity of the process for deriving new lexical items (cf. Kastovsky 1969; Adams 1973: 37; Tournier 1985: 198; Quirk et al. 1985: 1558; Bauer & Huddleston 2002: 1642; Plag et al. 2009, among others).

In this book, the conditions for canonical conversion are defined as follows (cf. Marchand 1963a: 176, Cetnarowska 1993; Kerleroux 1999; Valera 2014, 2015, among others):

i. It involves at least two lexemes, which belong to two different word-class categories that can be identified in context or use. The change in word class is reflected in the change in the inflectional paradigm and syntactic function of the lexemes (Valera 2015: 322).
ii. There are no formal or phonological distinctions between the lexemes, that is, they are formally identical (described in terms of an identity operation in Bauer 1983: 32).
iii. The lexemes are morphologically related: one is the base of the process and the other is derived from the former.

---

[7] For a discussion on the relations proposed in the literature for the relationship between conversion pairs and related cases, see Valera & Ruz (2021).

iv. The lexemes, or the senses they express, are semantically related. This connection has been most typically explained in terms of the lexemes sharing their core meaning or their most prototypical or salient aspect (cf. Sanders 1988: 157; Crocco Galèas 1990; Twardzisz 1997; Kövecses & Radden 1998; Dirven 1999; Radden & Kövecses 1999; Schönefeld 2005; Kopecka 2013: 357; Martsa 2014: 452–453; Rainer 2014: 348–349, among others), but extended senses may allow for conversions too.
v. There is directionality between the lexemes in that one or various of their senses may serve as a base for new converted senses in the other pair (cf. Plank 2010).

In relation to the latter two criteria, this study aims to support the idea that the lexemes in conversion pairs may be interrelated such that, for example, some of the senses of the noun may act as bases for the creation of new related senses in the verb, and vice versa. This may lead to chains of semantic derivations between lexemes, and to the identification of new senses in both directions between a pair. This study is thus in line with Plank's (2010) claim that directionality should be studied at the level of sense and not of lexeme.

2.4 The issue of directionality

The term *directionality*, as understood in this book, refers to the possibility of new lexemes to be formed from already existing lexemes in a language. As Iacobini (2000: 866) describes it, "[t]he principle of directionality recognises a relationship between two morphological items (a base and a derived word) in which one is characterized with respect to the other because of the adding of extra meaning together with the adding of phonic material". This principle applies in this study except for the latter condition, which does not apply in all cases, for example, in canonical conversion or back-formation.

Thus, directionality is here considered to be present in the various semantic-extension mechanisms or lexeme-creation processes in a language, that is, it is not exclusive to the process of conversion. This is in line with Kastovsky's (2005: 41) claim that derivational processes in present-day English are "necessarily directional". However, different degrees of importance are given to directionality in the various approaches to conversion. Section 2.4 is organized as follows:

i. Section 2.4.1. focuses on views on the need to establish a direction between conversion pairs.
ii. Section 2.4.2. is on difficulties in the study of conversion directionality.

2.4.1 Is there a need to establish directionality?

There is a debate as to whether there is a need to establish directionality in the first place. This is partly because directionality is given different degrees of importance in the various approaches to conversion. Under some approaches, directionality has no relevance (2.4.1.1.), other linguists recognize it but claim that it is difficult to determine (2.4.1.2), while another group of linguists argues that directionality in conversion may have varying importance (2.4.1.3).

2.4.1.1 Directionality as irrelevant

An analysis of directionality is rejected in approaches to conversion in terms of multifunctionality or underspecification (and therefore, as root-based). Within these approaches, it is argued that roots in English are unspecified for word class and, thus, that the same neutral lexical element can surface as various linguistic functions depending on the context of use, so an analysis of directionality has no place. Similarly, under approaches which treat the phenomenon as inflection, an analysis in terms of directionality does not make sense (cf. Myers 1984; Josefsson 1997; Giegerich 1999, all cited in Bauer & Valera 2005: 9).

The direction of conversion has also been claimed to be irrelevant synchronically. For instance, Bergenholtz & Mugdan (1979) argue that synchronically there is no priority in the meanings or uses of the lexemes in different syntactic contexts. It has been pointed out, however, that in derivation in general "[...] one is almost always able to make an intuitive statement about the direction of derivation, and about the word-class affiliation of the base underlying a derivative without great difficulty" (Kastovsky 1976: 26). In fact, Kastovsky highlights the importance of introducing the base of a process as containing the appropriate word-class affiliation and not as categorially indefinite for linguistic description, also in conversion, for example, *clear*^{V} meaning 'to cause to become *clear*^{ADJ}', with emphasis on the semantic aspect of the process. This typically accepted claim may be the reason why, in approaches that describe conversion as non-directional, the semantic connection between the lexemes in conversion is highlighted, or even an analysis in terms of semantic rules has been posited. For instance, Ljung (1977) claims that no derivational or directional relation holds between members of converted pairs, for example, *comb*^{V} : *comb*^{N} or *saw*^{V} : *saw*^{N} in an equation of such conversions to cases of exonym-endonym pairs such as *dig*^{V} : *spade*^{N} (Ljung 1977: 169–71, and references therein). The author argues that in such conversions the verbs are not semantically dependent on the nouns because one can carry the actions denoted by the verbs with other objects (for instance one can comb one's hair with the fingers), and that the instruments in these cases are simply strongly associated with the actions. However, Ljung later admits a strong semantic connection between conversion terms to the extent that, if the semantics of the instrument are extended, the meaning of the verb may be extended too (1977: 174), which leads to an analysis of these cases in terms of "fully productive instrument-verb-creating rules which permit the extension of instrument-denoting nouns into verbs expressing the use of these nouns" (cf. Ljung 1977: 178). Similarly, Lieber (1980), who proposes that both members of a conversion pair are equally listed in the lexicon as basic or derived and can belong to different word-class categories depending on the context of use, argues against a directional syntactic rule of conversion, on the arguments that it leads to the proliferation of zeroes or of directional rules in conversion. Yet, the author recognizes "directional semantic rules" between the terms, which she describes in terms of redundancy rules (Lieber 1980: 187–188, 203–206). In fact, Lieber (1980: 203) states that an analysis of the semantics of conversion is, in principle, independent from their syntactic analysis of conversion, and that "[...] the semantic analysis can involve directionality without arguing in any way against the non-directionality of the syntactic analysis".

2.4.1.2 Directionality as unpredictable

An analysis of conversion as a directional process in terms of *bidirectionality*, or *multidirectionality* has been proposed too. Leech (1981: 224–225), for instance, bases his argument on conversions for which an analysis of both directions could be possible. Similarly, Umbreit (2010) follows a cognitive approach based on word families, L2 acquisition and speakers' judgements, and proposes that, because some cases remain unclear, a bidirectional understanding of lexical motivation is better suited to account for all kinds of motivational pairs. Motivational relations can nevertheless display a certain tendency towards one direction, so Umbreit (2010: 323–324) presents directionality as a continuum.

Similarly, some authors recognize directionality but have claimed that it is virtually impossible to tell a direction between formally identical pairs because of the number of irregularities found in the lexicon (Langenfelt 1933, cited in Marchand 1963a: 178; Jackendoff 1974), or it is difficult for the polysemy involved (cf. Twardzisz 1997, who regards motivation in conversion as "[...] a complex multi-directional sanctioning phenomenon"). The semantic complexity in conversion may be one of the reasons why some authors may have chosen to ignore the issue of directionality, focusing on other aspects of the process, or have directly excluded conversion from their analyses.

2.4.1.3 Directionality as relevant

The research by several other authors explicitly or implicitly assumes the existence of directionality in conversion. This is especially so in studies which regard conversion as a process with a morphological and semantic relation between lexemes. However, dissimilar importance has been paid to the issue of directionality also among authors who recognize it.

For instance, Štekauer (1996), who takes an onomasiological approach, recognizes the issue in conversion but regards directionality as secondary and focuses on other aspects of the process, for example, the phonological differences between the conversion pairs.

Other linguists have paid special attention to the issue of directionality, either by proposing some criteria or by discussing the relevance of the criteria typically proposed in the literature to assess directionality between conversion pairs (cf. Marchand 1963a, 1963b, 1964, 1969; Adams 1973; Kastovsky 1976; Clark & Clark 1979; Kiparsky 1982; Sanders 1988; Cetnarowska 1993; Plag 1999, 2003; Iacobini 2000; Bauer & Valera 2005; or Valera 2014, among others; cf. Section 2.5).

Furthermore, several authors have carried out empirical studies in English and other languages to test some of the criteria to assess directionality. This has been done:

i. with the aim to test and discuss the applicability of the criteria in the literature (among others, Bladin 1911; Hertrampf 1932, cited in Marchand 1963a: 178; Biese 1941; Jespersen 1949; Don 2004; Balteiro 2007; Plank 2010; Umbreit 2010; Bram 2011; Kisselew et al. 2016; Lohmann 2017; Tribout 2020; Iordăchioaia et al. 2020; Ševčíková 2021), or
ii. with the intention to classify conversions in related studies, for example, with a focus on the semantic patterns typically expressed by conversion. In this regard, see, among others, Valera (2017), with a focus on the diversity of semantic changes between conversion pairs, Valera (2020), on the semantic patterns in noun/verb conversion in English, Valera (2023), on a comparative study of the semantic patterns in English and Spanish conversion, Mititelu et al. (2023), on the meaning of zero verbs and zero nouns, and Hledíková & Ševčíková (2024), on a comparative study of the semantics between nouns and verbs in Czech and English from a paradigmatic and a cognitive approach.

It is here considered that analyses that deny directionality, or claim that it is irrelevant and thus simplify the analysis and representation of the pairs, for example, not requiring the assignation of a base or derivative, dismiss the relevance of a directional approach to conversion for linguistic description in areas such as morphology, syntax, lexical semantics, and pragmatics. This is because these analyses do not account, among others, for the possible motivations or constraints on conversion, the semantic relations found, frequency effects, etc. Conceptualizations of conversion as bidirectional or multidirectional dispose of the so-called chicken and egg question, finding support in the lack of clear evidence for a preferred direction of conversion, either from historical, semantic, or statistical analyses. However, such approaches also disregard the semantics of the process, the formal complexity (when relevant), or its quantitative aspects, for example, frequency of use.

This study supports an analysis of conversion as directional. Specifically, the issue of directionality in conversion is approached from a synchronic perspective, and it is argued that directionality should be studied with special attention to the semantics of the process.

The main reasons why directionality is an issue in conversion are mentioned in Section 2.4.2, and some difficulties for the study of directionality in conversion are presented in Section 2.4.3.

2.4.2 Why is directionality an issue in conversion?

Even though directionality is central to most approaches to lexical semantics and word formation, it is most typically in conversion where it has been pointed out as a controversial issue. This is partly due to the formal aspects of the process, and particularly also because of the contradictions between the various methods to decide on directionality in conversion (cf. Section 2.5).

In word-formation analyses, conversion has often been described by analogy with overt word-formation processes, especially with affixation. This is because both processes share the same function, that is, that of creating new lexemes and concepts to address the needs of a community of speakers (cf. Trnka 1969: 184; Sanders 1988: 155; Payne 1997: 8, cited in Valera 2014: 155; Ungerer 2003: 563). In fact, as brought up by Ungerer (2003: 534–535) "[…] the grammatical function of suffixation has been so pervasive that it has led to the inclusion of conversion in the morphological paradigm by postulating a process of zero derivation".[8] However, the fundamental difference between the two processes lies primarily in formal grounds. This is because word-class changing affixation seems to reflect the structural patterns of a language in that an affix is typically added to a simpler lexeme (which is the base of the lexeme-formation process) for the creation of a more complex derivative lexeme, for example, *direction*^{N} (base) + *-al* (suffix) > *directional*^{ADJ} (derivative). In contrast, in English conversion, both the base and the derivative are formally identical, the process being formally unmarked. Conversion has been described as "le procede le plus simple" ('the simplest process'

8 Even if the processes are typically paralleled in their functionality or output, it has been discussed that the range of formations by affixation does not cover all the cases by conversion (cf. Sanders 1988: 168).

[my translation]) (Kerleroux 1999: 100), but it is precisely this formal simplicity of conversion which makes an analysis in terms of directionality challenging.

It must be noted, however, that directionality is not always straightforward in processes other than conversion, for example, in *reconsideration*^{N} (*re-* + *consideration*^{N} or *reconsider*^{V} + *-ation*) (cf. Plag 2003: 2.4, on multiple affixation), or, for example, in *asymmetric*^{ADJ} (*symmetry*^{N} > *symmetric*^{ADJ} > *asymmetric*^{ADJ}, or *symmetry*^{N} > *asymmetry*^{N} > *asymmetric*^{ADJ}) (cf. Iacobini 2000: 869, on cases of double motivation). In back-formation, for example, *editor*^{N} > *edit*^{N}, directionality is also an issue partly because the complexity of the lexemes does not reflect the direction of the derivation, the process being anti-iconic (cf. Marchand 1963b, on directionality in back-formation; see also Iacobini 2000: 872–874 for difficulties in the analysis of other "problematic" phenomena, specifically, back-formation, clipping, subtraction, and truncation).[9]

This book is in line with the literature that stresses the relevance of directionality in the description of present-day English word formation, lexical semantics and, particularly, in the description of conversion.

2.4.3 Difficulties in the study of directionality

When approaching the issue of directionality, several difficulties may arise. Some of them are discussed in the following subsections, specifically:

i. Section 2.4.3.1 briefly comments on the implications of considering conversion as word-based or not,
ii. Section 2.4.3.2 is on the difference between a diachronic and a synchronic approach to directionality, and
iii. Section 2.4.3.3 discusses the importance of an analysis of directionality at the level of sense instead of lexeme.

2.4.3.1 Conversion as root-, stem-, or word-based

One of the difficulties of conversion is whether it is root-based, stem-based, or word-based. This usually varies depending on the language under study.

In English, at least under synchronic approaches that consider conversion a lexeme- or word-formation process, conversion is typically accepted as word-based, and thus a directional analysis makes sense. This is the view here too, although

9 Interestingly, references often point to semantics as the solution. For instance, Iacobini (2000: 870) mentions that "[...] processes which do not formally express the direction of derivation nevertheless respect it semantically, and [...] cases which seem to contradict the principle of directionality, as does back-formation, can be reinterpreted just in the light of this principle".

this book uses the term *lexeme* instead of *word* and considers that the term *lexeme-based* is more precise (following Iacobini 2000: 868). A view of conversion as root-based may thus be discarded in this study (cf. Section 2.4.3.1).

It should be noted, however, that even if conversion is accepted as occurring between lexemes, the possibility of a smaller number of cases having a root-based origin is not discarded. In this regard, it has been argued that both a root-based formation and a word-based formation do not necessarily exclude one another, at least in English (cf. Don 2023: 7).

2.4.3.2 Diachronic vs synchronic analysis

Another difficulty in the study of directionality in conversion comes from considering directionality from a synchronic or from a diachronic perspective (cf. Section 2.5 for various criteria used to determine directionality in the literature, both from a synchronic and from a diachronic approach).

While directionality has been claimed to be relevant for diachronic analyses, it has been indicated as relevant and "convenient" in synchronic descriptions of conversion too (Quirk et al. 1985: 1558). It has been pointed out, however, that approaching conversion from these two perspectives often gives contradictory results (Marchand 1963a: 180; Adams 1973: 40; Cetnarowska 1993: 37–39; Bauer & Valera 2005: 11; Bram 2011: 90, among others). This is fundamentally because the two approaches focus on different aspects of the phenomenon. Specifically, diachronic analyses are concerned with the historical development of the lexemes in a language, that is, how words were introduced or created in a language, whereas the focus in synchronic analyses is rather on the semantic relation and sense development between the pairs as in present-day English.

This study takes a synchronic approach to directionality in conversion. Pairs of lexemes that may not be considered conversion from a diachronic approach but that have the same result (cf. Valera 2015: 324), for example, because of diachronic levelling, may be considered conversion in a synchronic approach.

2.4.3.3 Directionality at the level of lexeme vs sense

Conversion has typically been studied according to semantics at the level of lexeme, even if the role of senses has often been highlighted in the literature on derivation. For instance, Marchand (1964: 12) makes the claim that "[a] word may be a derivative in one sense and not in another. Both verb and substantive may follow separate trends of semantic development that are not necessarily paralleled by the other pair member". This is similar to the implications of Quirk et al.'s (1985: 1529) claim that "[c]onversion shows lexicalization having specific sense orientation, in that only a particular sense of a word may be converted to another word class". Thus, it is here considered pertinent to study specifically which of the senses of a base is converted.

Even more relevant for this study is Plank's (2010) study on conversion in the German example *fett*^{ADJ}/*Fett*^{N}/*fett-*^{V} 'fat', which shows that conversion operates over senses and that directionality may differ depending on which of the senses of the lexemes are at play.[10] Plank (2010: 87) emphasizes that directionality should be studied at the level of sense and not of lexeme, because several bases and several derivatives may exist within the same polysemous lexeme according to the senses of the input and the output. Plank also notes that the issue of directionality may pose a problem where lexical asymmetries can be established with some degree of conviction too, and questions standard assumptions about the integrity of lexemes:

> Instead of taking for granted that semantic complexity invariably motivates the same directions of morphological derivation for all relevant lexical items and across all languages, it is an empirical issue to determine, for particular derivational oppositions and for particular semantic subsets of senses, whether asymmetries are diachronically stable or unstable and crosslinguistically uniform or diverse. (Plank 2010: 87)

Research has recently emphasized the relevance of an analysis of conversion by senses (among others, Valera 2017, 2020, 2023; Iordăchioaia et al. 2020; Ševčíková 2021; Iordăchioaia 2022; Ševčíková & Hledíková 2022; Hledíková & Ševčíková 2024; cf. also Ruz & Cetnarowska 2023, for an analysis of directionality by senses in English affixation). It must be noted, however, that the difficulty of an analysis of directionality at the level of sense has often been pointed out too. For instance, Valera (2015: 328) claims that identifying the base and the derivative by senses rather than by lexemes

> [...] multiplies the difficulty inherent in the identification of directionality in conversion, but is consistent with the relative independence of senses within lexemes as regards their use in word-formation, or at least with the fact that derivation can pick up on a specific sense for creation of a new word and not others within the same lexeme.

Most likely the difficulty of such an analysis is the reason why some authors who have approached directionality, and who have looked at the semantics of the pairs, have done so only to a limited extent, typically disregarding the polysemy of the lexemes and focusing only on the core or central sense expressed by the

10 Note that, although it may be argued that Plank's (2010) paper relies on the analysis of a single example, the analysis of this case clearly supports the points raised in the paper, which may apply to other cases and to other languages.

pairs. This book underlines the crucial role of senses in derivation and follows Plank's (2010) claim that directionality should be studied by senses.

2.5 Criteria to determine directionality

When authors have approached the issue of directionality in conversion, they have done it from various perspectives, and this has led to contradictory results in some cases. Marchand (1963a: 180) shows "[h]ow completely different the etymological and historical aspect is from the derivational one" with the example *moan*, the noun (c. 1225) being recorded earlier than the verb (16th c.). Thus, the noun is the base from a diachronic perspective, but it is analysed as the 'act of moaning' by derivational criteria with a focus on the semantics of the terms, the noun thus being regarded as a derivative from the verb (cf. also Adams 1973: 40 for examples of how senses do not seem to indicate the same direction as OED attestation dates). Contradictory analyses regarding the directionality of specific pairs are available in the literature too. For instance, as noted by Sanders (1988: 158), while Quirk & Greenbaum (1973: 441) analyse the pair *cover* as Verb-to-Noun, Clark & Clark (1979: 770) analyse this case as the opposite direction, Noun-to-Verb (cf. also Cetnarowska 1993: 37–39 on equivocal results between the criteria).

Even if there are pairs for which no agreement (regarding their direction) is found between various authors, a series of criteria proposed in the literature make it possible to identify the direction of derivation in most cases (Iacobini 2000: 871). The criteria posed in the literature for the identification of directionality in conversion are introduced in Sections 2.5.1–2.5.7, with a recapitulation in Section 2.5.8.

2.5.1 Historical criteria

An approach to the issue from a diachronic perspective proposes to determine directionality on the basis of historical evidence (cf. the studies by Bladin 1911; Hertrampf 1932, cited in Marchand 1963a: 178; Biese 1941; Jespersen 1949: Ch. VII, VII; Tournier 1985; Štekauer 1996; Balteiro 2007, among others). Specifically, authors who take this approach choose to rely on first-attestation dates for the pairs, that is, whether a lexeme was first recorded as noun or as verb. Other information about their origin from etymological dictionaries has also been considered, for example, information about the cultural factors that may have influenced the creation of the pairs, the influence of analogy or of similar words, their status as borrowings, innovations, etc.

A diachronic approach is relevant for the description of the history of a language, that is, how words are introduced in a language at a specific time and in a specific context, but such analysis proves problematic in various respects:

i. The sources for language analysis are limited, and the dates of first attestation may not necessarily reflect the lexemes' creation and usage in a language because, as Biese (1941: 11) emphasizes research has revealed that "[...] a number of words can be ante-dated". This is for words for which attestation dates are not clearly indicated, for example, rare words and when both lexemes go back to Old English and it is not possible to establish which lexeme was used first at the time.
ii. It is particularly difficult to decide on directionality for pairs attested around the same short-span of time, historical dictionaries not telling in many cases which lexeme precedes the other in usage, because the first attestation dates are sometimes too close (Marchand 1963a: 177, 1969: 297; Adams 1973: 40). It has been emphasized that "[c]onversion mates may have occurred in written texts at the same time, especially if they were borrowed from French or Latin" (Cetnarowska 1993: 24), and that, in these cases, the arbitrary assumption in that the base is the one which has cognates in Germanic languages (Marchand 1963a: 177–178). For the same reasons, it is sometimes difficult to establish a precedence for very recent coinages just based on attestation dates.
iii. Language is not static: new usages emerge for already existing lexemes, and new words are created every day, based on the need of a community of speakers and on the influence of other languages or cultures, among other things. In this regard, as pointed out by Plag (2003: 108; cf. also Cruse 1986: 133), "[...] complex semantic changes may overwrite the original direction of conversion", that is, new senses may emerge or disappear for specific pairs, and the directionality may be reversed over time, or may differ for the various senses of the lexemes. A diachronic approach may not reflect the speakers' intuitions, and a synchronic analysis has been suggested as a more decisive indicator.

A diachronic account has thus been discarded here, in agreement with claims that it is based on extralinguistic information or has little heuristic value to begin with (Iacobini 2000: 870; Valera 2020: 326), and that such an account should be discarded in a synchronic approach. This is because it may not capture the current directionalities or sense relations between conversion pairs, in other words, "[...] etymological and historical estimates may not correspond to present-day judgments" (Cetnarowska 1993: 24).

2.5.2 Intuition criterion

Other authors appeal to native intuition to decide on a directionality in conversion (cf. Adams 1973, who uses intuition as the primary criterion, and considers other criteria too when intuition fails; Bergenholtz & Mugdan 1979; Clark & Clark 1979, on innovations by conversion; or Umbreit 2010, among others). This approach relies on the native speakers' or proficient users' judgments to decide which member of a pair is the base and which one is the derivative, assuming that the directionality may be determined by the semantic or syntactic properties of the words involved, or by the frequency or familiarity. Intuition has also been used as a secondary criterion too, for example, by Biese (1941), who resorts to intuition when historical information fails to indicate a direction, on the grounds that "[...] an ordinary speaker would be able to state which use, the nominal or the verbal one, is to be regarded as the original function of the word" (1941: 5).

Intuition, as well as other approaches that focus mainly on the semantics of the pairs, seems to be in line with the idea that directionality in conversion should be "[...] examined without any preconceptions adopted from the analysis of the older stages of the language" (cf. Trnka 1969: 185; cf. Section 2.5.6 for synchronic semantic criteria). The main advantage of an approach that relies on intuition is its easy applicability, as no external evidence or data are required. Indeed, such an approach can identify general tendencies or patterns, as perceived synchronically. The main drawback is that intuition is subjective, and inconsistencies may be found in its applicability as different speakers of a language, perhaps influenced by factors such as the context of use or register, their culture, dialect, etc., may disagree on the same conversion pair.

2.5.3 Morphological and phonological criteria

Another proposal has been to approach the issue of directionality by considering formal aspects in the pairs: morphological and phonological ones. The assumption is that structural or formal differences can be found between lexemes, and these differences point to their basic or derived character.

In this regard, Marchand describes a series of criteria to establish a "derivational relationship" between back-derived words (1963b) and words unmarked by derivational morphemes (1963a, 1964). Among the criteria of external form or "formal criteria", Marchand (1964: 15–19) lists the following:[11]

i. The phonetic shape of the lexemes: "[a] certain phonetic shape may put a word in a definite word class" (Marchand 1964: 16), for example, the characteristically nominal ending *-ment* in *document*.
ii. The stress placement found in the lexemes, which Marchand (1964: 17–19) signals as indicative of a derivational relationship between unmarked lexemes, wording out various possibilities, for example, *'export*^{N} vs *ex'port*^{V}, to show the derived character of the noun, as verbs are typically stressed on the final syllable.

---

[11] The examples in this section are taken from Marchand (1964).

iii. The morphological type of the lexemes may also be "[...] indicative of the primary or derived character of composite words" (Marchand 1964: 16), for example, because there are a large number of compound nouns of the types *snowball* (N+N) or *blacklist* (ADJ+N) in comparison to verbs.

The application of these criteria has been explored in studies on conversion in various languages. For instance, Hayes (1981), cited in Kiparsky (1982), or Kiparsky (1982) use level ordering, focusing on the (ir-)regularities and differences in stress patterns in English noun/verb conversion in disyllabic pairs (while taking semantics also into account). More recently, Lohman (2017), presents an empirical study of how phonological cues of nouns and verbs can be used to tell the directionality of noun/verb conversion in English (for words that are at least two syllables in length). The paper also discusses the relations of phonological properties with other criteria commonly employed to ascertain directionality.

For languages other than English, several authors have laid emphasis on formal characteristics: Don (1993, 2004) with a focus on the (ir-)regularities and complex syllabic structure for noun/verb pairs in Dutch, Rodrigues (2009) on differences in thematic vowels and stress patterns in noun/verb conversion in Portuguese, or Tribout's (2020) tests of morphological criteria (nominal gender and verbal inflection in French, along with other criteria, except that with inconclusive results).[12]

The advantage of an approach to directionality based on formal distinctions is that it uses easily-applicable, objective criteria. The main drawback is probably that, at least in English, the criteria mentioned do not apply to all cases of conversion and, thus, the directionality of pairs which do not show formal characteristics, that is, certain endings, stress differences, etc., remains unresolved. Furthermore, counterexamples are found (cf. Bram 2011: 85–86). Specifically regarding Aronoff's (1976) distributional criterion based on morphological types (or similarly Marchand's 1964 criterion of morphological type), it remains unclear how big the differences in the distribution of the types should be, the criterion not being applicable where a similar distribution is found. Also, as Rainer (1993: 52) remarks, it remains to be determined if this criterion mirrors psychological reality. Finally, like diachronic criteria, formal criteria do not account for the semantics in conversion and may not reflect the lexeme's usage.

2.5.4 Structural criteria

Another approach to directionality relies on finding parallel cases of overt derivation. This has typically been referred to as the "overt analogue criterion"

[12] It seems that formal criteria may be more easily applicable or provide dissimilar results for various other languages, for the characteristics that conversion has in each language.

(cf. Sanders 1988: 160–161, in its restricted version, 164–165 for the generalized version of this criterion, and references therein): "One word can be derived from another of the same form in a language (only) if there is a precise analogue in the language where the same derivational function is marked in the derived word by an overt (nonzero) form". According to this account, the verb *pattern* would be derived from the noun (*pattern*^{N} > *pattern*^{V}), because the relation can be paralleled to the one in cases such as (*drama*^{N} > *dramatize*^{V}).[13]

However, this criterion for the identification of "zero derivation relations" is not applicable in all cases. This is because, as noted by Sanders (1988: 167), it may be the case that various analogues are found and "[...] that one analogy suggests that function A is derived from B and another analogy that function B is derived from A", for instance:[14]

(3)	a.	*cover*^{N}	>	*cover*^{V} 'put cover(s) on'
		chain^{N}	>	*enchain*^{V} 'put chains on'
	b.	*cover*^{V}	>	*cover*^{N} 'instrument for covering'
		cleave^{V}	>	*cleaver*^{N} 'instrument for cleaving'

In cases like (3), the overt analogue criterion is not useful for the identification of directionality between the lexemes involved. This is because analogous pairs for which a Noun-to-Verb direction (3a) or a Verb-to-Noun direction (3b) can be found in the English language, and it remains unclear too how strong the parallelism with overt derivations must be to claim a specific directionality. Furthermore, overt derivation analogues do not seem to cover all the meanings or patterns identified in conversion (Sanders 1988: 168), that is, sometimes no overt parallel cases are found at all.

I agree, thus, with the claim that even though the overt analogue criterion "[...] can be appropriately construed as a useful heuristic principle and even as a sufficient condition for the recognition of zero derivation relations, it cannot be construed as a necessary condition for the recognition of such relations in all cases" (Sanders 1988: 156, 171). Sanders also notes that the overt analogue criterion is incomplete, because semantic and pragmatic relations are not considered.

13 Example taken from Kiparsky (1982: 5).
14 Example (6) is adapted from Sanders (1988: 167).

When analogues do not offer conclusive results, Sanders (1988: 171–174) mentions other possible criteria for recognizing zero-derivation relations:

i. diachrony, specifically, whether one of the functions precedes the other in history, but he mentions precedence in the process of language acquisition by individual speakers too, and recognizes the problems of such an approach for justifying synchronic analyses (1988: 171),
ii. markedness relations, according to which "[...] a typologically marked function of a word would always be taken to be derived from the corresponding unmarked function of a word" (1988: 72), for example, languages other than English seem to have *bottle*^{N} but not *bottle*^{V}, or the verbal counterpart is marked, for example, Sp. *botella* ('*bottle*'^{N}) and the corresponding verb marked by derivation *embotellar* ('*bottle*'^{V}), although admittedly further research is needed in this respect, and
iii. what Sanders (1988: 173–174) refers to as "some sort of dependence criterion" or a criterion of "semantic-pragmatic dependence", based on Marchand (1969, cf. Section 2.5.6 in this book), which, in fact, he considers to be crucial. Although Sanders recognizes the latter criterion as "complex" in application, for example, because of the possibility of relations of mutual dependence between the lexemes involved, it being difficult to ascertain one direction of dependence in all cases, the author still emphasizes its usefulness where the overt analogue criterion fails to give any results about derivational relatedness.

2.5.5 Contextual or paradigmatic criteria

Various contextual or syntactic aspects have often been used in the literature for the identification of directionality in some cases, specifically:

i. inflectional paradigms: It is typically accepted that, if a verb is irregular and the corresponding noun is regular, the verb is the base of the process, for example, *find*^{V} > *find*^{N}; if the noun is irregular and the verb is regular, then the noun is the base, for example, *man*^{N} > *man*^{V} (cf. Myers 1984: 58; Kiparsky 1997; or the description in Cetnarowska 1993 or Plag 2003, among others; see also Don 2004 for Dutch; Rodrigues 2009 for Portuguese; or Tribout 2020 for French, where its applicability seems limited). This criterion does not apply to all cases of conversion in English. Furthermore, it has limited applicability as regards new formations, which tend to be regular (Cetnarowska 1993: 36, and references therein), so it would apply best in the study of older conversions,
ii. syntactic environment: Similarly, syntax has been used to ascertain directionality on the observation that derivatives by conversion may retain features of the base lexeme or inherit its argument structure or valency. For instance, Ginzburg et al. (1979) and Kilby (1984), as described in Cetnarowska (1993:

33–34), claim that a noun can be regarded as deverbal when it occurs with modifying noun phrases which represent the subject or the object of the activity, for example, *John* **visited** *his friends* > *John's* **visit** *to his friends*. Other authors who have looked at the argument structure or the valency of verbs and nouns and have described that derivatives may reflect the bases' argument realization are, among others, Grimshaw (1990), Rappaport Hovav & Levin (1998), Alexiadou & Grimshaw (2008), Iordăchioaia (2019), with a focus on nominalizations from particle verbs of the type *to bail out* > *the bailout*, Iordăchioaia et al. (2020) and also, specifically in relation to the issue of directionality, Ševčíková (2021), which considers valency alongside other criteria. However, the applicability of this criterion is limited (Cetnarowska 1993: 33). Interestingly, Ševčíková (2021: 114) claims that the division in the interpretation of nouns with valency frame as deverbal and those with lack of valency frame as the reverse "[…] is not intuitively acceptable with many of the nouns". The reasons refer to shifts in the meaning of the nouns, the choice of a specific theory, or the limited coverage of the valency dictionary used in her study, and

iii. derivational paradigms: The role of the derivational relations or paradigms formed for each of the lexemes has also been emphasized. This approach considers that the lexeme that gives rise to a larger number of derivatives by affixation is the base. The main drawback here, as noted in Cetnarowska (1993: 32), is that some affixes can attach to both nominal and verbal bases. Thus, *-y* can form denominal adjectives with the sense 'full of N, abounding in N, characterized by N', for example, *hairy*, as well as deverbal adjectives with the meaning 'inclined or apt to V', for example, *sticky* (Marchand 1969: 352, in Cetnarowska 1993: 32). Interestingly, Cetnarowska (1993: 32) notes that, in order to determine the directionality of the process where suffixes can attach to several bases, "[…] it may be necessary to consider in detail the semantic interpretation of the derivative". Note also that some conversion pairs may not have any derivatives at all (Adams: 1973: 38), hindering the identification of directionality by this method.

2.5.6 Semantic criteria

The semantic criteria used in the literature are typically those described by Marchand (1963a, 1963b, 1964, 1969) as *content criteria*:[15]

i. semantic dependence (hereafter SD): Marchand (1964: 12) claims that "[t]he word that for its analysis is dependent on the content of the other pair member is necessarily the derivative", for example, the verb *saw* is analysed

[15] This book refers to Marchand's content criteria as "semantic criteria". The examples in this section are taken from Marchand (1964).

as denominal because it uses the content of the noun in its definition (*saw*^{N} ‘a cutting instrument with a blade, having a continuous series of teeth on the edge’ > *saw*^{V} ‘to cut with a saw, use a saw’). Similarly, in the case of *whistle* (*whistle*^{N} ‘instrument used for whistling’ < *whistle*^{V} ‘forcing the breath through the teeth or compressed lips’), the noun is analysed as deverbal because the verb does not use the contents of the noun for its definition while the noun does use the contents of the verb. SD is taken as the most relevant criterion to define directionality between unmarked terms by Marchand, who claimed that “[t]he most important [criterion] is that of semantic dependence, as it is as often as not sufficient in itself to solve the question of derivational relationship while the other criteria have a more or less concomitant character” (Marchand 1964: 10). Similar claims can be found in the literature (cf. Quirk et al. 1985: 1558; Cetnarowska 1993: 24–25; Iacobini 2000: 870, where SD and SR are the two most relevant criteria). For instance, Quirk et al. (1985: 1558) emphasize their treatment of conversion as a process now available for extending the lexical resources of a language, by claiming that “[…] often the semantic dependence of one item upon another is sufficient ground for arguing its derivational dependence”, and show this with paraphrases,

ii. restriction of usage (hereafter RU): Marchand (1964: 13) claims that “[i]f one word has a smaller range of usage than its pair member, it must be considered the derivative” and lists various possibilities:
    1. one of the words is not generally accepted while the other is common, for example, *author*^{N} is generally used, while the counterpart *author*^{V} is not so widely used,
    2. the use of one of the pair words is restricted to certain nominal or verbal forms, while the other pair word does not show any restrictions of usage, for example, *amend*^{N}, which Marchand mentions as taking only plural form and in the phrase *make amends*, while its counterpart *amend*^{V} shows no restrictions,
    3. one of the terms is used only as a half-serious word, while the other is unrestricted, for example, *burgle*^{V} (semifacetious word) < *burglar*^{N}, and
    4. one of the words is restricted to literary or poetic usage, while the counterpart is used generally or colloquially, for example, *hunger*^{V} < *hunger*^{N}.

iii. semantic range (hereafter SR): Marchand (1964: 14) observes that “[o]f two homophonous words exhibiting similar sets of semantic features the one with the smaller field of reference is the derivative”. This implies that the lexeme with the more specific meaning is the derivative, as it is typically assumed that only some of the senses of the base are converted, or that a converted lexeme does not carry with it the semantic range it had in the word-class category from which it is converted (cf. Quirk et al. 1985: 1560), for example, *cheat*^{V} > *cheat*^{N}, the noun meaning ‘one who cheats (habitually)’, while the verb does not mean ‘to be a habitual cheat’, and

iv. semantic pattern (hereafter SP): Marchand (1964: 15) claims that "[c]ertain words have characteristic meanings which mark them as derivatives". The author lists a series of sense group characteristics of deverbal (e.g. *cheat*^{N} 'one who cheats (habitually)' < *cheat*^{V}) and denominal derivatives (e.g. *baby*^{V} 'treat as a baby' < *baby*^{N}; further groups are also exemplified in his 1963a paper; cf. also the sense groups in Marchand 1969).

Note that Marchand (1964: 13) highlights the fact that one word having a smaller range of usage than its pair member may be expressed in terms of frequency too. This observation has led other authors to study directionality in conversion based on the frequency of the pairs involved (cf. Section 2.5.7).

The relevance of these semantic criteria as well as other criteria typically proposed for directionality have been discussed in the literature (cf., among others, Trnka 1969; Aronoff 1976; Cetnarowska 1993; Katamba 1993; Rainer 1993; Plag 1999, 2003; Iacobini 2000; Balteiro 2007; or Bram 2011). However, these criteria were not put to test until quite recently, when some authors have used semantic criteria in their analyses of directionality, alone or in combination with other criteria.

For instance, Balteiro (2007), although regarding etymological information as primary in her analysis, uses semantic criteria too, SD, SR, SP and frequency of occurrence (which she names RU). She argues that, although SD solves 95 % of cases, this should be taken with caution (2007: 124) for two reasons:

i. this criterion does not differentiate conversion from what is not, and
ii. this criterion does not allow to differentiate senses that were transferred at the time of the conversion and those acquired later by sense influence, which is irrelevant synchronically anyway.

SP has very similar results to SD. However, the criteria are applied at the level of lexeme, and not of sense, while a bidirectional or unidirectional label is assigned to each pair based on the OED. Balteiro's application of the criteria, specifically of SR, remains unclear. It seems that for SR, the author looks at senses in dictionaries, but the method is not described in detail, even if she acknowledges the difficulties in the analysis of SR in several cases.

Bram (2011) uses attestation dates (AD) as the criterion to set the direction in conversion and then tests frequency (in various corpora) and semantic criteria too to see if the indicated directionality correlates to the one provided by diachronic criteria. The semantic criteria studied (SD, SR) are applied at the level of lexeme, as only core or central senses are considered. These criteria seem to give limited results, and their correlations are below the 75 % cut-off point they establish. For instance, the correlation found in Bram's study between the criteria AD/SD is 32.7 % for Verb-to-Noun conversion, 53.7 % for Noun-to-Verb with different dates, and 73.3 % for Noun-to-Verb with the same dates; the correlation between AD/SR is of 70.5 % for Verb-to-Noun conversion, 45.1 % for Noun-to-Verb with different dates and 63.8 % for Noun-to-Verb with the same dates.

However, I argue that attestation dates should be discarded in a synchronic approach to language description, and that, as languages are constantly changing, new senses may emerge and the directions between pairs may change too. Probably the fact that a synchronic and a diachronic approach are combined, or that the criteria are tested at the level of lexeme justify Bram's view that the criteria have limited results. Also, when attestation dates or etymological information is used regardless of senses, the possibility of the direction between pairs being reverted is overlooked (for instance there may be cases for which original senses are no longer in use).

Kisselew et al. (2016) also investigate whether distributional information on the semantic specificity of the terms and their frequency can predict the direction in noun/verb pairs. Again, they take historical precedence as the standard of directionality and then consider frequency and semantics, while the criteria are tested at the level of lexeme too.

On a sample of French conversion, Tribout (2020) tests the criterion of SP, together with other diachronic and formal criteria. Regarding the analysis of SP, which is also applied at the level of lexeme, the author concludes that, except for the privative pattern, which can only be found in Noun-to-Verb conversion, SP does not allow for the identification of directionality in conversion, because all the semantic categories have counterparts in the opposite direction (Tribout 2020: 200).

More recently, Ševčíková (2021) looked at semantic dependency, together with other criteria such as morphographemic alternations, noun valency, and the number of verbs for each noun in a sample of Czech. Ševčíková observes differences between suffixless nouns in Czech expressing (non-)actional semantics arguing for two different groups: one based on a verbal root, and one based on a base noun or nominal root.

Other studies with a focus on various aspects of conversion use semantic criteria for the classification of directionality too, even when the focus is not on directionality. For instance, Valera (2014) notes that certain authors use the semantic criteria to tell directionality when providing examples in their description of conversion. Similarly, Bauer & Valera (2015), Valera (2020 on semantic patterns by senses in noun/verb conversion in English), and Valera (2023: 162 on the semantics of noun/verb conversion in English and Spanish), or Díaz-Negrillo & Fernández-Alcaina (2023 on the semantic distribution of low-frequency denominal verb formations in English), all assess directionality based on semantic dependency. Iordăchioaia et al.'s (2020) study of zero nominals (from MANNER and RESULT verbs) looks at semantic readings, together with attestation dates and etymological information, stress shift, and their frequency in the OED, to identify the extent to which nominals realize argument structure, or block stress shift, and they investigate the various readings of the nouns associated with the base MANNER and RESULT verbs.

The advantage of semantic criteria is that they can be applied systematically to most cases, while being less subjective than an approach to the pairs based solely on the speaker's intuition. This is because dictionaries or similar sources and widely accepted semantic classifications are typically used to test these criteria. These criteria also have the advantage of typically corresponding to the speaker's intuitions. However, as noted by Sanders (1988: 174) "[i]t remains to be determined [...] to what extent this criterion of semantic-pragmatic dependency can be generalized to less clear and less prototypical cases of multiple function and thus to what extent it can serve [...] as an appropriate basis for the recognition of zero derivation relations in all languages".

The main drawbacks of a synchronic approach to the semantics of pairs related by conversion are that the semantic criteria proposed in the literature are not always clearly or consistently applied, and that the synchronic approach is more time-consuming as compared to others (at least when applied at the level of sense). It must also be mentioned that lexicographic information may sometimes be inconclusive or misleading, and that different resources may represent lexemes and their senses differently.

The difficulty in the application of the criteria has been recognized by most authors, and the added difficulty of considering senses too (cf. Valera 2015: 328). This is partly for the polysemy of the lexemes involved and partly because of the mutual dependence sometimes found between the pairs, it being difficult to establish a unique direction in some cases, that is, a noun may be semantically dependent on the verb, and the verb may be semantically dependent on the noun as regards their definitions, for example, *saw*^{V} has been claimed to be definable as 'the instrument prototypically used for sawing things' and *saw*^{N} as 'to cut with a saw' (Sanders 1988: 174, cf. also Katamba 1993: 120). Furthermore, it has been claimed that "[...] we can adjust the definition of semantically-related words in accordance with our intentions" (cf. Štekauer 1996: 128) and thus lack objectivity (Umbreit 2010: 310).

2.5.7 Quantitative-distributional criteria

Last, some authors have pointed to quantitative-distributional criteria for the identification of the base and derived term in a conversion pair. These criteria are based on measurable frequency of occurrence or register distribution data. The assumption is that the base is more frequent or occurs more generally (in a larger number of registers) than the derivative (cf. Marchand 1963a, 1964; Bybee 1985, 1988: 133–134; Plag 2003).

Some authors have studied the frequency of lexemes to identify directionality between formally identical pairs in combination with other criteria (among others, Balteiro 2007; Bram 2011; Kisselew et al. 2016). However, as far as we know, this criterion has not been applied at the level of sense, partly for the difficulty of classifying polysemous pairs semantically, and because this information cannot be extracted from corpora easily.[16]

Balteiro, for instance, uses a relatively small corpus, *The International Corpus of English* (ICE), with about one million words, to measure frequency differences between pairs at the level of lexeme. She admits that her corpus size is a problem, and a larger dataset should be analysed (Balteiro 2007: 129).

Bram (2011) retrieves frequency data from various corpora, specifically, the *Brown Corpus*, the BNC and *Lancaster-Oslo/Bergen* (LOB) Corpus, to measure the agreement between the directions provided by attestation dates and by the frequency of the pairs in various corpora. As is natural, more pairs are found in the larger corpora, the BNC. The frequency is, however, also established at the level of lexeme.

Kisselew et al. (2016) also measure frequency at the level of lexeme in two large corpora, the BNC and ukWaC. Interestingly, both Bram (2011) and Kisselew et al. (2016: 97) establish frequency as a poor predictor of directionality for Verb-to-Noun conversion.

The advantage of these criteria is that they are empirical, measurable, and objective, while they require data from sources such as corpora. Such criteria, however, may present several issues in application. At a general level, as mentioned by Štekauer (1996: 129), frequency depends on the sources used, the corpus to analyse conversion pairs should thus be representative and large enough to offer reliable results, and it should include texts from a variety of registers for differences in usage to be found. The same applies when considering register usage.

It should be noted that, when considering the frequency of occurrence of a pair of lexemes, unrelated uses (mistakes and homonyms) should be discarded first. Moreover, it is relevant to mind the various senses that the pairs may

---

16 Although not on directionality, Lara-Clares & Thompson (2019) and Lara-Clares (2023) are relevant methodologically as the focus is on the meaning, frequency, and register distribution in a sample of nominal competition in English.

present. Thus, I argue that the results of any study which has not considered these issues are inconclusive. Indeed, other authors have admittedly not included the criterion of frequency of occurrence in their data analyses for the difficulties in its application. For instance, Ševčíková (2021: 107) does not apply the criterion of frequency of occurrence because the corpus used in her study, SYN2015, "[...] is not disambiguated for word senses and the frequency scores extracted would necessarily relate to all senses of polysemous items, which would make an adequate analysis impossible". More specific issues may appear too, for example, when pairs, or their senses, have a very low frequency of occurrence, or when their frequency of occurrence is very close. In such cases, directionality cannot be decided.

More generally, the frequency of occurrence or register usage data may not reflect the synchronic state of the language, or the actual directionality, as extra-linguistic factors may play a role in the frequency or register use of the terms. In this regard, it has also been mentioned that frequency can change over time (Umbreit 2010: 309) but I argue that directionality can change too. For these reasons, frequency has been regarded as having only limited reliability.

2.5.8 Recapitulation

This section describes the criteria available in the literature to tell directionality in conversion:

i. The diachronic criteria of attestation dates and etymological information from dictionaries to determine the chronological priority of the pair members were presented in Section 2.5.1,
ii. The proposal to rely on speaker intuition to decide which pair member is base was discussed in Section 2.5.2,
iii. Criteria based on morphological and phonological aspects between the pairs such as stress shift, morphologic type and type distribution of the lexemes were described in Section 2.5.3,
iv. A structural criterion consisting in finding parallel cases in overt derivation was presented in Section 2.5.4,
v. Contextual (syntactic) or paradigmatic criteria were examined in Section 2.5.5., for example, to consider (ir-)regularities in the inflectional paradigm of the pairs, and their syntax to determine if the lexemes have, for example, inherited the argument structure or valency from the pair, or to consider the word families or derivational paradigms emerging for each of the lexemes,
vi. a synchronic semantic approach proposing to rely on semantic evidence to determine the directionality in conversion pairs was considered in Section 2.5.6. Specifically, the criteria proposed are to look at the semantic

dependence between the lexemes, their semantic range, whether they show restrictions in usage, or whether they use semantic patterns typically identified for each of the pairs, and

vii. the quantitative criteria relying on the frequency of the lexemes or their register usage in corpora are presented in Section 2.5.7.

As described in Sections 2.5.1–2.5.7, the criteria are not without problems. When approaching directionality, authors have either focused on a single criterion, for example, Biese (1941), who relies on attestation dates in the OED, or they have used a combination of criteria from various approaches (see "mixture-based" approach in Bram 2011: 88 et passim). In fact, some authors have argued that using a combination of various criteria to determine directionality is more advantageous because it can capture the complexity of conversion and account for various aspects. However, when criteria have been combined, authors seem to prioritize one of the criteria over the others.

It is here argued that a mixed approach may not resolve ambiguous or controversial cases, where evidence from various criteria may indicate opposite directions or be inconclusive. Although approaching directionality by using both synchronic and diachronic criteria will capture the complexity of the process, the linguist should first decide where their interest lies and decide which criteria to use accordingly: in a diachronic approach (that is, in the historical precedence of the terms) or in a synchronic account to language description (with a focus on directionality as perceived today, or on the semantic patterns involved in conversion). It has been emphasized that a diachronic analysis of conversion is sometimes against present-day intuition and usage of the terms (see, for instance, Cetnarowska 1993: 24).

Remarkably, previous studies seem to have approached directionality at the level of lexeme. This is here argued to affect the results because, as is widely acknowledged, the senses involved between pairs of derivationally-related lexemes may develop differently, or senses in use may influence one another. Thus, various relations between the senses may be overlooked by an analysis of directionality at the level of lexeme (by considering just the most central or core sense for each lexeme of the conversion pairs).

In this book, a synchronic approach to the issue of directionality in conversion is taken, as the interest lies here in the sense relations between the terms in present-day English, and specifically, in the applicability of various synchronic criteria at the level of sense.

CHAPTER 3

Methodological approach

3.1 Resources: Dictionary and corpus

This is an experimental study that relies on database evidence to evaluate the relevance of various criteria for directionality described in the specialized literature, and their applicability at the level of sense. Specifically, this study relies on two main resources for data collection:

i. OED2 and OED3,[17] and
ii. BNC.

The OED is the data source of this study for retrieval of semantic information because it is the main lexicographical reference of the English language. The work on the dictionary started more than 150 years ago, and nowadays the OED offers a detailed account of the history, meaning and usage of over 500,000 words and phrases from across the English-speaking world.[18] It provides historical information and includes obsolete senses, which may prove relevant for proper understanding of the connections within the words and word families under study, and also synchronic information and senses that are in use in present-day English, the dictionary being revised and extended at regular intervals. The OED is used as a source of semantic information, specifically for the study and classification of the senses associated with the lexemes under study (cf. Section 3.2.2). The use of other dictionaries was discarded, unless required for senses not represented in the OED, to avoid a biased representation of the senses of each word.

[17] OED2 refers to the second edition of the dictionary, published in 1989, and OED3 refers to the third edition, which is an ongoing project that began in the 1990s. Updates adding new or revised words are published quarterly as part of the OED3.

[18] Cf. <https://www.oed.com/information/about-the-oed?tl=true>.

This study combines the use of dictionary and corpus data. The corpus used in this study is the BNC (Davies 2004–), a ca. 100-million-word database of spoken and written English of the late twentieth century (1960–1993).[19]

The BNC consists of texts from a variety of sources and (see Section 3.2.4.6 for specification of how register information was considered). It is considered large enough to be used as a representative sample of synchronic English use, and yet a manageable source of data compared with larger corpora, such as the *Corpus of Contemporary American English* (COCA).

These two properties are relevant because this piece of research on the applicability of the criteria on conversion entails analysis of the concordances for a sample of lexemes by senses. Also, the BNC has the advantage that it is a static corpus. Although a regularly updated corpus would allow the inclusion of neologisms and recent uses of words, this could also distort the results, as regards the usage of lexemes or their inclusion.

The BNC is used in this study to collect all the concordances available for the lexemes in the data sample described in Section 3.2.1 for research on their semantics according to the senses represented, their register use, and their frequency of occurrence. The data were collected with *Sketchengine*,[20] and the BNC version selected was the version using English CLAWS5.[21] This version was selected after manual checking of a random sample of lexemes in the two versions available in *Sketchengine*, because the overall frequency of the terms checked was closer to the one provided by the frequency list of *CQPWeb*,[22] also by UCREL, which is the basis for collection of the conversion sample (Section 3.2.1). While the data differed from those in the frequency list, no major differences in terms of frequency of occurrence were found in the analysis of the lexemes in any of the two versions available.

3.2 Procedures for the analysis of directionality

Section 3.2 describes the methodological procedure followed for the study of directionality in a sample of English noun/verb conversion, specifically:

i. Data sampling of formally identical and semantically related noun/verb pairs is described in Section 3.2.1.
ii. The issues found during sense classification of the sample's concordances

---

19 Cf. <https://www.sketchengine.eu/british-national-corpus-bnc/>.
20 Cf. <https://www.sketchengine.eu>.
21 Cf. <https://www.sketchengine.eu/english-claws5-part-of-speech-tagset/>.
22 Cf. <https://cqpweb.lancs.ac.uk>.

are listed in Section 3.2.2, specifically difficulties in the use of corpora (Section 3.2.2.1) and the use of dictionary information (Section 3.2.2.2).

iii. The semantic categories used for the classification of the senses identified in the sample in this study are presented in Section 3.2.3, both for derived senses and base senses.

iv. The use of several of Marchand's (1964) criteria for directionality at the level of sense to a sample of noun/verb English conversion is described in Section 3.2.4, specifically the criteria of SD (Section 3.2.4.1), RU (Section 3.2.4.2), SR (Section 3.2.4.3), SP (Section 3.2.4.4), FO (Section 3.2.4.5), and RR (Section 3.2.4.6). Even though the criteria were described in further detail in the previous chapter (cf. Section 2.5), a brief recapitulation of each, as described by Marchand, is given within each of these subsections for convenience.

3.2.1 Data sampling

As mentioned, the data corpus used in this study is based on the BNC. At the outset, a corpus query processor (*CQPWeb*),[23] was used for retrieval of the entire lemmatized frequency list of the BNC (XML edition), that is, a list of all lemmas in the corpus together with their part-of-speech tag (POS)[24] and their frequency of occurrence. The retrieved list consisted of 659,465 lemmas.

The aim was to select a sample of formally identical lexemes, tagged both as verbs and nouns in the BNC frequency list. The compilation of this list's formally identical items relied on a tool using simple matching search syntax/query (cf. the description in Ruz 2025). Thus, by running a matching test or list crossing, a list of all lemmas tagged as both word-class categories (VERB and SUBST in the lemmatized frequency list) was generated, along with their frequency of occurrence as each category.

The BNC lemmatized frequency list contained mistakes, even if the annotation accuracy is high. Hence, the list extracted was found to include mistakes too, even if the list of matching noun/verb pairs was generated after removing terms which contained either numbers or symbols at their beginning or end and which are, thus, not actual words (for example *p4/t3* (1/2),[25] *camp-crp/cytr* (1/1), *5-* (1/7)). Entries containing spaces, symbols or numbers within (for example *check module*

---

23 Available at <https://cqpweb.lancs.ac.uk>.

24 This book refers to POS as *word-class categories* or simply *categories*. Note also that the categories SUBST and VERB are referred to as noun and verb.

25 The frequency of a term as noun/verb is given between brackets and in this order, following the information in the BNC lemmatized list extracted from *CQPWeb*.

(2/1), *x'pert* (1/3), *d'ye* (40/10), *drtf1/e2f* (7/40)) were discarded using *Excel* searches and conditional formatting rules.

Even after this step, when a stratified sample of noun/verb pairs was obtained from the list, it was found that nearly half of the pairs selected were not actual cases of noun/verb conversion, most mistakes being found for lexemes with low frequency of occurrence as one word-class category or the other, so manual screening became necessary at a later stage. Examples manually cleared out from the list are provided below:

i. Terms not attested as verb in the BNC: *slogan* (801/1), *batt* (92/1)
ii. Terms not attested as noun in the BNC: *dron* (18/38), *shear* (120/140), *rouse* (49/407), *sede* (6/7)
iii. Terms wrongly tagged as verb in the BNC: *beem* (1/1), *cloy* (4/3)
iv. Terms wrongly tagged as noun in the BNC: *narrate* (1/1), *brisk* (1/1)
v. Cases of inflection and/or affixation, when the affix is analysable in English (indicated as affixation in the OED): *unwrap* (1/49), *philosophise* (2/3), *rediscount* (10/11), *undersold* (5/6), *classified* (6/1)
vi. Compounds and neoclassical compounds, for the entirely different directionality patterns they may use: *housebreak* (1/9), *giftwrap* (4/7), *mindblast* (1/1), *handbag* (665/1, used metaphorically), *electrocoat* (1/1), *biotype* (7/2)
vii. Foreign and OE words (when used in a foreign/OE language context): *comunicación* (1/1, Spa), *sonare* (1/1, Ita), *tombe* (1/1, Fr), *Baumgarten* (7/1, Gr), *drinke* (1/1, OE), *lufe* (9/1, OE)
viii. Words used metalinguistically: *coerce* (2/187), *drat* (2/23)
ix. Misspellings: *wex* (1/1, for *wax*), *skool* (8/2), *controll* (6/1), *suprise* (8/21), also expressions: *godammit* (1/4), *sonuvanitch* (1/1)
x. Acronyms: *YSD* (1/1), *WIIW* (1/1), *SAD* (1/1)
xi. Brand names: *demacort* (1/1), *alkylate* (1/9), *logitek* (8/2)

The data sample was then restricted to lexemes with frequency 1,000 in the BNC, as one word class or as the other. The alternative would have been to extract a stratified sample of the complete list, so terms of all frequencies were included. This option was discarded for higher manageability, that is, because including terms with a higher frequency of occurrence would result either in a less detailed semantic study, or in a study of fewer terms.

To which extent the decision to exclude terms with frequencies higher than 1,000 may have an impact on the directionality results remains unclear. The assumption is that no substantial differences would be found as regards, for example, the directionality patterns found. A sample including terms with frequencies up to 1,000 is here considered adequate to study directionality in present-day English conversion, and to test the applicability of the criteria.

Table 1 presents the distribution of nouns and verbs after the frequency of occurrence was restricted to include the range 1–1,000.

Table 1: Raw frequency distribution of the screened list of terms attested as noun (N) and verb (V) in the BNC up to frequency 1,000

Frequency distribution (raw)	N	%	V	%
Freq. 1	26	1.3%	104	5.1%
Freq. 2–5	127	6.2%	245	12.0%
Freq. 6–10	109	5.3%	196	9.6%
Freq. 11–50	375	18.4%	502	24.6%
Freq. 51–100	285	14.0%	244	11.9%
Freq. 101–250	484	23.7%	366	17.9%
Freq. 251–500	330	16.2%	238	11.7%
Freq. 501–750	243	11.9%	120	5.9%
Freq. 751–1,000	63	3.1%	27	1.3%
Total	2,042	100%	2,042	100%

The screened list (that is, containing pairs of lexemes in which both lexemes involved had a frequency of use of up to 1,000 occurrences) consists of 4,084 lexemes grouped as 2,042 pairs.

A first stratified sample of the list was obtained with 52 lexemes grouped as 26 pairs, that is, one lexeme every 160 was selected from the list of terms ordered by the frequency of the noun, and another lexeme every 160 was selected from the list ordered by the frequency of the verb. For higher objectivity, the sampling interval started at 5, an aleatory number obtained from Excel's random function. The sample selected in this first stage made ca. 1.3% the screened list. The sample was enlarged by systematic doubling to keep the frequency ranges, so the sample remained representative of the frequencies included. Around 2.5% was analysed after the first sample doubling, ca. 5% after the second, and ca. 10% of the screened list after the third (one lexeme every 20 in each of the lists). A complete list of the data analysed in this study in alphabetical order is provided in Appendix A.3, together with their final frequency of occurrence as verb and noun, after manual discard of unrelated examples, etc. (cf. 3.2.2).

3.2.2 Sense classification of the concordances

The first stage of data analysis was a manual classification of the concordances for each term according to the semantic information in the OED. For this purpose, all concordances for each sampled term were extracted, as mentioned in Section 3.2.1, from the BNC version tagged by CLAWS available in *Sketchengine*. This tool allows intuitive, simple searches and, thus, quick concordance extraction via an advanced query by 'lemma' and by 'part of speech' covering all word forms of a lemma as a specific POS. The concordances obtained were classified manually according to the senses available in the OED. Concordance sense classification was intended for a clearer picture of current usage, in terms of frequency and register. Sense classification is described in further detail in Sections 3.2.2.1 and 3.2.2.2, covering corpus- and dictionary-derived issues, respectively.

3.2.2.1 Corpus-derived issues

This section lists a series of issues arising during semantic classification of concordances. The cases listed, if disregarded, may have an impact on the results. They should be considered carefully if the goal is the analysis of frequencies and usage, and especially if the analysis is at the level of sense.

Although wrong annotation is initially not expected to influence, for example, overall frequency or register distribution for most of the terms included in the sample, these variables may influence the results as relevant differences for some of the pairs, terms, or their senses, for example, if numerous wrong tags are found, especially if the frequency of the lexemes is low. The following lists some of the issues that arose during sample processing:

i. Wrongly tagged instances of nouns and verbs were recategorized and included in our analysis under their correct word class, for example, (4) tagged in the BNC as a noun was relisted in the sample as a verb, and (5) tagged in the BNC as a verb instance was relisted as a noun, for instance:

(4) *He* **bombards/n** *the brandy with a violent infusion of soda from the large siphon.*
(5) *Soon he was hammering on the door,* **thud/v** *after thud, a noise fit to wake the dead.*

ii. Noun-premodifying adjectives wrongly tagged as nouns (6) or verbs (7) were recategorized and discarded, for instance:

(6) *The tiny eel was almost transparent, except for the jet black, pin* **prick/n** *eyes.*
(7) *It's possibly the most outrageous place anywhere in the Mediterranean, full of weird and wonderful people,* **stilt/v** *walkers, street markets, pavement cafés, and bars in which you just sit and watch a world you have never seen before walk […]*

iii. Premodifying *-ing* forms (intensifiers) were discarded, for example:

(8) *More than once they saw a passer-by,* **soaking/v** *wet, shout threats and curses at an open window.*

iv. Proper nouns in the sample wrongly tagged as verbs (9) were recategorized and discarded, for instance:

(9) **Bray/v** *cleverly lobbed the third from a penalty corner, before Lister scored the goal of the day.*

v. Metalinguistic occurrences tagged as nouns (10) or verbs (11) to which no sense of the word-class category can be ascribed were discarded, for example:

(10) *You will not find words like* **skive/n** *and naff in most dictionaries (or if you do they will be marked 'dialectal' or 'colloquial') [...]*
(11) *OA as in old, goat, boat,* **soak/v**, *poke, Oates, voter.*

vi. Acronyms tagged as nouns (12) or wrongly tagged as verbs (13) were discarded, for instance:

(12) *At the Hinkley C Inquiry this issue was pushed to the fore by the Severnside Campaign Against Radiation* (**SCAR/n**).
(13) *internal Strengths and Weaknesses of the organisation and the Opportunities and Threats to the organisation (hence* **SWOT/v**).

vii. Speaking mistakes, misspellings or unclear occurrences, (14), (15) and (16) respectively, were discarded, for example:

(14) *They know which one Richey actually is, since the above cutting (ha ha) suggests that The* **Scar/n**, *sorry, Star, are a tad confused.*
(15) *Full colour on every page! Dazzling,* **hug/v**?
(16) *[...] seek berries, shaste mooratoogs,* **purl/v** *i da paety loch an swittle taes.*

The sample includes also cases that are complex to analyse consistently and/or ambiguous (-ed, -ing and other plurivalent units). Because they may have an impact on the results, especially regarding the frequency of occurrence for the lexeme's senses in use, these cases are described in this section too. Among the complex or ambiguous cases, terms in *-ed* or *-ing* are most frequently found, for their difficult word-class categorization. The corpus includes numerous *-ed* and *-ing* occurrences as verb realizations in the participle forms. However, some of these are adjectivalizations or nominalizations. The challenging separation between adjectives, nouns and verbs used in the participle form relied on a series of syntactic and semantic tests (cf. Ruz 2025 for exemplification of the application of these tests).

Specifically, *-ed* adjectives and *-ing* nominalizations were recategorized as their corresponding word-class category and discarded. Ambiguous occurrences were included as verbs and marked with an asterisk * for concordances in which a verb periphrasis is recoverable, and for which both a verbal (for instance PROCESS/ACTION) and an adjectival interpretation (for instance STATE, as in (17)–(20)), or a verbal and a nominal interpretation (for instance RESULT, as in (21)–(23)) are possible, for instance:

(17) *[...] then the sandpaper or phosphorous paper,* **pasted/v** *ready beforehand, is applied and pressed on so that it sticks fast.* (OED sense 2*)

(18) *The dust allergy means that Will has to be bedded on paper, and his hay always has to be* **soaked/v**. (OED sense 5*)

(19) *From hides we watched skimming house martins, skulking/v moor hens,* **skidding/v** *coots, a hovering kestrel, [...].* (OED sense 5*)

(20) *Many of these are small, one- or two-person outfits, snack kiosks and the like. But there are signs of* **blossoming/v** *entrepreneurial spirit.* (OED sense 2*)

(21) *At home, record sounds like a door shutting, car starting, plane going over, bird* **chirping/v**, *dog barking, baby crying, [...].* (OED sense 1*)

(22) *[...] Some designs leave gaps for two wheeled traffic, to avoid the danger of* **skidding/v**, *[...].* (OED sense 3b*)

(23) *However, it is best to avoid continuous harsh braking which may just result in locking the wheel and* **skidding/v**. (OED sense 3*)

A last case worth mentioning is that of nouns in attributive position. These were categorized as nouns and marked as *PREM*, as in (24). Only where the term as an adjective is commonly used and recognized in English (that is, when the term appears as an adjective in dictionaries and conveys adjectival meaning different from the noun's senses recorded in the OED, as in (25)) were the concordances marked as adjectives and discarded:

(24) *Varnish stains: as well as using dyes, wood can also be coloured using* **varnish/n** *stains. These are clear varnishes to which either dyestuffs or transparent pigments, or both, have been added.* (OED sense 1c PREM)

(25) *He tossed a single* **crimson/n** *rose on to her oak coffin.* (PREM ADJ)

3.2.2.2 Dictionary-derived issues

Manual classification of the concordances was not without problems. Some of the issues found derive from the use of dictionaries for sense analysis.

First, sense classification by concordance allowed analysis of homonymous lexemes for their inclusion or exclusion in the sample according to whether an available converted pair is also recorded in the BNC, or not. Homonyms were found for ca. 35 % of the pairs in the sample (n=72 pairs), specifically, various homonymous entries were found for ca. 31 % of nouns in our list (n=69) and for ca. 20 % of verbs (n=45), but homonymous pairs were not always represented in both sources. After classification of the concordances, 30 homonymous converted pairs were found in both the OED and the BNC and thus included in our study.[26] During the analysis of homonymy, the following cases were found:

i. Various entries are available in the OED for one of the terms in our list, either the verb or the noun, while only one entry is available for the counterpart. In this case, concordances were classified according to the senses in the various entries recorded in the OED, but only the entries with a related counterpart were retained for subsequent analysis of the directionality criteria, and the entries for which no related converted counterpart was found were discarded (see Section 3.2.4 for a description of the application of the criteria in this study), for instance:

(26) *Pinion*: for the term *pinion*, five separate nominal entries are listed in the OED (N1, N2, N3, N4, N5), three of which are recorded in the BNC. In contrast, there is only one verbal entry in the OED (V), and all the occurrences in the BNC refer to this. In this case, the occurrences that relate to terms for which no converted pair is found are discarded. This is important, as it may have an influence on register distribution and frequency (both overall and by sense).

ii. Various entries are available in the OED for both terms in the sample list. In this case, the concordances were classified according to the senses in the various entries in the OED, and this resulted in the inclusion of various homonymous converted pairs when several related lexemes were recorded in the BNC concordances, as in (27), or in the inclusion of just one pair of lexemes, if no related counterparts are recorded in the BNC or just a pair was represented, as in (28), for instance:

(27) *Graf*: entries N1, N2, N3, N4, N5 and V1, V2, V3, V4 are available in the OED, and the concordance classification shows senses relating to all the entries except for N2, so eight lexemes are attested, and four related pairs are thus included: N1/V1, N3/V2, N4/V3 and N5/V4. The entry discarded, N2, is marked as obsolete in the OED.
(28) *Cork*: various entries are available in the OED, N1, N2, N3, N4, N5 and V1, V2, V3, V4 but only senses of entries N1 and V1 are attested in the concordances and, thus, only one pair is included.

Unrelated occurrences were discarded as described after sense classification. The classification of the concordances by sense proved relevant during data selection

[26] The list of pairs analysed in this book, with specification of homonymy and information on the actual noun/verb frequency data after exclusion of mistakes and unrelated concordances, and recategorization of the concordances as their correct word-class category is given in Appendix A.3.

and may allow for a comparison of the meaning, frequency or register use between each of the homonymous pairs.

Some of the issues encountered concerning the representation of the lexemes in the OED are discussed next. It must be noted first that many lexemes of the sample list show polysemous entries in the OED, with numerous senses and subsenses. Procedurally, Arabic-numbered senses (e.g. 1, 2, 3, etc.) were used for sense classification, and subsenses (e.g. 1a, 1b, 1c, etc.) were used when relevant too.

A difficulty that is to be expected from any large lexicographical source concerns sense representation. In this study, sense representation was found to be unequal in a few cases in the OED, as evidenced during the analysis of the SR (see Section 3.2.4.3). Just to provide an example, in the converted pair formed by the noun *slaver*^{N1} (senses in (29)) and the verb *slaver*^{V} (senses in (30)), the nominal subsense *1a* seems to match the verbal sense *1*, while the nominal subsense *1b* matches the verbal sense *4* and its subsenses:

(29) *Slaver*^{N1}
1. a. Saliva or other fluid issuing from the mouth; drool. Also: †excessive appetite (obsolete). Cf. slobber n. 2a.
b. figurative. Insubstantial or worthless language; nonsense, flattery, impertinence. Now chiefly British regional.

(30) *Slaver*^{V}
1. intransitive. Of a person or animal: to let saliva run from the mouth; to drool, slobber. Also with the mouth, etc. as subject. Also: †to crave food (obsolete).
4. figurative. a. intransitive. To utter meaningless, lustful, or sycophantic words; to show excessive admiration or desire; to fawn over; to lust after. [...]
b. transitive. To utter (words) in a meaningless, lustful, or fawning manner. [...]
c. transitive. To kiss, caress, or speak to (a person) in a lustful or fawning manner; to flatter.

In this case, if both senses are attested in the BNC, they are considered as separate senses in both noun and verb (that is, a literal and a figurative sense).

Another difficulty was that some concordances did not fit any of the senses in the OED entries. This is because some typically very specific or slang senses, especially those that seem to have started to be in use recently may not have been recorded in the OED.[27] When the concordances did not match any of the senses listed in the OED for a specific lexeme, the procedure was as follows:

[27] The opposite can also be the case, that is, newer senses recorded in the OED may not be attested in the BNC as it is a corpus from the late twentieth century.

i. if a related sense is found in the other pair, then it was marked, for example, as in (32) "Sense added based on context. V, 10 (related to crank N1, sense 6)" (see 31), and a simple definition was provided "to take/snort drugs", and
ii. in the rare case that no corresponding related sense is found in the pair senses and the concordance does not match any of the listed senses, external sources were consulted (as in (33) for which an extra sense (sense 3) was created based on various entries from *urbandictionary*,[28] a source which typically includes slang and specific senses), because the OED entries for the noun *swoon* did not include a CAUSER interpretation. For consistency, a new sense was created in both cases.

(31) OED entry crank N1, sense 6:[29] "Draft additions March 2006. slang (originally U.S.). An amphetamine drug, esp. methamphetamine."
(32) Sense added based on context. V, sense 10 (related to crank N1, sense 6): "to take/snort drugs", for example, "*You get smack cut with all kinds of shit. A geezer down in Catford once mixed smack with flour. Imagine* **cranking/v** *up with that! Flour and water's an adhesive, innit? You don't want glue in your veins, do ya?*" (BNC)
(33) *swoon*^{N}, sense 3 (added): "A person usually male who is very attractive." / "A word mainly used on the internet or chatrooms. This is usually addressing males but maybe for females too. It is used when there is a hot/sexy/cute boy that someone would "swoon" over. [...]" (<https://www.urbandictionary.com/define.php?term=Swoon&page=3>), for example, "*with Matey's assistance, 'I have heard of the ladies' sewing circle accused of many things, but never of bringing on a* **swoon/n**. *Resisting them, rather, is the usual belief?*" (BNC).

Addition of these related senses occasionally led to the inclusion of a pair. For example, the terms *kerf*, *brig* and *frisbee* were included in the sample even if no counterpart as one of the word classes was recorded in the OED. In the three cases, there was no verb, but were included because an unambiguous verb use related to the noun senses is available in the BNC.

3.2.3 Semantic categorization of the senses

This study specifies the semantic categories expressed by the noun/verb pairs for the identification of directionality patterns between the lexemes, or whether there is a difference in the applicability of the criteria across categories. The senses identified

[28] <https://www.urbandictionary.com/>.
[29] Sense *6* is the Arabic-number given in this study for the specific sense cited, which appears as a draft addition to the entry in the OED. The decision to continue classifying the senses added as draft additions, or senses found in the BNC which are not recorded in the OED, like sense *10* in example (32) above, was taken for easier analysis of the criteria and classification of the concordances by sense.

for each lexeme in our sample were assigned a semantic category each. This categorization concerns both derivative and base senses.

Derivative senses were classified according to the categories listed in the literature for semantic analysis in conversion. Table 2 presents the semantic categories used for the semantic classification of denominal verbs in this study,[30] and Table 3 presents the semantic categories used for deverbal nouns.

Table 2: The semantic categories for Noun-to-Verb conversion (adapted from Plag 1999: 9; Bauer et al. 2013: 285; plus EFFECTIVE and DIRECTIONAL from Rainer 1993: 239; Valera 2023: 158–161; and DURATION from Clark & Clark 1979: 773)

Semantic category	Paraphrase	Examples
CAUSATIVE	'to make N, to cause to become N'	*orphan*
INCHOATIVE	'to become N'	*gel*
INSTRUMENTAL	'to use N, to perform an action with N'	*hammer*
LOCATIVE	'to make sthg to go to/in/on N'	*archive*
DURATION	'to carry an action during N'	*summer*
ORNATIVE	'to make N go to/in/on sthg, to provide with N'	*marmalade*
PERFORMATIVE	'to do N'	*tango*
PRIVATIVE	'to remove N'	*skin*
RESULTATIVE	'to make into N'	*package*
SIMILATIVE	'to do/act/make in the manner of or like N'	*chauffeur*
STATIVE	'to be, act as N'	*landmark*
EFFECTIVE	'to create, produce or bring about N'	*kitten*
DIRECTIONAL	'to go or move towards N'	*nightclub*

The categories MANNER OF MOTION and SOUND EMISSION listed in Bauer et al. (2013: 285) are not included in Table 2:

i. SOUND EMISSION, because verbs motivated onomatopoetically are not denominal, for example, *wuff*, and
ii. MANNER OF MOTION, because it appears as a subtype of other categories.

In this line, Lieber's (2004: 91) "motional meaning[s]" for denominal verbs are viewed here as the result of the combination of various categories, and are classified in our sample as follows:

[30] Cf. also Díaz-Negrillo & Fernández-Alcaina (2023).

i. Senses expressing the motional meaning 'move in x manner' are classified as SIMILATIVE_MANNER OF MOTION, for example, "*Monster cars* **sharked** *past, the cluster of Wall Street skyscrapers loomed [...]*" (BNC),
ii. Senses expressing the motional meaning 'move using x' are classified as INSTRUMENTAL_MEANS OF MOTION, for example, "*We were told not to do this, told not to come here, told to* **sledge** *and throw snowballs and make snowmen all we wanted [...]*" (BNC), and
iii. Senses expressing the motional meaning 'move at x location', for example, *quarterdeck* (Lieber 2004: 91), although not found in our sample, would be classified as LOCATIVE_MANNER OF MOTION.

Table 3: The semantic categories for Verb-to-Noun conversion (Plag 1999; Bauer et al. 2013: 286; plus PROCESS in Bauer 1983: 185, for nominalizations in *-ation*)

Semantic category	Paraphrase	Examples
EVENT	'the act/event of V-ing'	*surrender, catch*
ACTION	'the action of V-ing'	*fight, review*
INSTANCE	'an instance of V-ing'	*belch, frown*
PROCESS	'the process of V-ing or being V-ed'	*rot*
PRODUCT	'the thing that is created/comes into being by V-ing'	*tear*, as in '[...] making the *tear* worse'
RESULT	'the outcome of V-ing'	*divorce*
STATE	'the state of V-ing or being V-ed'	*regret, hope*
INSTRUMENT/MEANS	'the thing used for V-ing'	*cure, clog*
LOCATION	'the place where one/sthg V-s or is V-ed'	*dump, seat*
DIRECTION	'the direction or path of V-ing'	*decline, ascent*
AGENT	'one who V-s'	cook, flirt
PATIENT	'the thing V-ed, thing affected or moved by V-ing but not created'	*purchase, kill*
MEASURE	'how much is V-ed', 'measure of the degree to which sthg in V-ed'	*pinch, weight*

Derivative senses were sometimes classified as expressing more than one semantic category, or a combination of them, for example, the verbal categories CAUSATIVE/RESULTATIVE often appear in combination, for the difficult separation between the two.[31] Nominal categories that have also been found difficult to dissociate are, for example, ACTION/EVENT, ACTION/INSTANCE, and RESULT/STATE.

For the classification of base senses, ontological types or categories were used. Ontological categories are considered appropriate for the semantic classification

[31] Note, however, that according to Rainer (1993, cited in Plag 1999: 125), CAUSATIVE verbs are deadjectival and RESULTATIVE verbs are denominal.

of base senses in conversion because, as claimed in Schulte (2015: 4.1), ontological categories have been used in linguistic research from very different backgrounds and are candidates for universally accepted classifications. Specifically, the classifications by Dixon (2005) and Levin (1993) were used to classify base verb senses. For nouns, the classifications by Szymanek (1988), Dixon (2005), Lieber (2004); Murphy (2010), Haselow (2011), and Schulte (2015) were used.

3.2.4 Application of Marchand's (1964) criteria in conversion

This section describes and exemplifies the application of each criterion in the sample of noun/verb conversion-related terms. Based on the principle that word meaning must consider the role of senses, each criterion was applied at the level of sense. This entails sense classification of the BNC concordances for each lexeme, based on the sense information from the OED.[32] For convenience, a short description of the criteria by Marchand is provided within each subsection. Note that the semantic criteria are presented following the order in Marchand (1964) and are followed by the related criteria of FO and RR.

3.2.4.1 Semantic dependence (SD)

In this study, Marchand's (1964) criterion of SD was dealt with according to the OED senses. Marchand (1964: 12) claimed that "[t]he word that for its analysis is dependent on the content of the other pair member is necessarily the derivative", for example, *knife*^{N} > *knife*^{V} 'to V with a *knife*'.

After the manual classification of the BNC concordances of each lexeme into senses (following the sense information in the OED), the criterion of SD was measured. It may be worth recalling that, regarding the OED sense classification, Arabic-numbered senses (for example, 1, 2, etc.) were considered, and subsenses (represented by alphabetical letters, for example, 2a, 2b, etc.) were only considered when relevant. Also, the criterion was applied to the senses that appear in use in the BNC. In the application of SD, each sense was marked as follows:

i. Not showing SD (–) to the conversion-related senses, for example, *anagram*^{N} "1. A transposition of the letters of a word, name, or phrase, whereby a new word or phrase is formed." does not show SD to its verbal counterpart.
ii. Showing SD (+) to the conversion-related pair's senses, for example, *anagram*^{V} "2. intr. To make anagrams". Added senses, that is, senses which do not appear represented in the OED, were also marked as showing SD based on definitions in other sources. For instance, sense 2 for *swoon*^{N} is not represented in the OED and was added after checking several entries

[32] The meaning of the lexemes was checked in the OED at different intervals of time during the period 2020–2023.

in *urbandictionary*:[33] "A person usually male who is very attractive." or "A word mainly used on the internet or chatrooms. This is usually addressing males but may be for females too. It is used when the is a hot/sexy/cute boy that someone would "**swoon**" over. Or in other words drool fall in love with tap etc.". This sense was interpreted as showing SD (+).

iii. Additionally, the label (+?) is used for senses interpreted as showing SD towards the base but where this may be debatable. For instance, *tack*^{V5}, is defined in the OED as "transitive. = tackle v. 3. (to harness a horse) Usually with up. Also intransitive". Even though it does not directly refer to the related noun *tack*^{N7}, it is interpreted as "to put a tack^{N} to a horse". Also noted as showing SD but not as clearly (+?) is *swot*^{N}, for which an additional sense is identified in context:

(34) *[...] Techniques "at the bell" are four (1) living with the headlines and main outlines of your subject by the use of* **swot/n** *cards; (2) rehearsing old papers (or papers concocted from textbook examples) under examination conditions, with [...]* (BNC)

In this context, "swot cards" are understood as cards used to study, and thus the noun is interpreted as referring to the action of the verb "intransitive. To work hard at one's studies; to 'bone up'. Also transitive, to 'get up', 'mug up' (a subject); more rarely, without up." (OED). This sense was added, because the senses corresponding to the noun in the OED did not include it: "1. Work or study at school or college; in early use spec. mathematics. Hence gen. labour, toil." and "2. One who studies hard". Only sense 2 in the OED and the added sense are attested in the BNC.

iv. A question mark (?) is reserved to cases where definitions do not clearly show SD and deciding on an analysis of SD as (+) or (–) is questionable based on the OED definitions alone, for example, *aggregate*^{V} "1. a. transitive. To gather into one whole or mass; to collect together, assemble; to mass." and the more directly related sense of *aggregate*^{N} "1. A complex whole, mass, or body formed by the union of numerous units or particles; an assemblage, a collection". In this case, both the nominal and verbal senses were marked as unclear because an interpretation of the verb as the base (V_GROUP EXISTENCE_HERD) and the noun as the RESULT of the action is most likely, and yet, based on the definition alone, the noun may be analysed as basic too (N_THING_MASS) and the verb as RESULTATIVE 'to gather into a N'.

The SD analysis for the senses was then contrasted between pairs, which also allowed for cases where various directions were involved (based on the SD criterion analysis) to be identified. Whether a sense is analysed as clearly showing SD (+) or interpreted as showing SD but with some doubt (+?) is not expected

33 <https://www.urbandictionary.com/define.php?term=Swoon>.

to be an issue. This is because the analysis of SD is later contrasted by related senses. If one of the members in a pair is marked as showing SD (+) or showing SD with some doubt (+?), this is interpreted as indicating a directionality if the related sense is marked as not showing SD (–), however, if the related sense is also marked as showing SD, the analysis of directionality is unclear between the senses.

Table 4 presents the pair *fuss*^{V}/*fuss*^{N} as illustration of the analysis of the criterion of SD in this study.

Table 4: Analysis of the criterion of SD at the level of sense for the conversion-related pair *fuss*$^{N/V}$

Lexeme	(OED) sense	Semantic category	SD (+/–/?/+?)	Related senses
fuss^{N2}	1. a. *A bustle or commotion out of proportion to the occasion; a needless or excessive display of concern about anything; ostentatious or officious activity.* [...]	ABSTRACT CONCEPT	–	
fuss^{N2}	2. *A state of (more or less ludicrous) consternation or anxiety.*	STATE	–	
fuss^{N2}	3. [< **fuss v.**] *One who* **fusses.**	**AGENT**	+	V, 1, 2
fuss^{V}	1. *intransitive. To make a* **fuss;** *to be in a bustle; to busy oneself restlessly about trifles; to move fussily (about, up and down, etc.).*	**EFFECTIVE**	+	N2, 1
fuss^{V}	Added sense: 1 ext. *Said of other things, not people.*	TRANSF. NATURE SIMILATIVE		
fuss^{V}	Added sense: 1b. *'To* **fuss** *over': to pay excessive attention to or concern for something.*	EXT_SIMILATIVE MANNER		
fuss^{V}	2. *transitive. To put into a* **fuss;** *to agitate, worry; to bother about trifles. Also to fuss up (? dialect): to flatter, treat with fussy politeness.*	**CAUSATIVE/ RESULTATIVE**	+	N2, 2

As can be seen in Table 4, three senses of the noun are attested in the BNC, of which two senses do not seem to show SD to the verb (marked with a minus sign (–)), while one of those senses (3) shows SD to the verb (+), as the counterpart verb is used in the definition of this sense (in bold) "*One who* **fusses.**", and also, clear reference to the verb entry is made, a derivation direction even being indicated in this case "[< **fuss v.**]". On the other hand, two senses of the verb are attested (although sense 1 develops presents transferred or extended senses itself too, hence marked in grey, and for which no SD is analysed as it is assumed that the SD analysis is the same as in the main sense). Of these two senses, both are analysed as showing SD to the N, because the counterpart noun is used in the definition of the senses (also in bold).

The criterion of SD in this pair is interpreted as indicating a bidirectional sequence of the type Noun-to-Verb-to-Noun (N>V>N), where the noun senses 1 and 2 are bases, the verb creates two directly related senses to the nominal senses as shown in column *Related senses*, and then a new sense is created for the noun in relation to any of the senses of the verb, as represented in Figure 6, with specification of the semantic category for each sense:

$N^{\text{ABSTRACT CONCEPT}} \rightarrow V^{\text{EFFECTIVE}}$

$\rightarrow N^{\text{AGENT}}$

$N^{\text{STATE}} \rightarrow V^{\text{CAUSATIVE / RESULTATIVE}}$

Figure 6: Exemplification of related categories for the pair *fuss*$^{N/V}$.

3.2.4.2 Restrictions of usage (RU)

Regarding the criterion of RU, Marchand's standpoint is that "[i]f one word has a smaller range of usage than its pair member, it must be considered the derivative" (1964: 13). Marchand listed various possibilities for RU, repeated here for convenience (1969: 13–14), specifically:

i. for one of the words not to be generally accepted while the other is commonly used (RU1),
ii. for a word to be restricted to certain forms as one of the word classes while it is not restricted as the other (RU2),
iii. for a word to be used as half serious or semifacetious (RU3), or
iv. to take a literary or poetic use (RU4).[34]

For a more detailed description of RU types, cf. Section 2.5.6. In the study of the applicability of the criteria for directionality, the criterion of RU was measured at the level of sense, based on OED information. Independently of the type of RU identified, the senses in our sample were classified as:

[34] Figurative and extended senses were quantified as restrictions in this study only in some cases: if a sense contrasts with the related sense in the counterpart lexeme in that just one of the senses can only be used figuratively while the counterpart has a general use, then the figurative sense would be analysed as restricted (+). If a specific sense covers the use of the related sense in the counterpart lexeme and additionally it is described as with the possibility of a figurative interpretation, then this is not counted as restricted (–), because this specification would rather widen the SR of the sense in question (Ruz & Cetnarowska 2023: 14).

i. Not showing RU (–), for example, *soak*^{V} "a. To lie immersed in a liquid for a considerable time, so as to be saturated or permeated with it; to become thoroughly wet or soft in this manner."
ii. Showing RU (+), for example, *soak*^{N} "1. c. dialect. A piece of marshy, swampy ground."

The criterion of RU was then analysed by comparing the related senses in the sample pairs, and by considering the total number of senses showing any restrictions for each pair according to the OED.

Table 5: Restrictions of usage in the pair *skive*$^{N3/V3}$ (OED). Sense restrictions appear in grey font

Lexeme	OED sense no. and definition	Semantic category	RU (+/–)	RU type	nSen +RU
skive^{N3}	2. *colloquial (chiefly British). b. An instance of avoiding work or a duty by staying away or leaving early. Frequently in on the skive.*	INSTANCE	+	RU1	1/1
skive^{V3}	2. *transitive. Originally U.S. College slang. To avoid (work or a duty) by leaving or being absent; (now) esp. to play truant from (school). Now chiefly British colloquial.*	V_ACTION_ AVOID	+	RU1	2/2
skive^{V3}	3. *colloquial (chiefly British). a. intransitive. Originally Military slang. To avoid work or a duty by staying away or leaving early; to shirk; (sometimes) spec. to play truant from school. Also with off (in prepositional phrase specifying the activity, duty, etc.).*	V_ACTION_ AVOID	+	RU1	

Table 5 exemplifies the analysis of RU for the pair *skive*$^{N3/V3}$. The table specifies the application of the criterion of RU in this study with the pair *skive*$^{N3/V3}$. Restrictions are marked in grey font in the second column, which provides the OED senses. The fourth column, *RU*, specifies whether a sense is restricted (+) or not (–). The restriction type according to the ones listed by Marchand (1964) is specified in the fifth column, *RU type*, and the number of restricted senses out of the total number of senses in use for each lexeme is specified in the last column *nSen +RU*. In the example pair *skive*$^{N3/V3}$, this criterion does not indicate a directionality, as all senses in use are marked as restricted.

3.2.4.3 Semantic range: Qualitative analysis (SR)

Regarding the criterion of SR, Marchand (1964: 14) argues that "[o]f two homophonous words exhibiting similar sets of semantic features the one with the smaller field of reference is the derivative", for example, *convert*^{V} > *convert*^{N} 'one who has been converted to a religion/belief'. SR is measured in this study based on a qualitative analysis or comparison of the senses for the lexemes in the conversion sample.

The analysis of SR is exemplified for the pair *whimper*[N/V] in Table 6, for which it is interpreted as "≈", that is, as similar, with few differences.

Table 6: Semantic range (SR) for the pair *whimper*[N/V]

Lexeme	OED senses	Sense	SR
whimper[N]	1. a. A feeble, broken cry, as of a child about to burst into tears; a fretful cry expressive of complaint or grief.	1	≈
	b. A similar cry of dogs, etc.	2	
	c. transferred. Of inanimate things.	3	
	2. not with a bang but a whimper: see bang n.1 2b.	4	
whimper[V]	1. a. intransitive. To utter a feeble, whining, broken cry, as a child about to burst into tears; to make a low complaining sound. / b. figurative. To complain pulingly; to 'whine': esp. for, after, †to something. / c. transitive. To utter or express in a whimper.	1	
	2. intransitive. Of an animal, esp. a dog: To utter a feeble querulous cry.	2	
	3. Of running water or the wind: To make a continuous plaintive murmur. Also transitive.	3	

The possible interpretations of the SR of a pair are as follows:

i. The pair has a similar SR (≈), as in *whimper*[N/V] above. Although the noun presents an extra phrasal use, it is unclear whether this sense is relevant for the directionality thus the lexemes were analysed as showing a similar SR. Or, for example, *hex*[N/V], the nominal use referring to "[a] magic spell or curse." and the verb with a PERFORMATIVE interpretation "intransitive. To practise witchcraft. Also transitive, to bewitch, to cast a spell on."
ii. One of the lexemes has a wider SR (>), for example, *bayonet*[N] > *bayonet*[V]. In this case, the nominal senses refer principally to "a stabbing instrument" (INSTRUMENT) and are also metonymically extended to refer to "military force" and to "soldiers armed with the instrument", and (figuratively) extended to refer to people or other instruments with a similar function/motion. The verb only presents an INSTRUMENTAL sense "1. transitive. To stab or pierce with a bayonet."
iii. One of the lexemes has a slightly wider SR, or the lexemes' SR is closely similar (≳), for example, *dwarf*[N] ≳ *dwarf*[V]. In this case, the noun shows more specific extended senses in use, while the verb senses are more general.

Because considering the number of senses as indicative of directionality does not prove a useful method in a pilot study (cf. Ruz 2025: Section 3.3.3.3), the criterion of nSen was not studied for the directionality sample. This is partly because:

i. The representation of senses in the OED is not consistent (cf. Section 3.2.2.2). This is also the case, for example, in *whimper*$^{N/V}$ (see Table 6 above), for which a comparison of the nSen of the lexemes based on the Arabic-numbered senses provided in the OED alone lists two senses for *whimper*^{N}, while *whimper*^{V} shows three senses. After sense re-numbering (under column *Sense* in the table), *whimper*^{N} could be interpreted as taking four senses, while *whimper*^{V} would take three senses.
ii. The extent to which a difference in the number of senses between a pair, be it wider or narrower, may serve to indicate a difference in the SR of the lexemes is unclear.

3.2.4.4 Semantic pattern (SP)

Regarding the criterion of SP, Marchand (1964: 15) stated that "[c]ertain words have characteristic meanings which mark them as derivatives", for example, *father*^{V} 'to act as a father'. The criterion of SP was also measured at the level of sense based on OED information in the study of the applicability of the criteria for directionality in a sample of noun/verb conversion. Specifically, the BNC concordances are assigned a sense, and the senses in use are marked as follows:

i. Not showing a SP typical of a derivative (–), for example, *beep*^{N} "The sound made by a horn on a motor car or other vehicle; a short high-pitched sound such as is emitted by an echo-sounder, a radar device, etc. Also attributive."
ii. Showing a SP typical of a derivative (+), for example, *beep*^{V} in both of its senses "1. transitive. To sound (a horn); to make (something) emit a short high-pitched sound; to indicate by sounding beeps.; 2. intransitive. To emit beeps."
iii. Additionally, senses may be classified as showing SP but where this is debatable (+?). For instance, sense 3 for *chaperon(e)*^{N} "3. b. transferred. One who escorts; guide, conductor." is marked as showing SP to the verb sense "1. transitive. To act as chaperon to (a young lady); to escort." but with doubts (+?). This is because it is interpreted as showing a SP typical of a derivative "one who Vs" expressing the semantic category AGENT. However, it may be argued that, as the OED indicates, it is transferred from the main sense of the noun "3. a. figurative. A person, esp. a married or elderly woman, who, for the sake of propriety, accompanies a young unmarried lady in public, as guide and protector.", and thus not related by conversion, but simply an extension within the same word-class category. The verb sense is marked as showing SP (+) to the noun sense 3a, marked as not showing SP.
iv. The label (?) is reserved for senses for which an analysis of SP is unclear for example, *hoax*^{N} "1. b. concrete. One who is a deception, 'a fraud'." (AGENT), which may simply be an extended use from the nominal sense "1. a. An act of hoaxing; a humorous or mischievous deception, usually taking the

> form of a fabrication of something fictitious or erroneous, told in such a manner as to impose upon the credulity of the victim.", which however shows SP to the verb sense "transitive. To deceive or take in by inducing to believe an amusing or mischievous fabrication or fiction; to play upon the credulity of".

As in the analysis of SD, whether a sense is analysed as clearly showing SP (+) or interpreted as showing SP but with some doubts (+?) is not expected to be an issue because the analysis is later contrasted by related senses, within the pairs of lexemes. Table 7 exemplifies the analysis of the criterion of SP for the pair *fuss*^{V}/*fuss*^{N}.

Table 7: Analysis of the criterion of SP at the level of sense for the conversion-related pair *fuss*$^{N/V}$

Lexeme	OED sense no. and definition	Semantic category	Paraphrase	SP (+/–/?/+?)
fuss^{N2}	1. a. *A bustle or commotion out of proportion to the occasion; a needless or excessive display of concern about anything; ostentatious or officious activity.* [...]	ABSTRACT CONCEPT		–
fuss^{N2}	2. *A state of (more or less ludicrous) consternation or anxiety.*	STATE		–
fuss^{N2}	3. [< **fuss v.**] *One who* **fusses.**	**AGENT**	One who Vs	+
fuss^{V}	1. *intransitive. To make a* **fuss**; *to be in a bustle; to busy oneself restlessly about trifles; to move fussily (about, up and down, etc.).*	**EFFECTIVE**	To make a N	+
fuss^{V}	Added: 1 ext. *Said of other things, not people.*	TRANSF. NATURE SIMILATIVE		
fuss^{V}	Added: 1b. '*To* **fuss** *over': to pay excessive attention to or concern for something.*	EXT_SIMILATIVE MANNER		
fuss^{V}	2. *transitive. To put into a* **fuss**; *to agitate, worry; to bother about trifles. Also to fuss up (? dialect): to flatter, treat with fussy politeness.*	**CAUSATIVE/ RESULTATIVE**	To put into a N (STATE)	+

As can be seen in the table, three senses of the noun are attested in the BNC, two of which senses do not show a SP typical of a derivative (–), and only one of the senses (3) shows a SP typical of a derivative paraphrased as 'One who Vs'. On the other hand, two senses of the verb are attested in the BNC, both showing a SP typical of derivatives, the first sense paraphrased as 'To make a N', and sense 2 as 'To put into a N (STATE)'.

3.2.4.5 Frequency of occurrence (FO)

As previously noted, Marchand (1964) mentions frequency of occurrence (hereafter FO for the criterion) too in relation to RU, such that, if a word is less commonly used than its counterpart, then, this may be expressed in terms of frequency. In this study, FO is analysed as a separate, though clearly not unrelated criterion. Specifically, a comparison of the frequency of occurrence of the senses involved in each pair is carried out. Normalized frequencies (NF, here referring to the number of occurrences of a lexeme per million tokens) are used.

Regarding FO, it must be noted again that, if a reliable comparison of the frequency of the lexemes or of their senses in use is the goal, a revision and classification of the concordances ought to be made first (with special consideration of the issues mentioned in Sections 3.2.2.1 and 3.2.2.2). In a comparison at the level of sense, the reason is clear, but even for a comparison of the frequency of occurrence by lexemes, a revision of the concordances is necessary. This need is clear in cases where various homonymous lexemes are available, but the overall frequency of lexemes may vary to a certain extent even regardless of homonymy. See for instance the examples of Tables 8 and 9.

Table 8: Exemplification of the variation of the raw frequency of some terms of the sample after concordance reclassification for the effect of homonymy

Term/Pair	Noun initial freq.	Verb initial freq.	Noun revised freq.	Verb revised freq.
graft	185	187	210	162
graft$^{N1/V1}$			122	147
graft$^{N3/V2}$			11	1
graft$^{N4/V3}$			52	9
graft$^{N5/V4}$			25	5
mace	77	12	87	2
mace$^{N5/V3}$			5	2
mace^{N1}			19	
mace^{N2}			62	
mace^{N4}			1	
mash	103	129	126	106
mash$^{N1/V1}$			122	95
mash^{N2}			1	
mash^{N}			3	
mash^{V2}				1
mash^{V3}				10

Table 8 shows three examples where the lexemes' frequency varies after concordance reclassification and identification of homonyms. For *mash*, for instance, corpus frequency data indicates that the verb (n=129) is more frequent than the noun (n=103). After revision and reclassification of the concordances, however, not only is the noun (n=126) more frequent than the verb (n=106), but some of the concordances are identified as examples of unrelated homonymous lexemes and are thus discarded. Unrelated homonyms may have a more relevant effect on the included pair frequency in other cases, for example, *mace*, the frequency of the pair being reduced to five nominal occurrences and two verbal occurrences after the exclusion of unrelated examples. The picture changes also in the case of *graft*, both because some concordances wrongly tagged as noun or verb are reclassified, and because various related pairs are found and thus included separately in the analysis.

Table 9: Exemplification of the variation of the raw frequency of some terms of the sample after concordance reclassification

Term	Noun initial freq.	Verb initial freq.	Noun revised freq.	Verb revised freq.
barter	83	109	121	71
pinion	29	19	21	27
varnish	334	99	358	75
vow	320	630	327	623

Table 9 shows examples of the variation in the frequency of lexemes after reclassification of the concordances, for pairs for which homonymy does not play a role. It seems that the variation in lexeme frequency after a reclassification and revision of the concordances does not change the overall picture for most cases in the sample, for example, *varnish*$^{N/V}$ or *vow* $^{N/V}$, where the interpretation is that the noun is still more frequent than the verb in the case of *varnish*$^{N/V}$, and the verb remains more frequent than the noun for the pair *vow* $^{N/V}$. However, instances can be found in which the picture does change, for example, in the analysis of FO at the level of lexeme, *barter*^{V} is more frequently used than *barter*^{N} according to the frequencies given by the corpus, or *pinion*^{N} is more frequently used than its counterpart *pinion*^{V}. Revision and reclassification of the BNC concordances for each lexeme shows that the case is otherwise. Note that raw frequencies are provided as this is just an example, and that more specific results concerning the criterion of FO and its application are provided in Section 4.2.6.

The application of the criterion at the level of sense was then carried out by comparing the frequency of each of the senses for each lexeme and their relation(s). This was possible, as each BNC concordance was classified according to the OED senses.

A final relevant aspect is that it remains unclear whether the difference in the frequency of occurrence by sense pairs is significant or not.

For a more reliable interpretation of the data, a Chi-squared test (χ^2) was performed using the Excel function *CHISQ.TEST*. This test fits here as it allows to statistically assess whether the observed differences between pairs are significant ($P < 0.05$) or are due to random variation ($P > 0.05$), providing a more robust data-driven approach to evaluating frequency differences.

3.2.4.6 Range of registers (RR)

For the criterion of RR, this study uses the BNC register distribution data to study the range of registers covered by the senses of each lexeme. The base hypothesis is that the derived lexeme and their senses would cover a smaller range of registers than the base (cf. Marchand 1964: 14).

RR was measured as a quantitative criterion at the level of sense. For this purpose, all concordances for each lexeme were extracted from the BNC alongside the metadata of their register usage. Specifically, RR was initially compared between lexemes/senses following:

i. Lee's (2001) proposed classificatory scheme, which groups the BNC registers into twelve main groups or "super genres" (2021: 57–58).
ii. "David Lee's classification" information extracted from the BNC, which classifies BNC concordances into 71 registers or genres, for example, *W_fict_prose*, *W_non_ac_soc_science*, *S_interview_oral_history*, *S_brdcast_news*, etc. This information allows the classification of the concordances into written vs spoken modes, and into specific registers (for example *fiction*) or subregisters (for example *prose*), when relevant.

Once the concordances were extracted and classified by senses, the range of registers covered by each sense/lexeme was calculated, together with the frequency for each of the registers in use for each sense/lexeme. Calculations were carried out with Excel and Python, in *Google Colaboratory*,[35] for easier extraction of the registers in use for each of the senses and their frequency. An example of the organization of the data by sense and register is provided in Table 10 for the three various lexemes in use for the term *sledge*.

[35] Also known as *Google Colab*, or simply *Colab*, this platform is introduced by Bisong "as an alternative platform to quickly spin up a high-performance computing infrastructure running Jupyter notebooks for rapid data science and data modeling tasks" (2019: 64). This platform can be accessed for free at <https://colab.research.google.com/>.

Table 10: Register classification of *sledge* by senses. The absolute frequency of each register is under column number four *Freq*.

W-class	Mode	David Lee's classification	Freq.	Lee's (2001) classification	Sense	OED entry, sense
V	Written	W_fict_prose	1	W_fict	2	V1, 2
V	Written	W_fict_prose	5	W_fict	4	V2, 2
V	Written	W_misc	3	W_other	4	V2, 2
V	Spoken	S_conv	1	S_other	4	V2, 2
V	Written	W_ac_nat_science	1	W_ac	4	V2, 2
V	Spoken	S_brdcast_discussn	1	S_brdcast	4	V2, 2
V	Written	W_misc	1	W_other	6	V3, 1
V	Written	W_newsp_other_report	2	W_newsp	6	V3, 1
V	Written	W_pop_lore	2	W_other	6	V3, 1
N	Written	W_ac_humanities_arts	1	W_ac	1a	N1, 1a
N	Written	W_biography	1	W_other	1a	N1, 1a
N	Written	W_fict_prose	1	W_fict	1a	N1, 1a
N	Written	W_non_ac_humanities_arts	1	W_non_ac	1a	N1, 1a
N	Written	W_pop_lore	1	W_other	1a	N1, 1a
N	Spoken	S_conv	1	S_other	1a	N1, 1a
N	Spoken	S_interview_oral_history	1	S_interv	1a	N1, 1a
N	Written	W_instructional	2	W_other	1a	N1, 1a
N	Written	W_misc	2	W_other	1a	N1, 1a
N	Written	W_news_script	2	W_other	1a	N1, 1a
N	Written	W_newsp_other_reportage	3	W_newsp	1a	N1, 1a
N	Written	W_ac_humanities_arts	2	W_ac	1c	N1, new
N	Spoken	S_conv	1	S_other	2a	N2, 1a
N	Written	W_ac_humanities_arts	6	W_ac	2a	N2, 1a
N	Written	W_ac_nat_science	2	W_ac	2a	N2, 1a
N	Written	W_ac_polit_law_edu	1	W_ac	2a	N2, 1a
N	Written	W_ac_medicine	1	W_ac	2a	N2, 1a
N	Written	W_biography	2	W_other	2a	N2, 1a
N	Written	W_fict_poetry	1	W_fict	2a	N2, 1a
N	Written	W_fict_prose	66	W_fict	2a	N2, 1a
N	Written	W_misc	71	W_other	2a	N2, 1a
N	Written	W_newsp_brdsht_nat_misc	1	W_newsp	2a	N2, 1a
N	Written	W_newsp_other_social	1	W_newsp	2a	N2, 1a
N	Written	W_non_ac_humanities_arts	2	W_non_ac	2a	N2, 1a
N	Written	W_pop_lore	10	W_other	2a	N2, 1a
N	Written	W_biography	2	W_other	2a	N2, 1a
N	Written	W_biography	5	W_other	3a	N2, 2a

(Continued)

Table 10: *(Continued)*

W-class	Mode	David Lee's classification	Freq.	Lee's (2001) classification	Sense	OED entry, sense
N	Written	W_fict_prose	2	W_fict	3a	N2, 2a
N	Written	W_misc	2	W_other	3a	N2, 2a
N	Written	W_non_ac_humanities_arts	2	W_non_ac	3a	N2, 2a
N	Written	W_non_ac_nat_science	1	W_non_ac	4	N2, 3
N	Written	W_biography	5	W_other	3a	N2, 2a

Following the information in Table 10, the conclusion would, for example, be that the lexeme *sledge*[N1] has a wider register use compared to its counterpart *sledge*[V1], because the noun appears in various written and spoken texts in the BNC, while for the verb a single register is found. This may be as a result of the difference in the frequency of occurrence of the lexemes in the pair, or the other way around. In many cases, however, it remains unclear whether the difference in the range of registers covered by pairs is significant or not, and, thus, to which extent the results of RR can be considered reliable for directionality. Fisher's exact test was selected to test whether the difference in RR between the pairs is significant. This is because Fisher's exact test is claimed to be more reliable for the estimation of statistical significance (p-values) for small-size categorical data, where a Chi-squared test (as applied for FO, cf. Section 3.2.4.5) could be inaccurate (Brezina 2018: 113). This test was carried out with Python, in Google Colab.

However, the applicability of this test to our data remains unclear. When Lee's classification into twelve registers was tested, Fisher's exact test indicates a significant difference between 4.87 % of the pairs, possibly because the register classification only uses twelve categories, and this test is not reliable to decide whether the difference is significant or not. When the BNC's David Lee's classification into 71 registers is considered, Fisher's exact test indicates a significant difference between 40.3 % of the pairs of senses: As a more fine-grained register classification is used and the categorical data are bigger, the test indicates that there is a statistically significant difference between the register use of a larger number of pairs. Consequently, results are presented in subsequent sections only for RR according to David Lee's corpus retrieval classification. For a more detailed comparison of the results of RR according to the two classifications (into twelve and into 71 registers), see Ruz (2025).

3.3 Distribution of senses into orders of derivation

This book bases the study of directionality on the level of sense. Thus, for the relevance of the criteria used in assessing directionality, senses were first systematically arranged, related, and ascribed a direction of derivation. Sense organization is based on their denotation, which typically coincides with the analysis of the criteria of SD and SP. However, even when the direction based on the criterion of SD or SP is unclear, a direction is ascribed based on a semantic interpretation. When the senses of the pairs refer to each other and a semantic arrangement is unclear, two analyses were undertaken: Each lexeme was presumed to be the base in each analysis, in order to see which analysis proves relevant for each criteria, and whether these would indicate the same direction or not, for example, in *whoop*$^{N/V}$, where SD and SP are marked as unclear, but FO, RU, or RR may indicate a direction.

The distribution of senses into orders of derivation results in the following picture for the 226[36] pairs of lexemes of the sample:

i. Of the total of 1487 senses analysed for the lexemes, 488 senses are either nominal or verbal senses categorized as base or extended senses within the same lexeme (N^0 or V^0),[37] and to which no senses of the counterpart lexeme are directly connected,[38] for example (cf. Table 11):

(38) *jog*^{V} OED sense 1a "a. transitive. To shake or move (a heavy body) with a push or jerk; to throw up with a jerk; to shake up".

---

36 Two entries from the initial list obtained (*incense* and *queer*) were removed because, despite the seeming derivational connection, the OED does not give enough evidence to justify their conversion (on the same footing meaning degree of certainty) as the rest of the entries.

37 For easier data representation, sometimes directions are formalized with specification of level of derivation, for example, $N^1{>}V^2$ or $V^1{>}N^2$ vs *Noun-to-Verb* or *Verb-to-Noun* in D2, respectively.

38 By "senses related *directly* by conversion" this study means senses which are analysed as deriving from a specific sense in the pair lexeme, for example, the following sense for the noun and the verb *belch* are analysed as directly related by conversion:

(35) *belch*^{V} (SOUND EMISSION)
"1. intransitive. To void wind noisily from the stomach through the mouth, to eructate." (OED), for example, "*Manolo* **belched**, *and excused himself.*" (BNC)

(36) *belch*^{N} (INSTANCE/RESULT)
"1. An eructation." (OED), for example, "*He leered at Robyn, and masked a* **belch** *with the back of his hand.*" (BNC)

This is by contrast with senses derived within one of the lexemes, for example, the following verb sense:

(37) *belch*^{V} (MANNER OF SPEAKING)
"2. transitive. To ejaculate, to give vent to; to vent with vehemence or violence (words, feelings). [...]" (OED), for example, "*The thin man sniffed. 'Don't you think you ought to be asking some?' 'I am a qualified physician,'* **belched** *the other. 'I know the answers.'*" (BNC)

ii. 211 senses are nominal or verbal senses marked as extended within the same lexeme in order one (N^1 or V^1), and eight are extended senses in order two (N^2 or V^2). Directly related senses in the counterpart lexeme are found for 27 of the extended senses (12 %). That is, senses initially not directly associated with a particular base sense (in N^0 or V^0) but analysed as emerging (for instance by sense extension) within the presumed derivative by conversion are found to further derive senses in the counterpart (base) lexeme too, for example (cf. Table 13):

(39) *holler*^{N} OED sense 3 "3. spec. in the Southern States of America, a work-song." (ABSTRACT_MUSIC/PRACTICE)
> *holler*^{V} OED sense 3 "Also: to sing a 'holler' (see holler n.1). Occasionally transitive." (PERFORMATIVE)

iii. 798 senses were related in the first derivational order (D1), that is, the criteria were compared for 399 sense pairs (N^0>V^1 or V^0>N^1), for example (cf. Table 11):

(40) *jog*^{V} OED sense 4 "4. a. intransitive. To walk or ride with a jolting pace, 'to move with small shocks like those of a low trot' (Johnson); to move on at a heavy or laboured pace, to trudge; hence, to move on, go on, be off. *More recently, to run at a gentle pace (esp. as part of a 'keep-fit' schedule).*" (EXT_MANNER OF MOTION)
> *jog*^{N} OED sense 2 "2. (a) The act of jogging or moving mechanically up and down. *(b) The act of jogging along (see jog v. 4)*; a slow, measured walk, trot, or run; also transferred, for example, of the rhythm of the verse." (ACTION/EVENT)

iv. 134 senses were related in the second derivational order (D2), that is, 67 pairs of senses (expected direction: N^1>V^2 or V^1>N^2), for example (cf. Table 12):

(41) *picket*^{N} OED sense 4 "a. Military. A small detachment of troops, sent out to watch for the approach of the enemy (also as outlying picket), or held in quarters in readiness for such duty and to guard against sudden attack (also as inlying picket); any detachment of troops sent out to perform a particular duty. Also: a single soldier so employed. Cf. out-picquet n. Earliest in picket guard n. at Compounds 2. In the British Army Regulations spelt piquet. / b. Military colloquial. Short for picket duty n. at Compounds 1b." (HUMAN_COLLECTIVE)

> *picket*^{V} OED 3b "3. Military. b. transitive. To post (soldiers, etc.) as a picket; (also) to occupy, watch, or guard as a picket. Also figurative and in extended use." (CAUSATIVE/SIMILATIVE)
> *picket*^{N} OED 5b "[...] (in singular): the act of doing this, or the blockade so formed." (EVENT)

Tables 11 to 13 below exemplify sense distribution by orders of derivation for the pairs *jog*$^{N/V}$, *picket*$^{N/V}$, and *holler*$^{N/V}$:

Table 11: Sense distribution for *jog*$^{N/V}$ (senses related by conversion appear in the same row)

V⁰ sense	Semantic category	N¹ sense	Semantic category
1a	CAUSATIVE_MANNER OF MOTION		
1b fig	EXT_FIG_CAUSATIVE_MANNER OF MOTION		
2a	CAUSATIVE_MANNER OF MOTION		
2b	EXT_FIG_CAUSATIVE_MANNER OF MOTION	1 fig	FIG_ACTION/INSTANCE/EVENT
3	MANNER OF MOTION		
4	EXT_MANNER OF MOTION	2	ACTION/EVENT
4c	EXT_FIG_MANNER OF MOTION		

Table 12: Sense distribution for *picket*$^{N/V}$ (senses related by conversion appear in the same row)

N^0 sense	Semantic category	V^1 sense	Semantic category	N^2 sense	Semantic category
1a	ARTEFACT	1b	INSTRUMENTAL		
3a	EXT_ARTEFACT				
4	HUMAN_COLLECTIVE	3b	CAUSATIVE/SIMILATIVE	5b	EVENT
5	EXT_HUMAN_COLLECTIVE	4	SIMILATIVE	5c	INSTRUMENT

Table 13: Sense distribution for *holler*$^{N/V}$ (senses related by conversion appear in the same row)

V^0 sense	Semantic category	N^1 sense	Semantic category	V^2 sense	Semantic category
1	MANNER OF SPEAKING	1	ACTION/INSTANCE		
		3 (ext/base)	ABSTRACT_ MUSIC/PRACTICE	3	PERFORMATIVE

As the tables show, the distribution of senses into orders of derivation allows for the identification of senses for which no counterpart sense is found (in grey). These senses add to the SR that the lexemes can cover. However, these do not show SD specifically towards any of the senses in the related pair, or a SP typical of a derivative. Thus, only related senses between the pairs are contrasted to identify a direction based on SD, SP, RU, FO, or RR.[39]

39 For the criterion of FO senses are checked for possible cases, for example, where the frequency of occurrence of extended senses is higher than that of the related lexemes.

3.4 Methodological remarks

It may be argued that the results of the criteria for directionality may differ if different corpora are used. True as this may be, largely as a result of the influence of the type and quality of any data source, only changes for a minor number of pairs concerning, for example, FO or RR, or even the SR covered may be expected. This is especially relevant for pairs identified as restricted in use, for example, dialectal, slang, specialized, etc. No significant changes are expected for widely used pairs.

Similarly, the choice of the dictionary may influence the analysis. In this study, the OED was selected as it captures a wide variety of meanings. Use of other resources to analyse senses may affect the outcomes. Still, the combination of both dictionary and corpus data in this study is intended to assist a more comprehensive analysis of the lexemes' senses.

The bias that the above might cause is similar to differences in sample selection or analysis approach, for example, in that:

i. If all concordances of the pairs are considered, as in this study, less common or specialized senses can be identified too. Use of a threshold allows for a more manageable analysis, but it potentially omits senses used less frequently. In this study, many senses with low frequency of occurrence were found. Thus, the inclusion of all senses in use is considered relevant for directionality synchronically (even if extended senses which may not be key for directionality are included too). Admittedly, the method used in this regard has limitations, because manual classification of the concordances into senses is time-consuming, and this is partly why lexemes with a frequency higher than 1,000 were not included in our sample too.
ii. Differences may be found between an analysis at the level of lexeme, that is, by considering core senses, and at the level of sense. Further variation may be expected in higher frequency words, such that they might exhibit a wider range of polysemy. In this study, pairs for which both lexemes present only one sense, as well as polysemous lexemes are represented. Still, as the sample is, by definition, limited, it is not expected to be representative of all the patterns that are possible in conversion.
iii. Differences may be found between an analysis of senses in use and an analysis of all senses, in use or not. Because this study focuses on directionality synchronically (cf. Section 2.4.3.2), lexical history, or obsolete senses (that is, senses not attested in the BNC) are discarded. If these were included, the analysis of directionality would differ for some pairs as regards, for example, the criteria of SD, SP, or SR or, even more generally, the sense distribution into orders of derivation.

Regarding point ii. above, a key aspect of this study is that directionality is researched at the level of sense. Previous research has focused on directionality in conversion at the level of the lexeme (cf. Balteiro 2007 to some extent; Bram 2011; Kisselew et al. 2016, among others). This study aims to test if the semantic and quantitative-distributional criteria prove applicable when applied by senses, and to what extent they do, if at all.

The standpoint is that the results differ according to whether lexemes are analysed as a whole or by senses. This methodological difference is apparent in that, whereas a lexeme analysis (that is, with focus on core senses) leads towards an analysis of conversion in terms of unidirectionality, a sense analysis allows:

i. for the identification of multiple directions for the same pair of lexemes (which may be due to the influence of other lexemes), and, specifically,
ii. for the identification of recursive derivation in conversion.

Regarding point iii. above, it has been found that a diachronic and a synchronic approach to directionality in conversion often lead to contradictory results (Section 2.4.3.2, and references therein). This is because the interest lies in different issues: the former looks at the origin of words in a language, while the latter focuses on sense relations in present-day English. Thus, inconsistencies between, for example, historical criteria (etymological information or attestation dates) and semantic or distributional criteria (the criteria tested in this study) are expected to differ regarding the direction(s) they identify for lexeme pairs. The low consistency found in previous research on directionality between some of the criteria may partly reflect this, together with the issues that the criteria and their application may present too. It is argued here that some of the criteria cannot be compared, because they look at different aspects of language, for example, it does not make sense to compare FO and AD (dates of first attestation), unless a historical corpus with information of the use of senses over time is used. And even then, the analysis would not be free from the constraints associated with the use of dictionaries.

Partly also concerning differences in the approach taken, it was mentioned that directionality may change over time (cf. Section 2.5.7).[40] What is meant by this claim is that the first order of derivation direction identified for a pair may change, for example, because the original sense in one of the pairs may

---

[40] This is in relation to Umbreit's (2010: 309) claim that frequency of occurrence can change over time as the semantic range of base and derived terms may change.

disappear (i.e. it is no longer in use). Note that this applies only within a synchronic approach to directionality, and especially one which considers senses.

While senses in the first order of derivation may no longer be in use, and, thus, may not affect the analysis of directionality, this issue is not exclusive to the senses in the first order of derivation. Sometimes, gaps are found in recursive sense derivation too, which increases the complexity of the directionality analysis in polysemous pairs. This may be for two reasons:

i. senses, base or derived may become obsolete, but the senses directly related in the counterpart lexeme may still be used, or
ii. the specific sense may not be represented in the corpus employed. If this were the case, and because the corpus used in this study contains about a 100 million words, the misrepresentation of a sense is most probably linked to the sense being in restricted use.

Examples (42) and (43) are senses identified for the verb *prick*^{V} and marked as derivative senses based on their semantics (SD or SP), but for which no related senses were attested in the BNC, even though they are represented in the OED (senses (44) and (45), respectively).

(42) *prick*^{V} (one occurrence in the BNC)
sense 5b "†b. intransitive. Archery. To shoot at a mark or prick (prick n. 19); (figurative) to aim at. Obsolete." (OED), for example, "*Prussian muskets* **pricked** *fame from the wood's edge, but the shooting was at too long a range and only one French horse tumbled into the wheat.*" (BNC)

(43) *prick*^{V} (one occurrence in the BNC)
sense 20 "a. transitive. To write or set down (music) by means of pricks or notes; (also) †to write music in (a book) (obsolete). Also intransitive: to write or mark out musical notation. Now chiefly historical." (OED), for example, "*[...] lyrics rendered on the wild side in a predictably debauched drawl; sparse, uneasy music* **pricked** *by the ghosts of previous drug mythologists Lou Reed, Nick Cave, Nico and The Jesus And Mary Chain [...]*" (BNC)

(44) *prick*^{N} (sense not identified in the BNC)
sense 19 "VI. In archery. 19. a. A mark aimed at when shooting an arrow, esp. the centre of the target or the area immediately around the pin (pin n.1 2b); the bullseye; (hence) a target, esp. one at a fixed distance, having such a central mark. Now rare. Contrasted in the latter sense with butt n.7 2 and rover n.2 1a. / †b. twelve (also twenty-four) score prick: a target with a mark in the centre placed 240 (or 480) paces distant, the regular distance at which shooting at the prick was practised. Obsolete." (OED)

(45) *prick*^{N} (sense not identified in the BNC)
sense 3b "b. A mark or dot used in musical notation; (a) (in medieval music) a note; (b) (in later musical notation) a dot placed after a note or rest for various purposes. Obsolete. Cf. prick v. 20a." (OED)

The presumption is that these may be examples of ii. above because the senses:

i. seem to be very specific or in restricted use, most marked as obsolete or rare too, and
ii. present a low frequency of occurrence in the corpus, as only one instance for each sense was identified after concordance classification into the OED senses.

Another methodological decision taken, as described in Section 3.3., is to study the applicability of the criteria for the identification of directionality in conversion at the sense level, by an arrangement of the senses into orders of derivation. Precisely the latter point imposes the need for a presumed direction, but such a direction is only a methodological requirement that is subject to the results found over data analysis.

The identification of directionality based on semantic analysis can be biased, but subjective interpretations are prevented as far as possible in that the semantic analysis carried out in this study is based mainly on OED data, assisted by the usage that the lexemes take in context according to BNC concordances, whenever usage data is not available from the OED.

A key point of this analysis is that, even though the presumed derivational direction suggested between senses may not always be correct, the criteria used to assess directionality are then scrutinized and may prime the opposite derivational direction. Thus, the analysis is not inherently compromised by sense distribution into orders of derivations; if anything, sense distribution would identify the percentage of data for which the criteria and sense organization based on semantics align.

While sense classification into orders of derivation may admittedly introduce bias because semantic criteria are primed, especially the criteria of SD and SP, sense distribution into derivational paradigms is deemed best to test directionality criteria at the level of sense for several reasons:

i. the identification of directionality without any sense organization, for example, by counting the number of total senses that follow a criterion per pair member would lead to unreliable results,
ii. the approach used here accounts for polysemy, which is often a major difficulty in the identification of directionality,
iii. sense organization into derivational orders allows for the representation of subsequent derivation between the senses of the pair members, for example, *clamp*^{N} (INSTRUMENT) → *clamp*^{V} (INSTRUMENT) → *clamp*^{N} (RESULT). Subsequent derivation is observed for 46 pairs in our sample (20 %), for which a total of 67 pairs of senses were identified in the second order of derivation,
iv. this approach allows a more detailed analysis of senses and avoids issues from including extended or figurative senses whenever they do not show

SD or SP to senses in the counterpart lexeme (because figurative senses typically arise within the same lexeme, even if similar senses may be found in the pair member too), and

v. this approach allows for easier identification of pairs of senses by order of derivation.

Regarding point iv. above, and as has been described throughout, extended or figurative senses are sometimes identified and classified as extended within lexemes, and others in connection with senses in the other pair. A direction was analysed only in the latter case. This is in line with Valera's (2017) paper where he shows how sometimes figurative mechanisms give rise to conversion directly, while in others "[...] figurative extension by itself does not have any effect as far as conversion is concerned" (Valera 2017: 6–7). The implications of the sense distribution in this study are discussed next.

3.5 Implications of the sense organization

Section 3.5 comments on the implications of the sense organization used in this study to test the criteria. This study focuses on the direction(s) between noun/verb pairs for the senses classified by order of derivation. This has led to testing how well the criteria work to identify:

i. One direction between converted senses, if only one direction is identified by order of derivation, by one or more senses.
ii. Several directions, for example, where two more or less independent groups of senses are identified for the same lexeme.

This study identifies recursive sense derivation between the pairs of lexemes described as in subsequent orders of derivation, that is, the first or the second order of derivation (D1 or D2). And even if a single direction can often be identified for some pairs, this study does not support an analysis of conversion in terms of *unidirectionality*. In fact, the results show that several directions can be identified for 46 pairs (20.35 %), which is a fairly large number, especially as not all lexemes in our sample show polysemy.

The classification of senses into orders of derivation is here argued to be an effective method for the identification of directionality in conversion. This is especially relevant for polysemous pairs, where several directions may be found according to the senses at hand.[41] Although the classification of the senses may

[41] In this sense, derivational paradigms or networks seem suitable for the study of conversion, specifically of directionality and the semantic patterns that can be identified between paronymous lexemes (understood as in Cruse 1986, cf. the review in Valera & Ruz 2021).

cause bias, because it relies primarily on semantic criteria, this is just as in any approach that relies on sense analysis.[42]

More generally, the classification of senses into orders of derivation touches on the issue of whether conversion:

i. involves different lexemes as in derivation by affixation, or
ii. involves just a pair of lexemes.

The first interpretation of the direction relations between senses is plausible but entails an analysis under which the issue of the proliferation of zeroes would be at hand. Orders of derivation in this study are intended simply as a means for representation of the various directions in sense extension between a pair of lexemes, which is established here according to sense analysis. The proposal here is, thus, that:

i. directionality or relations in conversion are to be studied by senses, and
ii. whereas sense relations may be parallel to the relations found between several pairs of lexemes formed by affixation this is not necessarily the case in conversion, that is, directionality is here considered a property of senses within pairs of lexemes. The difference results from the fact that the semantic capacity of affixes is restricted while in conversion, because there is no formal mark signalling the change in word-class category, the semantic capacity of the lexemes is formally unlimited.

Under the approach adopted in this study, thus, the two representations for the pair *hoover*$^{N/V}$ in our sample,[43] in Figures 7 and 8 below have the same implications. The organization in Figure 7 was used because it allows for easier identification and analysis of the criteria in subsequent sense extension within pairs related by conversion. This is without implying the existence of several lexemes in conversion relations.

hoover^{N} (INSTRUMENT) → *hoover*^{V} (INSTRUMENTAL) → *hoover*^{N} (ACTION)

Figure 7: Directionality for three related senses of the pair *hoover*$^{N/V}$.

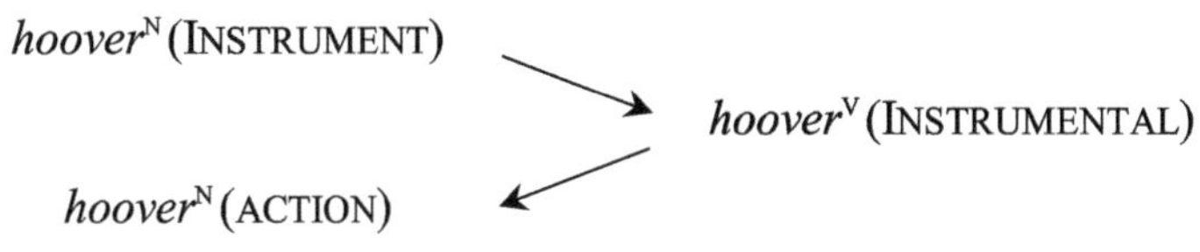

Figure 8: Directionality for three related senses of the pair *hoover*$^{N/V}$.

42 Note again, however, that the sense analysis relies on information from the OED and is not just based on intuition.

43 Note that only three of the senses identified for the pair are represented, but further derived and extended senses are found in the pair too.

Applicability of the criteria for directionality

4.1 Individual applicability of the criteria

The study of directionality in noun/verb conversion opens the door to a wide range of descriptive insights. Chapter 4 focuses on the key findings on the relevance of the criteria for directionality in a sample of present-day English noun/verb conversions, namely, SD, SP, SR, RU, FO and RR.[44]

4.1.1 Semantic dependence (SD)

Section 4.1.1 presents the results of testing SD at the sense level by comparing the senses by pairs to determine if one of the senses shows SD towards the related sense in the counterpart lexeme. The sense analysis classifies senses as: i) showing SD (+, and occasionally +? when the definitions used are not available from the OED and have been supplied ad hoc according to the concordances), ii) not showing SD (–), or iii) unclear (?; cf. Section 3.2.4.1. for specific examples of the application of the criterion). Several options are identified:

i. Noun-to-Verb direction, for example, *bale*^{N} (THING_ARTEFACT) does not show SD, only the counterpart verb sense (RESULTATIVE) is defined based on the noun:

(46) *bale*^{N} (–) (THING_ARTEFACT)
"A large bundle or package of merchandise, originally of more or less rounded shape; now, spec. a package closely pressed, done up in canvas or other wrapping, and tightly corded or hooped with copper or iron, for transportation." (OED), for example, "**Bales** *of carpet samples fill the pattern room in time for the deadline*" (BNC)

[44] In Chapters 2 and 3, the criteria appear following the order in Marchand (1964), but in Chapters 4 and 5, they do not:
i. The semantic criteria are described first, starting from SD (as the main criterion for Marchand 1964, then followed by SP, SR, and RU, according to their applicability.
ii. The quantitative-distributional criteria follow: first FO and then RR, also according to their applicability.

(47) *bale*^{V} (+) (RESULTATIVE)
"To make up into a bale or bales." (OED), for example, "*So he gave me a baler and I did all of Ork around about Birsay and Sanday and round the area here and* **baled** *their hay to them. And then he bought another baler and he worked with two balers.*" (BNC)

ii. Verb-to-Noun direction, for example, *nibble*^{V} (INGESTING) does not show SD, only the counterpart nominal sense is defined based on the verb. (ACTION/INSTANCE):

(48) *nibble*^{V} (–) (INGESTING)
"a. transitive. To take a small bite, or a series of small bites, at or from (a thing); to bite away gradually; to bite tentatively, delicately, playfully, or amorously. Also figurative and in extended use. In quot. a1500 perhaps: to make an attempt at." (OED), for example, "*He is sitting on the corner of the big table in the kitchen, nodding his head and* **nibbling** *a dry biscuit, as Shirley Esplin, the flautist, explains about her work to him.*" (BNC)

(49) *nibble*^{N} (+) (ACTION/INSTANCE)
"a. The action or an act of nibbling; a small, tentative, delicate, or amorous bite. Often used of the behaviour of fish in response to a lure, piece of bait, etc., whence the figurative use described at sense 1b." (OED), for example, *Henry did not have to see his thin anxious face, his nervous* **nibble** *at his lower lip or the furtive glance to left and right to know that [...]*" (BNC)

iii. Noun-to-Verb or Verb-to-Noun, when the definitions used are not available from the OED and have been supplied ad hoc according to the concordances (+?),[45] for example, *soak*^{N} sense 5b:

(50) *soak*^{N} (+?) (AGENT)
"5b. Fig. One who soaks (in various senses, based on context)" (my definition based on the BNC's concordances), for example, "*She was told – and believed – that the woman Charles once called 'my old* **soak**' *(because she absorbed all his worries) no longer tended to his demands.*" (OED)

iv. Unclear direction (?) because, even though a connection is established between the senses, none of them shows SD strongly as in *fathom*$^{N/V}$, or because both related senses show SD towards the other to some extent, so a direction cannot be established with certainty based on SD alone, as in *assart*$^{N/V}$:

[45] Whether a sense is marked as + or +? (showing SD) does not make a difference as for the final analysis because if the counterpart sense does not show SD (–), they are marked as pairs where a direction can be established.

(51) *fathom*[N] (?) (EXT_FIG_MEASURE)
"d. in plural. Depths. literal and figurative. Also in figurative expressions *fathoms deep, fathoms down*; cf. Compounds 2." (OED), for example, "*Elisabeth's feelings were in danger of becoming* **fathoms** *deep in torment.*" (BNC)

(52) *fathom*[V] (?) (FIG_SIMILATIVE)
"b. To get to the bottom of, dive into, penetrate, see through, thoroughly understand." (OED), for example, "*Loren was upstairs, engaged in that long getting-ready process that he'd never quite been able to* **fathom**." (BNC)

(53) *assart*[N] (?) (THING_ARTEFACT_MODIFIED LANDSCAPE or RESULT?)
"1. A piece of forest or waste land converted to arable use by clearing trees, bushes, etc.; a clearing in a forest." (OED), for example, "*He was often directed to see to the ploughing, tilling and sowing of* **assarts**, *waste and other lands belonging to the king in the forest [...]*" (BNC)

(54) *assart*[V] (?) (CAUSATIVE/RESULTATIVE)
"transitive. To convert (forest or waste land) to arable use by clearing trees, bushes, etc. Also occasionally intransitive" (OED), for example, "*the late Earl of Salisbury was convicted of having* **assarted** *2,300 acres of Brigstock Parks in 1604, destroying the vert and a thousand deer, and enclosing the parks.*" (BNC)

The results of the analysis of SD by senses for the 399 pairs of senses identified in the first order of derivation (D1), and the 67 pairs of senses identified in the second order of derivation (D2) are presented in Table 14.

Table 14: Results of SD by sense

		D1		D2	
SD by sense pairs		**nPairs senses**	**%**	**nPairs senses**	**%**
Applicable	Shows a direction (N>V or V>N)	316	79.2 %	55	82.09 %
Not applicable	Unclear	83	20.8 %	12	17.91 %

Overall, the results of the analysis of SD for pairs of senses are as follows:

i. Of the 399 pairs of senses identified in D1, SD indicates a direction (Noun-to-Verb or Verb-to-Noun) for 316 pairs (79.2 %), while a direction cannot be established by SD for 83 pairs (20.8 %).
ii. Of the 67 pairs of senses in D2, SD indicates a direction for 55 pairs (82.09 %), whereas a direction is not clear for twelve pairs (17.91 %).

Note that the results of the interpretation of SD for lexeme pairs in D1 and D2 were obtained from the total number of pairs of senses indicating one or the other direction for each pair of lexeme, for example, for *fathom*[N/V] two pairs of senses were identified, the direction identified for one of the pairs based on SD was Noun-to-Verb, whereas the direction between the other pair of senses was marked as unclear. Thus, for the lexeme pair *fathom*$^{N/V}$ the interpretation of the direction by SD is Noun-to-Verb.

The results for the 226 N/V pairs in this study after a sense analysis in D1 are shown in Table 15.

Table 15: SD: Results by lexeme pair according to a sense analysis in D1

				Total	
SD (D1)	**Direction**	**nPairs**	**%**	**nPairs**	**%**
Applicable	Noun-to-Verb	125	55.31 %	193	85.4 %
	Verb-to-Noun	67	29.65 %		
	Two groups of senses $N^0>V^1$ and $V^0>N^1$	1	0.44 %		
Not applicable	Unclear	33	14.6 %	33	14.6 %

A sense analysis of SD yields the following results for the 226 noun/verb pairs in the sample:

i. SD proves relevant to identify a direction for 193 pairs (85.4 %), as confirmed by one or more senses within the pair. Specifically, SD identified a Noun-to-Verb direction for 125 pairs (55.31 %) and a Verbto-Noun direction for 67 pairs (29.65 %). For one pair (0.44 %), that is, *fluff*$^{N/V}$, two groups of senses were identified for which SD indicates opposite directions: Some of the senses within the pair appear to be related to another lexeme (*fluff*^{V2}), as indicated in the OED, and this may have influenced the sense development within the pair, and
ii. SD does not prove relevant to identify a direction in 33 pairs (14.6 %).

The results in D2 are provided in Table 16, which also indicates if the direction identified is consistent with the direction assigned in D1 (+) or not (–).

Table 16: SD: Results by lexeme pair according to a sense analysis in D2

					Total	
SD (D2)	**Direction**	**Direction aligns with D1**	**nPairs**	**%**	**nPairs**	**%**
Applicable	$V^1>N^2$	+	22	47.83 %	40	86.96 %
	$N^1>V^2$	+	18	39.13 %		
Not applicable	Unclear	na	6	13.04 %	6	13.04 %

The results of the analysis of SD for the 46 noun/verb pairs showing related senses in D2 can be summarized as follows:

i. SD identifies a direction for 40 pairs (86.96 %). Specifically, 22 pairs (47.83 %) show Verb-to-Noun direction (V^1>N^2), which is consistent with the direction identified for the pair in D1 (N^0>V^1), and 18 pairs (39.13 %) show Noun-to-Verb direction (N^1>V^2), which is consistent with the direction identified for the pair in D1 (V^0>N^1).
ii. SD is not relevant for the remaining six pairs (13.04 %).

4.1.2 Semantic pattern (SP)

Section 4.1.2 offers the results of testing SP by comparing the senses in the pairs of lexemes to see if any of the senses shows SP towards another sense in the counterpart lexeme. The sense analysis classifies senses as showing SP (+, occasionally +?, as explained in Section 4.1.1), not showing SP (–) or as unclear (?) (cf. Section 3.2.4.4. for specific examples of the application of the criterion of SP). Several options are identified:

i. Noun-to-Verb direction, for example, *sludge*^{N} (SUBSTANCE/MATERIAL) does not show SP, only the counterpart verb sense (PRIVATIVE) is defined according to a pattern typical of a derivative:

(55) *sludge*^{N} (–) (SUBSTANCE/MATERIAL)
"2. a. Any earthy or slimy matter or deposit; a mixture of some finely powdered substance and water. spec. Such material formed as waste in various industrial and mechanical processes." (OED), for example, "*Thus fluorinated gases released into the air by chemical works can get into the sewers as liquids. They enter the* **sludge** *and are spread as fertiliser.*" (BNC)

(56) *sludge*^{V} (+) (PRIVATIVE)
"3. To clear from sludge or mud." (OED), for example, "*Gushers rose from disconnected water pipes, and the Dream matter* **sludged** *instantly.*" (BNC)

ii. Verb-to-Noun direction, for example, *whap*^{V} (CONTACT BY IMPACT) does not show SP, only the counterpart nominal sense is defined according to a pattern typical of a derivative. (INSTANCE):

(57) *whap*^{V} (–) (CONTACT BY IMPACT)
"2. a. transitive. To strike with heavy blows; to beat soundly, flog, thrash, belabour (a person or animal; rarely, an inanimate object). colloquial or vulgar." (OED), for example, "[…] *won't dare to charge the core unit with knights or other precious troops – if he does the Fanatics will come out and* **whap** *him as he moves.*" (BNC)

(58) *whap*[N] (+) (INSTANCE)
"An act of whopping; a heavy blow or impact; a bump." (OED), for example, "*It toppled over to the floor with a flat* **whap**! *and Jimmy backed off into the centre of the office as Duvall scrambled to his feet at last.*" (BNC).

iii. Unclear direction according to SP (?) because, even though a relation obtains between the senses, none of them shows SP as in *wanton*[N/V], cf. examples (59) and (60), or because both related senses seem to show a semantic pattern typical of a derivative to some extent, as in for example, *whoop*[N/V], cf. examples (61) and (62). Specifically, in (61) vs (62), the direction is marked as unclear, because the possibility for the noun sense to be the derivative (INSTANCE/RESULT) is as possible as for the verb sense to be the derivative (EFFECTIVE_MANNER OF SPEAKING).

(59) *wanton*[N] (?) (HUMAN+CHARACTERISTICS)
"2. A lustful or lecherous person; a person inclined to loose or unrestrained sexual conduct; a prostitute; spec. (with possessive) a (man's) mistress. Also (in a milder sense): a flirt." (OED), for example, "[…] *began on the prosecution side, convinced by what he called the 'orthodox belief that Mary was a* **wanton** *and a murderess*'" (BNC).

(60) *wanton*[V] (?) (MANNER OF ACTION)
"a. intransitive. To pass one's time carelessly; to go idly or heedlessly (up and down, over, through a place). Also with on. Now rare." (OED), for example, "[…] *Mr. Williams, sometimes take too much liberty with the world,* **wantoning** *in the sunbeams of a dangerous affluence.*" (BNC).

(61) *whoop*[N] (?) (INSTANCE/RESULT)
"1. A cry of 'whoop', or a shout or call resembling this, used to attract attention, as a summons, or to express derision, defiance, support or encouragement, etc., or (now usually) exuberant excitement […]" (OED), for example, "*Chaka Khan has been around forever, and recently her trademark* **whoops** *and screams have sounded a little forced.*" (BNC).

(62) *whoop*[V] (?) (EFFECTIVE_MANNER OF SPEAKING)
"1. a. intransitive. To utter a 'whoop!' or a cry or shout resembling this, typically in order to attract attention, as a summons, or to express derision, defiance, support or encouragement, etc., or (now usually) exuberant excitement. / c. transitive. With direct speech as object: to say or utter (something) with a whoop; to call out or yell excitedly." (OED), for example, "*A sense of adventure invaded the group, everyone* **whooping** *and yelling as they were flung between towers on their way to Athena Gardens* […]" (BNC).

The results of SP, presented in Table 17 were obtained according to the total number of pairs of senses indicating a Noun-to-Verb (N>V) or Verb-to-Noun (V>N) direction for each lexeme pair by order of derivation.

Overall, the results of the analysis of SP for pairs of senses by order of derivation are as follows:

i. Of the 399 pairs of senses identified in D1, SP indicates a direction (N^0>V^1 or V^0>N^1) for 323 pairs (80.95 %). A direction cannot be established for 76 pairs (19.05 %).
ii. Of the total of 67 pairs of senses in D2, SP identifies a direction for 62 pairs (92.54 %), while a direction is not clear for five pairs (7.46 %).

Table 17: Results of SP by sense

		D1		D2	
SP by sense pairs		**nPairs senses**	**%**	**nPairs senses**	**%**
Applicable	Shows a direction (N>V or V>N)	323	80.95 %	62	92.54 %
Not applicable	Unclear	76	19.05 %	5	7.46 %

The results of the interpretation of SP for the 226 N/V lexeme pairs in this study after an analysis by senses in D1 are shown in Table 18.

Table 18: SP: Results by lexeme pair according to a sense analysis in D1

				Total	
SP (D1)	**Direction**	**nPairs**	**%**	**nPairs**	**%**
Applicable	Noun-to-Verb	121	53.54 %	191	84.51 %
	Verb-to-Noun	69	30.53 %		
	Two groups of senses N0>V1 and V0>N1	1	0.44 %		
Not applicable	Unclear	35	15.49 %	35	15.49 %

SP yields the following results for the 226 noun/verb pairs in D1:

i. SP proves relevant to identify a direction for 191 pairs (84.51 %). Specifically, SP identified a Noun-to-Verb direction for 121 pairs (53.54 %) and a Verb-to-Noun direction for 69 pairs (30.53 %). As with the criterion of SD, two groups of senses were identified for one pair (0.44 %), *fluff*$^{N/V}$, for which SP indicates opposite directions, and
ii. SP is not relevant to identify a direction in 35 pairs in D1 (15.49 %).

The results of the analysis of SP in D2 are provided in Table 19, with indication of whether the direction identified is consistent with the direction in D1 (+) or not (–).

Table 19: SP: Results by lexeme pair according to a sense analysis in D2

SP (D2)	Direction	Direction aligns with D1	nPairs	%	Total nPairs	Total %
Applicable	$V^1>N^2$	+	25	54.35 %	43	93.48 %
	$N^1>V^2$	+	18	39.13 %		
Not applicable	Unclear	na	3	6.52 %	3	6.52 %

The results of the analysis of SP for the 46 noun/verb pairs showing related senses in D2 can be summarized as follows:

i. SP identifies a direction for 43 pairs (93.48 %). Specifically, 25 pairs (54.35 %) show Verb-to-Noun direction ($V^1>N^2$), which is consistent with the direction identified for the pair in D1 ($N^0>V^1$), and 18 pairs (39.13 %) show Noun-to-Verb direction ($N^1>V^2$), which is consistent with the direction identified for the pair in D1 ($V^0>N^1$).
ii. SD is not relevant for the remaining three pairs (6.52 %).

4.1.3 Semantic range: Qualitative analysis (SR)

Section 4.1.3. focuses on the results of a qualitative analysis of the criterion of Semantic Range (SR). In this study, the SR of a lexeme is compared to its pair member by considering the senses each lexeme has in use (that is, by senses attested in the BNC). This is because one can only comment on whether a lexeme has a wider or narrower SR than its paronymous lexeme, if the various senses they can take and their use are considered. Finally, the analysis of SR does not consider obsolete senses or, rather, senses that are not attested in the BNC.

The qualitative results of the analysis of the criterion of SR for the sample of English noun/verb conversion analysed in this study are presented in Table 20 as follows:

i. 'N>V' indicates that the noun shows a wider SR than its verbal counterpart, for example, *bayonet*^{N} denotes "[a] stabbing instrument of steel, which may be fixed to the muzzle of a musket or rifle; originally its handle was inserted in the mouth of the gun, but it is now secured by a circular band clasping the barrel [...]" (OED) (INSTRUMENT), for example, "*A soldier tried to shove a* **bayonet** *into his throat, but the steel buckled against his adam's apple superconductor.*" (BNC). Extended and metonymic senses are attested for the noun, whereas they are not for the verb (for *bayonet*^{V}), for which only the sense "1. transitive. To stab or pierce with a bayonet." (INSTRUMENTAL) is attested in the OED, for example, "*He was* **bayoneted** *to death by a soldier in front of two priests who had tried to protect him.*" (BNC)
ii. 'V>N' indicates that the verb shows a wider SR than its nominal counterpart, for example, *bonk*^{V} denotes a base sense "a. transitive. To strike

(something hard or unyielding), esp. with an audible, typically hollow-sounding, heavy thump; to bump, to bang" (CONTACT BY IMPACT), for example, "*[...] but one day I took I took a jelly out in a glass dish and it* **bonked** *this thing and the light came on again.*" and an extended slang sense "3. slang. a. transitive. To have sexual intercourse with (a person)." (OED) (EXT_CONTACT BY IMPACT), for example, "*In an ideal world you'd be able to meet someone at a bus-stop, go for a drink, take them home and* **bonk** *their brains out – and then go home to your girlfriend for dinner.*" (BNC). By contrast, in *bonk*^{N} only the related slang sense "3. slang. An act of sexual intercourse. Cf. bonk v. 3, bonking n. 2." (ACTION/EVENT) is attested in the OED, for example, "*[...] the usual rather silly collection of schematic cliches by David Hare, follows a similarly leaden pattern. There is the* **bonk** *on the floor, the bonk on the table, the bonk in the bed; lace-top stockings are discreetly displayed, [...]*" (BNC).

iii. 'N≳V' indicates that the noun shows a slightly wider or very similar SR than its verbal counterpart, for example, the SR of *umpire*^{N} and *umpire*^{V} is similar: a specialized use of the noun in law contexts is attested, for example, "*[...] but the courts have not seen the umpire procedure as an important factor, and the involvement of an* **umpire** *does not turn a reference to an expert into an arbitration.*" (BNC), while the verb presents SIMILATIVE senses which seem to cover only the general uses of the N, as arbitrator in a dispute, for example, "[...] *help in seeing why debates among Realists, Pluralists, and Structuralists in International Relations are so hard to* **umpire**." (BNC), or as a supervisor in games or contests, for example, "*The event, run by John Burgess formerly of Anstey County Junior School, was* **umpired** *by volunteers including members of the Alton Ants netball club.*" (BNC)

iv. 'V≳N' indicates that the verb shows a slightly wider or very similar SR than its nominal counterpart, for example, both *joust*^{V} and *joust*^{N} cover similar senses, but one instance of an obsolete sense of the verb is attested in the corpus too "†1. (?) To join, to ally oneself. Obsolete. rare." (OED) (SOCIAL INTERACTION), for example, "*THE EGLINTON TOURNAMENT Mounted knights in shining armour,* **jousting** *in the lists; lords and ladies clothed in raiment, [...]*" (BNC), so the SR of the verbs is interpreted as slightly wider.

v. 'V≈N' indicates that both lexemes in a pair show a similar SR, that is, their lexemes cover equivalent semantic reference, the difference lying in the categorial meaning alone, for example, independently of the number of senses, the pair *libel*$^{N/V}$ seems to cover a similar SR.

vi. Last, the label '?/other' indicates that the pair's SR is unclear, among other possible reasons, because the senses in use are influenced by senses of other lexemes, for example, in the pair *blind*$^{N/V}$, both terms present several senses related to the adjective each. Some of these senses are connected between the verb and the noun, but the SR between the pair is difficult to contrast. As a different example, the terms of *brood*$^{N/V}$ present several senses derived within the lexemes, but they are not easily connected.

The results of the qualitative analysis of SR for the pairs of lexemes studied are shown in Table 20.

Table 20: Results of a qualitative analysis of SR

SR	Direction	nPairs	%	Total nPairs	Total %
Applicable	N>V	67	29.65 %	112	49.56 %
	V>N	45	19.91 %		
Questionable applicability	N≳V	17	7.52 %	35	15.49 %
	V≳N	18	7.96 %		
Not applicable	N≈V	68	30.09 %	79	34.96 %
	?	11	4.87 %		

The results of the analysis of SR reveal the following:

i. For a large number of pairs (n=79, 34.96 %), the criterion does not prove relevant to decide on a direction between the pairs, either because their SR is equivalent (30.09 %), or because it differs to the extent that a comparison of the lexemes' SR is obscure (4.87 %), for example, for the influence of other lexemes in their sense development.

ii. The applicability of the criterion is questioned in 35 pairs (15.49 %). This is because the difference between the SR covered by the terms of the pair cannot be claimed to be different enough to decide on a direction.

iii. The criterion seems reliable only for 112 pairs (49.56 %), where the SR covered by the terms of the pairs is indicative of a direction.

4.1.4 Restrictions of usage (RU)

Initially, this study intended first to compare the total number of restricted senses that a pair of lexemes shows and then to analyse RU by considering specific senses. However, two types of analysis at the level of lexeme (considering senses) were discarded because they often led to the identification of an unreliable interpretation of the direction. Specifically, the tests discarded are:

i. the number of restricted senses by pair, and

ii. the percentage of restricted senses out of the total number of senses that a lexeme takes. compared to its counterpart.

See, for example, *barrack*$^{N/V}$, for which the following OED senses are attested in the BNC:

(63) *barrack*[N]
Sense 1b. (ARTEFACT/LOCATION) "'A straw-thatched roof supported by four posts, capable of being raised or lowered at pleasure, under which hay is kept.' Bartlett Dict. Americanisms 1848.", for example, "*On the earth floors of the leaking, palm-thatched* **barrack** *huts dotted around the vast plantation, [...]*" (BNC).
Sense 2. (ARTEFACT/LOCATION) "A set of buildings erected or used as a place of lodgement or residence for troops. [...] / d. (singular or plural). A large plain building or range of buildings, tenements, or flats in which a number of people are housed; also, any strikingly plain-looking building suggestive of a military barracks. [...] ", for example, "*He picked up the dead man's only possession, a straw mat, and together he and Dong dragged the body out of the* **barrack** *and through the mud towards the jungle half a mile away.*" (BNC)

(64) *barrack*[V]
Sense 2/1. (ORNATIVE/LOCATIVE) "2. intransitive. To lodge in barracks. / 1. transitive. To provide barracks for; to locate in barracks.", for example, "*The Reiksguard is* **barracked** *in the comparative comfort of Altdorf, and accompanies the Emperor on campaign and during diplomatic tours*" (BNC)

If RU is applied, the following data are obtained. For the pair *barrack*[N/V]:

i. An analysis of the numbers of senses (nSenses) showing RU whereby the pair with the higher number of senses with restrictions is the derivative yields a Verb-to-Noun direction.
ii. Similarly, an analysis of the number of senses showing RU out of the total number of senses for each lexeme yields, a Verb-to-Noun direction (N: 0.5; V: 0).

Table 21: RU analysis for *barrack*[N/V]

Lexeme	nSenses	–RU	+RU	Type
barrack[N]	2	1	1	RU1
barrack[V]	2	1		

Remarkably, both methods are misleading in that they lead to an incorrect interpretation: When the senses and their use are considered, the senses connected directly by conversion are not restricted in use. Also, the restricted nominal sense (1b) is recorded once in the BNC, while sense 2 is recorded 77 times, while the verb sense 2/1 is recorded twice in the BNC (which is probably a better indicator that the verb is not in wider use than the noun).

Thus, because a comparison of RU based on the number of senses showing restrictions in use proved problematic and easily led to the identification of a number of misleading analyses, RU is considered in this study specifically by a comparison between related senses in our arrangement into orders of derivation. Table 22 exemplifies the analysis for four pairs.

It presents the pairs' direction based on RU by pairs of senses in D1 for the lexeme pairs *anagram*$^{N/V}$, *bluster*$^{N/V}$, *quack*$^{N2/V2}$, and *slit*$^{N/V}$.

Table 22: Direction indicated by RU for pairs of lexemes after a comparison of the restrictions by pairs of senses in D1

	No relevance		Relevance		
Pair	BOTH (N+/V+)	NONE (N–/V–)	N>V (N–/V+)	V>N (N–/V+)	Direction
anagram$^{N/V}$	0	0	1	0	N>V
bluster$^{N/V}$	0	3	0	0	UNC
quack$^{N2/V2}$	2	0	0	0	UNC
slit$^{N/V}$	0	1	0	1	V>N

Table 22 indicates:

i. Whether sense comparison has no relevance to identify a direction, either because both the sense of the noun and the sense of the verb compared are restricted in use, or none of them is restricted.
ii. Whether sense comparison is relevant to identify a direction because one of the senses is restricted in usage and the related sense is not.
iii. The final outcome (Column six *Direction*) based on this information, for example, the direction is unclear (*UNC*) for the pair *bluster*$^{N/V}$ because all senses in the two pairs of senses related by conversion show restrictions (+), and it is indicated as Verb-to-Noun (*V>N*) for the pair *slit*$^{N/V}$ because, although there is one pair showing no restrictions of usage (–), the nominal sense in another pair shows restrictions while the counterpart verb sense is unrestricted.

The results of the analysis of RU by pairs of senses are provided in Table 23, by order of derivation.

Table 23: Applicability of RU by sense

		D1		D2	
RU by sense pairs		nPairs senses	%	nPairs senses	%
Applicable	Shows a direction (N>V or V>N)	90	22.56 %	22	32.84 %
Not applicable	Both + RU	76	19.05 %	21	31.34 %
	Both – RU	233	58.4 %	24	35.82 %

Overall, the results of the analysis of RU for pairs of senses are as follows:

i. Of the total of 399 pairs analysed in D1 (N^0>V^1 or V^0>N^1), RU identifies a direction for 90 pairs of senses (22.56 %), whereas direction cannot be established by RU for 309 pairs (77.44 %):
   a. in 76 pairs (19.05 %) because both senses show restrictions, and
   b. in 233 pairs (58.4 %) because none of the senses are restricted.
ii. Of the total of 67 pairs analysed in D2 (N^1>V^2 or V^1>N^2), RU identifies a direction for 22 pairs of senses (32.84 %), whereas direction cannot be established by RU for 45 pairs (67.16 %):
   a. in 21 pairs (31.34 %) because both senses show restrictions, and
   b. in 24 pairs (35.82 %) because none of the senses are restricted.

The results of the application of RU for lexeme pairs are provided in Table 24 for D1 and Table 25 for D2.

Table 24: RU: Results by lexeme pair according to a sense analysis in D1

				Total	
RU (D1)	**Direction**	**nPairs**	**%**	**nPairs**	**%**
Applicable	N^0>V^1	34	15.04 %	69	30.53 %
	V^0>N^1	35	15.49 %		
Not applicable	Unclear	157	69.47 %	157	69.47 %

Table 25: RU: Results by lexeme pair according to a sense analysis in D2

					Total	
RU (D2)	**Direction**	**Direction aligns with D1**	**nPairs**	**%**	**nPairs**	**%**
Applicable	V^1>N^2	+	10	21.74 %	16	34.78 %
	N^1>V^2	+	5	10.87 %		
	V^1<N^2	-	1	2.17 %		
Not applicable	Unclear	na	30	65.22 %	30	65.22 %

The results of the analysis of RU for the 226 noun/verb pairs by related senses in D1 can be summarized as follows:

i. RU identifies a direction only for 69 pairs (30.53 %). Specifically, 34 pairs (15.04 %) show Noun-to-Verb direction, and 35 pairs (15.49 %) show Verb-to-Noun direction.
ii. RU is not relevant for the remaining 157 pairs (69.47 %).

The results of the analysis of RU for the 46 lexeme pairs by related senses in D2 are as follows:

i. RU identifies a direction for 16 pairs (34.78 %). Specifically:
   a. ten pairs (21.74 %) show Verb-to-Noun direction ($V^1>N^2$),
   b. five pairs (10.87 %) show Noun-to-Verb direction ($N^1>V^2$).
   c. for one other pair, a Noun-to-Verb direction is identified based on RU ($V^1<N^2$). As specified in the table, for this pair the direction identified in D2 does not align with the direction identified in D1 ($N^0>V^1$).
ii. RU is not relevant for the remaining 30 pairs (65.22 %).

Based on these results, it remains unclear whether this analysis proves relevant for directionality.

4.1.5 Frequency of occurrence (FO)

Section 4.1.5 focuses on the results of the criterion of frequency of occurrence (FO) in a sample of noun/verb conversion pairs in the BNC. The results are provided for the applicability of FO at the level of sense. To this end, the BNC concordances were classified into the OED's noun/verb senses first, and wrongly tagged concordances were recategorized where relevant (cf. Section 3.2.2.1). Then, the applicability of FO was tested by comparing the frequency of occurrence of the lexemes' senses in the BNC after their distribution into orders of derivation.

Table 26 exemplifies the distribution of senses for the pairs *dupe*$^{N2/V2}$,[46] *lesion*$^{N/V}$, *scythe*$^{N/V}$, and *skid*$^{N/V}$, and their frequency.

Table 26: BNC's raw frequency of occurrence for the senses of *dupe*$^{N2/V2}$, *lesion*$^{N/V}$, *scythe*$^{N/V}$, and *skid*$^{N/V}$ by order of derivation. An asterisk is used for repeated senses, that is, related to more than one sense in the pair. The senses for each pair in the table (as N^0, V^1, N^2) are arranged according to the presumed direction based on their semantics. Senses in the same row are related by conversion. Senses in grey do not have a counterpart

Pair	N^0 sense	Raw freq.	V^1 sense	Raw freq.	N^2 sense	Raw freq.
dupe$^{N2/V2}$	1	5	1	1		
lesion$^{N/V}$	1	189	1	2		
	1 ext	1				
scythe$^{N/V}$	1	67	1b	24	2b	2
	1b	9				

[46] Note that the subscript in *dupe*$^{N2/V2}$ in the column *pair* and the description in the text do not refer to orders of derivation but to the number of the lexemes' entries as Noun and Verb in the OED.

Pair	N⁰ sense	Raw freq.	V¹ sense	Raw freq.	N² sense	Raw freq.
	1c	15				
	1*	67	2	28		
			2 fig	1		
skid[N/V]	1 fig	1				
	2	16				
	2 fig	23				
	3	9	3	196	4	48
			3 fig	2		

The results allow to compare directly related senses by conversion, for example, sense 1 for *dupe*[N2] is attested five times in the BNC while the counterpart (sense 1 for *dupe*[V2]) is attested once. This indicates a Noun-to-Verb direction based on the frequency of the senses. A direction is also clearly established for the pair *lesion*[N/V] because the noun sense is much more frequent (189 occurrences) than the verb sense (two occurrences) in the BNC.

More complex pairs are represented too because they are polysemous and because subsequent derivation can be found between the senses, as in *scythe*[N/V] and *skid*[N/V]: Both pairs show senses for which no directly derived sense is found and which in these cases do not seem to be relevant for a FO analysis (in grey font), but they differ regarding the direction indicated by FO. For *scythe*[N/V] the direction by FO, if we look at the senses in the first order of derivation, is as expected or aligns with the representation of senses into orders of derivation based on semantics ($N^0 > V^1$). By contrast, the direction shown by FO for *skid*[N/V] is the opposite ($V^0 > N^1$) and does not align with our semantic analysis.

For a more reliable data interpretation, a Chi-squared test (χ^2) was performed using the Excel function *CHISQ.TEST*. This test fits as it allows to statistically assess whether the observed differences between pairs of senses are significant ($P < 0.05$) or are due to random variation ($P > 0.05$), providing a more robust data-driven approach to evaluating frequency differences. The specific results of the Chi-squared test to analyse the observed differences between the related senses for the pairs exemplified above are shown in Table 27.

Table 27: Analysis of FO for *dupe*$^{N2/V2}$, *lesion*$^{N/V}$, *scythe*$^{N/V}$, and *skid*$^{N/V}$ based on a Chi-squared test. An asterisk is used for repeated senses, that is, related to more than one sense in the pair lexeme

Pair	N^0 sense	Raw freq.	V^1 sense	Raw freq.	N^2 sense	Raw freq.	Chi^2 (p-value)	Significant difference	Direction
dupe$^{N2/V2}$	1	5	1	1			0.10	No	$N^0>V^1$
lesion$^{N/V}$	1	189	1	2			1.02E-41	Yes	$N^0>V^1$
scythe$^{N/V}$	1	67	1b	24			6.56E-06	Yes	$N^0>V^1$
			1b	24	2b	2	1.60E-05	Yes	$V^1>N^2$
	1*	67	2	28			6.23E-05	Yes	$N^0>V^1$
skid$^{N/V}$	3	9	3	196			5.53E-39	Yes	$N^0>V^1$
			3	196	4	48	2.67E-21	Yes	$V^1>N^2$

Results of the analysis of FO were then obtained by considering the number of pairs of senses indicating either Noun-to-Verb (N>V) or Verb-to-Noun (V>N) direction for each pair of lexemes. The direction was established according to the FO sense analysis by orders of derivation. For the pairs in Table 27, for example, the direction in the first order of derivation would thus be interpreted Noun-to-Verb (no significant difference found between the sense pair) for *dupe*$^{N2/V2}$, Noun-to-Verb (with a significant difference found between pairs of senses) for *lesion*$^{N/V}$ and *scythe*$^{N/V}$, and Verb-to-Noun (with a significant difference found between sense pairs) for *lesion*^{N} *skid*$^{N/V}$.

The results of the analysis of FO by pairs of senses are provided in Table 28 below, by order of derivation.

Table 28: Direction by sense according to FO

FO by sense pairs		D1 nPairs senses	D1 %	D2 nPairs senses	D2 %
Applicable	N>V or V>N (significant difference (Y))	299	74.94 %	51	76.12 %
Not applicable	No significant difference (N)	90	22.56 %	15	22.39 %
	Unclear (same freq.)	10	2.51 %	1	1.49 %

The results of the interpretation of FO for the noun/verb pairs by senses are presented next. Specifically, Table 29 presents the results of FO in D1, and Table 30 presents the results of FO in D2.

Table 29: FO: Results by lexeme pair according to a sense analysis in D1

					Total	
	FO (D1)	**Direction**	**nPairs**	**%**	**nPairs**	**%**
Applicable	Significant difference (Y)	$N^0>V^1$	115	50.9 %	183	80.97 %
		$V^0>N^1$	58	25.7 %		
	Undecided (UND Y)	$N^0>V^1$	6	2.7 %		
		$V^0>N^1$	4	1.7 %		
Not app.	No significant difference (N)	$N^0>V^1$	20	8.8 %	38	16.81 %
		$V^0>N^1$	18	8.0 %		
	Unclear (same freq.)	N=V	5	2.2 %	5	2.21 %

A sense analysis of FO yields the following results for the 226 noun/verb pairs in D1 (cf. Table 29):

i. FO proves relevant to identify a direction in 183 pairs (80.97 %), as indicated by one or more senses with a significant observed frequency difference (Y/UND Y), as confirmed by a Chi-squared test. Specifically:
   a. A significant difference (Y) is found between the senses of 173 pairs: 115 pairs (50.9 %) signal a Noun-to-Verb direction, and 58 pairs (25.7 %) signal a Verb-to-Noun direction.
   b. For cases marked in the Table as *Undecided* (UND Y), a similar number of pairs of senses signal a significant difference but an opposite direction, so the direction was decided according to the analysis of the pair of senses with the higher frequency of occurrence within the pair of lexemes. Specifically, the direction thus identified was Noun-to-Verb in six pairs, and Verb-to-Noun in four pairs.

ii. In 38 pairs (16.81 %), the difference in the frequency of occurrence of the related senses within the pair is not statistically significant (N). This includes pairs in which two opposite directions are found (no statistically significant difference), and in which the direction is according to the pair of senses with the higher frequency (UND N). As the difference is not significant for these cases the criterion is considered as not applicable for directionality in this study.

iii. In the remaining five pairs (2.21 %), the direction remains unclear according to FO, because the senses have the same frequency of occurrence in the BNC, or because there seem to be two opposite directions as by different pairs of senses, but their frequencies are close.

Table 30: FO: Results by lexeme pair according to a sense analysis in D2

FO (D2)		Direction	Direction aligns with D1	nPairs	%	Total nPairs	Total %
Applicable	Significant difference (Y/UND Y)	$V^1>N^2$	+	24	52.17 %	38	82.61 %
		$N^1>V^2$	+	11	23.91 %		
		$V^1<N^2$	–	na	na		
		$N^1<V^2$	–	3	6.52 %		
Not applicable	No significant difference (N)	$V^1>N^2$	+	1	2.17 %	7	15.22 %
		$N^1>V^2$	+	3	6.52 %		
		$V^1<N^2$	–	2	4.35 %		
		$N^1<V^2$	–	1	2.17 %		
	Unclear	Same freq.	na	1	2.17 %	1	2.17 %

A sense analysis of FO yields the following results for the 46 noun/verb pairs in D2 (cf. Table 30):

i. FO proves relevant to identify a direction in 38 pairs (82.61 %), as confirmed by a Chi-squared test (Y/UND Y). Specifically, 24 pairs (52.17 %) signal a $V^1>N^2$ direction, and eleven pairs (23.91 %) signal a $N^1>V^2$ direction, the results aligning with those in D1. However, FO also identifies a $N^1<V^2$ direction for three pairs, which is unexpected as it does not align with the direction in D1.
ii. FO is not applicable to determine a direction in seven other pairs, as the frequency differences between the senses do not prove significant, and
iii. FO is not applicable to determine a direction in the remaining pair because the senses have the same frequency of occurrence in the BNC.

4.1.6 Range of registers covered (RR)

Section 4.1.6 presents the results of the analysis of the criterion of range of register (RR) in a sample of noun/verb conversion in English. Specifically, this section presents the quantitative results of RR at sense level by comparing the number of registers in which the lexemes' senses appear in the BNC after their distribution into orders of derivation.

Table 31 exemplifies the distribution of senses for the pairs *huddle*$^{N/V}$ and *scythe*$^{N/V}$, and the number of registers in which each sense appears according to the BNC's David Lee's classification for corpus data retrieval, which consists of 71 registers or genres.[47] The table also shows whether the difference between the number of registers covered by the senses is significant ($P < 0.05$) or not ($P > 0.05$), according to

[47] Cf. Ruz (2025) for further discussion of how the choice of a more or less fine-grained register classification may affect the results on the applicability of RR, when statistical significance levels are considered.

Fisher's exact test. Fisher's exact test was selected because as mentioned in Section 3.2.4.6, it has been claimed to be more reliable for the estimation of statistical significance for small-size categorical data (Brezina 2018: 113).

Table 31: Analysis of RR for *huddle*$^{N/V}$ and *scythe*$^{N/V}$ according to the BNC's classification into 71 registers. An asterisk is used for repeated senses, that is. related to more than one sense in the pair lexeme

Pair	V^0 sense	nReg	N^1 sense	nReg	V^2 sense	nReg	Fisher's exact test (p-value)	Significant difference	Direction
huddle$^{N/V}$	1	3	4	7			0.33	No	N^0>V^1
	6, 7	27	1a	9			0.0009	Yes	V^0>N^1
			1a	9	3	4	0.24	No	N^1>V^2
			2	6	3b	2	0.27	No	N^1>V^2
Pair	**N^0 sense**	**nReg**	**V^1 sense**	**nReg**	**N^2 sense**	**nReg**	**Fisher's exact test (p-value)**	**Significant difference**	**Direction**
scythe$^{N/V}$	1	14	1b	9			0.36	No	N^0>V^1
			1b	9	2b	1	0.02	Yes	V^1>N^2
	1*	14	2	10			0.50	No	N^0>V^1

The results of the analysis of RR were then obtained by considering the total number of pairs of senses indicating either Noun-to-Verb or Verb-to-Noun direction for each pair of lexemes and their use, by order of derivation. Thus, for example, the direction identified by RR in D1 would be Verb-to-Noun for the pair *huddle*$^{N/V}$, and the direction identified in D2 for the same lexeme pair is as expected or aligns with the direction found in D1 (N^1>V^2), although the difference in RR is not statistically significant for the sense pairs in D2.

The results of the applicability of RR for the 399 pairs of senses compared in D1 and the 67 pairs of senses compared in D2 are presented in Table 32, by order of derivation.

Table 32: Direction by sense according to BNC's David Lee's classification into 71 registers

RR by sense pairs		D1 nPairs senses	D1 %	D2 nPairs senses	D2 %
Applicable	N>V or V>N (significant difference (Y))	159	39.85 %	27	40.3 %
Not applicable	No significant difference (N)	206	51.63 %	36	53.73 %
	Unclear (same nReg.)	34	8.52 %	4	5.97 %

Overall, the results of the application of RR by pairs of senses are as follows:

i. In D1, RR may be taken as indicating a direction ($N^0>V^1$ or $V^0>N^1$) for 365 pairs (91.48 %). However, of those pairs, Fisher's exact test confirms a significant difference in 159 pairs of senses (39.85 %), while the difference is not statistically significant in 206 pairs of senses (51.63 %). When the latter is the case, the criterion of RR is not considered applicable. Furthermore, a direction cannot be established according to RR for 34 pairs in D1 (8.52 %) because the senses appear in the same number of registers in the BNC.

ii. In D2, RR identifies a direction for 27 pairs of senses (40.3 %), between which a significant difference is found. However, the difference between 36 other pairs (53.73 %) is not significant and thus RR does not prove applicable to identify a direction in those cases. The remaining four pairs of senses (5.97 %) appear represented in a similar nReg thus no direction can be established between those senses based on RR.

The results of the interpretation of RR by senses for the 226 noun/verb pairs in the sample pairs are presented in Tables 33 and 34, for D1 and D2 respectively.

Table 33: David Lee's classification (BNC): Results of RR by lexemes-pairs according to a sense analysis in D1. *nPairs* refers to the number of pairs of lexemes for which a specific direction is interpreted

					Total	
RR		**Direction**	**nPairs**	**%**	**nPairs**	**%**
App.	Significant difference (Y/UND Y)	$N^0>V^1$	76	33.63 %	116	51.33 %
		$V^0>N^1$	40	17.70 %		
Not app.	No significant difference (N)	$N^0>V^1$	50	22.12 %	96	42.48 %
		$V^0>N^1$	46	20.35 %		
	Unclear (same freq.)	N=V	14	6.19 %	14	6.19 %

Table 34: David Lee's classification (BNC): Results of RR by lexemes-pairs according to a sense analysis in D2. *nPairs* refers to the number of pairs of lexemes for which a specific direction is interpreted

						Total	
RR		**Direction**	**Direction aligns with D1**	**nPairs**	**%**	**nPairs**	**%**
Applicable	Significant difference (Y/UND Y)	$V^1>N^2$	+	14	30.43 %	23	50 %
		$N^1>V^2$	+	7	15.22 %		
		$V^1<N^2$	–	1	2.17 %		
		$N^1<V^2$	–	1	2.17 %		

RR		Direction	Direction aligns with D1	nPairs	%	Total nPairs	Total %
Not applicable	No significant difference (N)	$V^1>N^2$	+	11	23.91 %	21	45.65 %
		$N^1>V^2$	+	7	15.22 %		
		$V^1<N^2$	–	1	2.17 %		
		$N^1<V^2$	–	2	4.35 %		
	Unclear	Same freq.	na	2	4.35 %	2	4.35 %

A sense analysis of RR yields the following results for the 226 noun/verb pairs in D1 (cf. Table 33):

i. RR proves relevant to identify a direction in 116 pairs (51.33 %), as confirmed by Fisher's exact test (Y/UND Y). Specifically, a Noun-to-Verb direction is found for 76 pairs (33.63 %), and a Verb-to-Noun direction for 40 pairs (17.70 %).
ii. No significant difference is found between 96 pairs (42.48 %) and thus RR is not considered applicable to decide on directionality in these cases.
iii. RR is not applicable to determine a direction in the remaining 14 pairs (6.19 %) because the senses appear in the same number of registers in the BNC.

A sense analysis of RR yields the following results for the 46 noun/verb pairs in D2 (cf. Table 34):

i. RR identifies a direction for 23 pairs (50 %), as confirmed by a Fisher's exact test (Y/UND Y). Specifically, 14 pairs (30.43 %) signal a $V^1>N^2$ direction, and seven pairs (15.22 %) signal a $N^1>V^2$ direction, the results aligning with those in D1. However, RR identifies a $V^1<N^2$ for one pair and a $N^1<V^2$ direction for one pair, not aligning with the direction in D1.
ii. RR is not applicable to determine a direction in 21 pairs (45.65 %), as differences in the range of registers covered by the senses in the pair do not prove significant.
iii. RR does not identify a direction in the remaining two pairs (4.35 %) because the senses appear in the same number of registers in the BNC.

4.1.7 Comparison of the criteria individual applicability

The results presented in Sections 4.1.1–4.1.6 show that the extent to which the various criteria for directionality can be applied by sense is rather dissimilar. Results of the applicability of all the criteria by senses (independently of the order of derivation, that is, for the total of 466 pairs of senses analysed) are summarized in Table 35.

Table 35: Individual applicability of the criteria of SD, SP, RU, FO and RR for the 466 pairs of senses analysed

	Unclear				Applicable	
	Not applicable/ Unclear		No significant difference		SD indicates a direction (N>V or V>N)	
Criterion	nPairs of senses	%	nPairs of senses	%	nPairs of senses	%
SD	95	20.39 %	na	–	371	79.61 %
SP	81	17.38 %	na	–	385	82.62 %
RU	354	75.97 %	na	–	112	24.03 %
FO	11	2.36 %	115	24.68 %	350	75.11 %
RR	38	8.15 %	242	51.63 %	186	39.91 %

Table 36 puts together the directionality results of the semantic criteria for the pairs of lexemes after a sense analysis in D1, again showing the dissimilar degree of applicability of each criterion, and Table 37 does the same for D2. Note that SR is displayed only in Table 36 because the direction based on the semantic range covered was established considering all senses in use for the 226 pairs of lexemes, and thus it only makes sense to compare the results of the criterion to the direction identified by other criteria in D1.

Table 36: Directionality of the semantic criteria for the pairs by sense in D1. Not applicable includes cases where the differences found between the senses in the pairs are not significant (N) for the criteria of FO and RR

	Not applicable/ Unclear		Applicable						Total Applicable	
			Noun-to-Verb $N^{0}>V^{1}$		Verb-to-Noun $N^{0}>V^{1}$		Two groups $N^{0}>V^{1}$/ $N^{0}>V^{1}$			
Criterion	nP	%	nP	%	nP	%	nP	%	nP	%
SD	33	14.61 %	125	55.31 %	67	29.65 %	1	0.44 %	193	85.39 %
SP	35	15.49 %	121	53.54 %	69	30.53 %	1	0.44 %	191	84.51 %
SR (N)	79	34.96 %	84	37.17 %	63	27.87 %			147	65.04 %
SR (Y)	114	50.44 %	67	29.65 %	45	19.91 %			112	49.56 %
RU	157	69.47 %	34	15.04 %	35	15.49 %			69	30.53 %
FO	43	19.03 %	121	53.54 %	62	27.43 %			183	80.97 %
RR	110	48.67 %	76	33.63 %	40	17.70 %			116	51.33 %

Table 35 shows that the applicability of some criteria for determining directionality, for example, the semantic criteria of SD or SP is significantly higher compared to the applicability of other criteria, for example, RU.

Specifically, the tables show that the criterion of SD is applicable for 79.61 % of the pairs of senses identified for the noun/verb pairs in this study (371 pairs out of the 466 pairs in D1 and D2, cf. Table 35). In turn, this translates to the identification of directionality for 193 of the pairs of lexemes in the sample in D1, after the organization of senses by orders of derivation (85.39 %, cf. Table 36), the number of pairs analysed as Noun-to-Verb being higher than those showing Verb-to-Noun direction. Additionally, Table 37 shows that the directions identified by SD in D2 align with those in D1.

The results of SP are very similar. Out of the 466 pairs of senses in our sample, SP indicates a direction for 385 pairs (82.62 %, cf. Table 35). A direction can be established by lexemes based on the related senses in D1 for 191 of the pairs of lexemes in the sample (84.51 %). This criterion offers a very similar picture in the number of Noun-to-Verb and Verb-to-Noun pairs compared to SD (cf. Table 36). Similarly, the directions identified by SP in D2 align with those in D1 (cf. Table 37).

Table 37: Directionality of the criteria for the pairs based on a sense analysis in D2. Not applicable includes cases where the differences found between the senses in the pairs are not significant (N) for the criteria of FO and RR

	Not applicable/ Unclear		Applicable								Total applicability	
			Direction aligns with D1				Direction does not align with D1					
			$V^1>N^2$		$N^1>V^2$		$V^1<N^2$		$N^1<V^2$			
Criteria	nP	%	nP	%	nP	%	nP	%	nP	%	nP	%
SD	6	13.04 %	22	47.83 %	18	39.13 %					40	86.96 %
SP	3	6.52 %	25	54.35 %	18	39.13 %					43	93.48 %
RU	30	65.22 %	10	21.74 %	5	10.87 %	1	2.17 %			16	34.78 %
FO	8	17.39 %	24	52.17 %	11	23.91 %			3	6.52 %	38	82.61 %
RR	23	50 %	14	30.43 %	7	15.22 %	1	2.17 %	1	2.17 %	23	50 %

Similar results were expected in the overall applicability of these two criteria because these typically go together, in that, when a sense shows semantic dependence towards another sense in the derivative, it is often defined using a semantic pattern typical of a derivative too, while the definitions of base senses are often more elaborate (cf. thus *bayonet*[N] and *bayonet*[V] below):

(65) *bayonet*[N] (INSTRUMENT)
"2. a. A stabbing instrument of steel, which may be fixed to the muzzle of a musket or rifle; originally its handle was inserted in the mouth of the gun, but it is now secured by a circular band clasping the barrel [...]" (OED)

(66) *bayonet*[V] (INSTRUMENTAL)
"1. transitive. To stab or pierce with a bayonet." (OED)

Only for very few cases, just one of the other criteria was marked as showing a direction. When this is so, typically, the sense analysis was slightly more unclear, that is, marked as showing SD or SP with some doubt.

Regarding SR, Table 36 includes cases of questionable applicability in the results section (cf. Table 37) as applicable as SR (N), whereas only clear cases are included as SR (Y). Even if questionable cases are interpreted as indicating a direction, the criterion still has a lower applicability compared to SD or SP (147 pairs, 65.04 %). Also, if only cases where the SR of the pairs is more certain are considered relevant, the applicability of the criterion decreases (112 pairs, 49.56 %). However, even when the criterion applies, its relevance is questionable as the derivative is not necessarily always the pair member with the lower SR. This is because pairs of lexemes may follow different paths of development. The relevance of SR is further commented on in Section 4.3.3, when the consistency of SR and the other criteria tested in this study is compared, and in Section 5.4, showing examples of the relevance of SR in directionality.

RU proves applicable for a small part of the data, 112 pairs of senses out of the 466 pairs analysed in this study (24.03 %, cf. Table 35), which translates to the identification of directionality for 69 pairs out of the 226 pairs of lexemes in our sample (30.53 %) based on sense analysis in D1 (cf. Table 36). The applicability of the criterion is also low when senses in D2 are analysed (16 pairs, 34.78 %, cf. Table 37), and a case is found where the direction identified in D2 does not align with that in D1. The low applicability of the criterion results from the fact that for most pairs of senses in D1 and D2, either both (n=97, 20.82 %) or none of the senses (n=257, 55.15 %) show RU (cf. Table 37). Thus, it can be concluded that RU only proves applicable for very specific cases, when applied at the level of sense too. This is in line with the results of a pilot study on the applicability of the criteria in affixation (Ruz & Cetnarowska 2023: 27). Results of this criterion cannot be compared with results of previous research on directionality in conversion because, as far as we know, only Balteiro (2007) uses RU for directionality in English (note, however, that she interprets the criterion as FO is interpreted in this study).

As regards the quantitative-distributional criteria of FO and RR, Table 35 shows that FO proves applicable for a higher number of pairs of senses (350 pairs out of the total of 466 pairs analysed, 75.11 %), whereas the individual applicability of RR is lower (186 pairs, 39.91 %). Specifically, RR is not applicable when the pairs of senses compared cover the same number of registers in 38 pairs of senses (8.15 %), and the difference in the register usage between 242 pairs (51.63 %) is questioned as a directionality indicator because it did not prove statistically significant according to the Fisher's exact test performed. When the criteria are interpreted for the pairs of lexemes (Tables 36 and 37), FO and RR seem to offer a similar picture, but the applicability of FO is higher. Also, the directions identified by FO for two pairs in D2 (4.34 %) or by RR for three pairs in D2 (6.52 %) do not align with that identified by the criteria in D1.

If one were to assume that the direction signalled by the criteria is correct and, thus, that the criteria indicate the same direction (or at least for most cases), directionality should be established based on the semantic criteria of SD and SP. This is because these are the most applicable criteria, followed by FO, which proves also fairly applicable to decide a direction. A direction, however, cannot be established for a large part of the data based solely on the applicability levels of the criteria of SR, RU, and RR, and, thus, these should not be given priority in the study of directionality.

4.2 Cross-criteria consistency

Section 4.2 offers the results of the consistency across the criteria tested in this study by pairs of senses. Specifically:

i. Section 4.2.1 is on the consistency between SD and SP
ii. Section 4.2.2 is on the consistency between SD and SR
iii. Section 4.2.3 is on the consistency between SD and RU
iv. Section 4.2.4 is on the consistency between SD and FO
v. Section 4.2.5 is on the consistency between SD and RR
vi. Section 4.2.6 is on the consistency between SP and SR
vii. Section 4.2.7 is on the consistency between SP and RU
viii. Section 4.2.8 is on the consistency between SP and FO
ix. Section 4.2.9 is on the consistency between SP and RR
x. Section 4.2.10 is on the consistency between SR and RU
xi. Section 4.2.11 is on the consistency between SR and FO
xii. Section 4.2.12 is on the consistency between SR and RR
xiii. Section 4.2.13 is on the consistency between RU and FO
xiv. Section 4.2.14 is on the consistency between RU and RR
xv. Section 4.2.15 is on the consistency between FO and RR

Note that in subsections on the consistency of SR, FO and RR and other criteria, the tables show results according to two interpretations of the criteria (Y/N):

i. *SR(N)* includes cases for which a direction is identified according to SR but is questionable, that is, cases for which the SR between pairs was marked as close to similar (the semantic range covered by one of the pairs being slightly wider).
ii. *SR(Y)* counts only cases for which the SR was identified as wider (marked >) for one of the pairs.
iii. Similarly, *FO(N)* and *RR(N)* include all cases where a direction can be identified, that is, cases where the frequency of occurrence or the range of registers covered by one of the pair senses is higher than its counterpart's.
iv. *FO(Y)* and *RR(Y)* count only cases for which the differences were interpreted as significant after application of two statistical tests (a Chi-squared test for FO and a Fisher's exact test for RR).

4.2.1 Consistency between SD and SP

The results of the consistency between the criteria of SD and SP are presented in Table 38.

Table 38: Consistency between SD and SP by sense

				Total	
SD vs SP (D1)	**Direction**	**nPairs**	**%**	**nPairs**	**%**
Consistent direction	$N^0>V^1$	121	53.54 %	188	83.19 %
	$V^0>N^1$	67	29.65 %		
Inconsistent direction	SD (direction) vs SP (unclear)	4	1.77 %	6	2.65 %
	SD (unclear) vs SP (direction)	2	0.88 %		
Unresolved direction	SD/SP (unclear)	32	14.16 %	32	14.16 %

				Total	
SD vs SP (D2)	**Direction**	**nPairs**	**%**	**nPairs**	**%**
Consistent direction	$V^1>N^2$	22	47.83 %	40	86.96 %
	$N^1>V^2$	18	39.13 %		
Inconsistent direction	SP (direction) vs SD (unclear)	3	6.52 %	3	6.52 %
Unresolved direction	SD/SP (unclear)	3	6.52 %	3	6.52 %

As regards the consistency between SD and SP in D1, Table 38 shows that:

i. The criteria indicate the same direction in 188 pairs (83.19 %), specifically, they agree on a Noun-to-Verb direction in 121 pairs (53.54 %), and a Verb-to-Noun direction in 67 pairs (29.65 %).
ii. Only one of the criteria (SD or SP) identifies a direction in six other pairs (2.65 %).
iii. None of the criteria can be confidently analysed as indicating a direction in the remaining 32 pairs (14.16 %).

In D2, similar results are found:

i. A similar consistency rate is found between SD and SP: they indicate the same direction in 40 pairs (86.96 %), specifically, Verb-to-Noun ($V^1>N^2$) in 22 pairs (47.83 %) and Noun-to-Verb ($N^1>V^2$) in 18 pairs (39.13 %).
ii. One or both criteria cannot be confidently analysed as indicating a direction in the remaining six pairs (13.04 %).

4.2.2 Consistency between SD and SR

The results of the consistency between the criteria of SD and SR are shown in Table 39. Note that because SR is a criterion best applied by considering the overall senses that lexemes take, no analysis can be made as regards the senses in the second order of derivation (D2), thus only the directions identified by SD in the first order of derivation (D1) are compared.

Table 39: Consistency between SD (D1) and SR by sense

				Total	
SD vs SR	**Direction**	**nPairs**	**%**	**nPairs**	**%**
Consistent direction (Y)	$N^0>V^1$	54	23.89 %	85	37.61 %
	$V^0>N^1$	31	13.72 %		
Consistent direction (N)	$N^0>V^1$	12	5.31 %	18	7.96 %
	$V^0>N^1$	6	2.65 %		
Inconsistent direction	SD (direction) vs SR (unclear)	69	30.53 %	112	49.56 %
	SD (unclear) vs SR (direction)	24	10.62 %		
	Opposite direction (Y)	13	5.75 %		
	Opposite direction (N)	6	2.65 %		
Unresolved	SD/SR (unclear)	11	4.87 %	11	4.87 %

The results are as follows:

i. The criteria indicate the same direction in 103 pairs (45.58 %), specifically, a Noun-to-Verb direction in 66 pairs (29.20 %) and a Verb-to-Noun direction in 37 pairs (16.37 %). However, as represented in the table, if only the cases where SR can be taken as indicating a direction with a higher degree of confidence (Y), it can be observed that the criteria signal the same direction for 85 pairs (37.61 %), specifically, a Noun-to-Verb direction in 54 pairs (23.89 %) and a Verb-to-Noun direction in 31 pairs (13.72 %).
ii. The directionality results of the criteria of SD and SR disagree in 112 pairs (49.56 %). When this is the case:
   a. both criteria indicate opposite directions in 19 pairs (8.41 %),
   b. SD indicates a direction, but the analysis of SR is unclear in 69 pairs (30.53 %), and
   c. the direction based on SD is unclear, but SR indicates a direction in 24 pairs (10.62 %).
iii. None of the criteria can be confidently analysed as indicating a direction in the remaining eleven pairs (4.87 %).

Whenever the directionality established by an analysis of SR by senses is marked as unclear (N) the data are disregarded, and thus, the consistency between SR and other criteria decreases. Notably, however, the comparison of cases for which the criteria indicate opposite directions is not as expected: Whereas SR may be expected to disagree with SD especially when the semantic range covered by the senses of the lexemes is considered close to similar (N), the results show that, for a higher number of cases (13 pairs, 5.75 %), an opposite direction is found where SR is applicable (Y), that is, when a lexeme presents a wider semantic range than its related pair.

4.2.3 Consistency between SD and RU

The results of the consistency between the criteria of SD and RU are shown in Table 40, by orders of derivation. As regards the consistency of the criteria in D1, it can be seen that:

i. SD and RU indicate the same direction in 48 pairs (21.24 %), specifically, a Noun-to-Verb direction in 30 pairs (13.27 %) and a Verb-to-Noun direction in 18 pairs (7.96 %).
ii. The directionality results of the criteria of SD and RU disagree in 153 pairs (67.7 %). When this is the case:
   a. both criteria indicate opposite directions in 13 pairs (5.75 %),

b. SD indicates a direction, but the analysis of RU is unclear in 131 pairs (57.96 %), and
c. the direction based on SD is unclear, but RU indicates a direction in nine pairs (3.98 %).

iii. None of the criteria can be confidently analysed as indicating a direction in the remaining 25 pairs (11.06 %).

Similar consistency levels are found between SD and RU in D2:

i. The criteria indicate the same direction in twelve pairs (26.09 %),
ii. In the remaining 34 pairs (73.92 %), either one or both criteria cannot be confidently analysed as indicating a direction. Among these, the major number of pairs correspond to the group that is assigned a direction by SD while the direction by RU is unclear (27 pairs, 58.70 %).

Table 40: Consistency between SD and RU by sense

				Total	
SD vs RU (D1)	**Direction**	**nPairs**	**%**	**nPairs**	**%**
Consistent direction	N^0>V^1	30	13.27 %	48	21.24 %
	V^0>N^1	18	7.96 %		
Inconsistent direction	SD (direction) vs RU (unclear)	131	57.96 %	153	67.7 %
	SD (unclear) vs RU (direction)	9	3.98 %		
	Opposite directions	13	5.75 %		
Unresolved	SD/RU (unclear)	25	11.06 %	25	11.06 %
				Total	
SD vs RU (D2)	**Direction**	**nPairs**	**%**	**nPairs**	**%**
Consistent direction	V^1>N^2	6	13.04 %	12	26.09 %
	N^1>V^2	6	13.04 %		
Inconsistent direction	SD (direction) vs RU (unclear)	27	58.70 %	32	69.57 %
	SD (unclear) vs RU (direction)	4	8.70 %		
	Opposite directions	1	2.17 %		
Unresolved	SD/RU (Unclear)	2	4.35 %	2	4.35 %

4.2.4 Consistency between SD and FO

The results of the consistency between the criteria of SD and FO are shown in Table 41. The criteria indicate the same direction in 147 pairs (65.04 %) in D1, however, when significance levels are considered, the results are as follows:

i. A Chi-squared test identifies a significant difference between the senses of 127 pairs (56.64 %), specifically, a Noun-to-Verb direction is identified for 93 pairs (41.15 %) and a Verb-to-Noun direction in 34 pairs (15.04 %). For the remaining 20 pairs (8.85 %) no significant difference is found by FO, and thus, even if the results between the criteria may seem consistent, FO is deemed as not applicable for these cases.
ii. The consistency results are not relevant to decide on directionality as the criteria disagree in 78 pairs (34.51 %). When this is the case:
   a. both criteria indicate opposite directions in 43 pairs (19.03 %), and in 34 of those pairs, the FO differences prove significant.
   b. SD indicates a direction, but the analysis of FO is unclear in three pairs (1.33 %), and
   c. the direction based on SD is unclear, but FO indicates a direction in 32 pairs (14.16 %).
iii. None of the criteria give a direction for one remaining pair (0.44 %).

Table 41: Consistency between SD and FO by sense. Significance is indicated for FO (*Y/N*)

				Total	
SD vs FO (D1)	**Direction**	**nPairs**	**%**	**nPairs**	**%**
Consistent direction (Y)	N^0>V^1	93	41.15 %	127	56.19 %
	V^0>N^1	34	15.04 %		
Consistent direction (N)	N^0>V^1	9	3.98 %	20	8.85 %
	V^0>N^1	11	4.87 %		
Inconsistent direction	SD (direction) vs FO (unclear)	3	1.33 %	78	34.51 %
	SD (unclear) vs FO (direction)	32	14.16 %		
	Opposite direction (Y)	34	15.04 %		
	Opposite direction (N)	9	3.98 %		
Unresolved direction	SD (unclear) and FO (unclear)	1	0.44 %	1	0.44 %

				Total	
SD vs FO (D2)	**Direction**	**nPairs**	**%**	**nPairs**	**%**
Consistent direction (Y)	V^1>N^2	17	36.96 %	27	58.70 %
	N^1>V^2	10	21.74 %		
Consistent direction (N)	V^1>N^2	1	2.17 %	4	8.70 %
	N^1>V^2	3	6.52 %		
Inconsistent direction	Opposite direction (Y)	7	15.22 %	9	19.57 %
	Opposite direction (N)	2	4.35 %		
Unresolved direction	FO (Y) vs SD (unclear)	6	13.04 %	6	13.04 %

Similar results are found in D2:

i. SD and FO show consistent results for 31 pairs (67.39 %), specifically, the direction identified is Verb-to-Noun (V^1>N^2) for 18 pairs (50 %) and Noun-to-Verb (N^1>V^2) for 13 pairs (28.26 %). FO proves applicable in 27 of those pairs (58.70 %).
ii. For the remaining 15 pairs in D2 no consistency is found between the direction indicated by SD and FO: in six pairs because SD is unclear (13.04 %), and in nine pairs because they identify opposite directions (the difference in FO is significant in seven of those pairs, 15.22 %).

It might be expected that, if opposite directions were identified by the criteria, these would be cases where the difference in the frequency of occurrence is not statistically significant (N) and, thus, a direction cannot be claimed with confidence based on FO. However, contrary to expectations, the number of pairs where the criteria indicate opposite directions is quite large for cases where the difference in the senses' frequency of occurrence is statistically significant (Y) in both D1 and D2. The results cast doubts on the applicability of the criteria.

4.2.5 Consistency between SD and RR

The results of the consistency between the criteria of SD and RR are shown in Table 42. The comparison of SD with RR according to the BNC's retrieval classification into 71 registers shows that the criteria indicate the same direction in 135 pairs (59.73 %) in D1: a Noun-to-Verb direction in 93 pairs (41.15 %) and a Verb-to-Noun direction in 42 pairs (18.58 %). However, after a Chi-squared test was performed, results are as follows:

i. A significant difference is identified between the senses of 85 pairs (37.71 %), specifically, a Noun-to-Verb direction is identified for 59 pairs (26.11 %) and a Verb-to-Noun direction in 26 pairs (11.5 %). For the remaining 50 pairs (22.12 %) no significant difference is found by Fisher's exact test, and thus, RR is not considered applicable in these cases.
ii. The directionality results disagree for 88 pairs (38.94 %) in that:
   a. both criteria indicate opposite directions in 47 pairs (20.8 %),
   b. SD indicates a direction, but the analysis of RR is unclear in eleven pairs (4.87 %), and
   c. the direction based on SD is unclear, but RR indicates a direction in 30 pairs (13.27 %).
iii. None of the criteria give a direction for three pairs (1.33 %).

Table 42: Consistency between SD and RR by sense according to BNC's David Lee's classification into 71 registers. Significance is indicated for RR (Y/N)

				Total	
SD vs RR (D1)	**Direction**	**nPairs**	**%**	**nPairs**	**%**
Consistent direction (Y)	N^0>V^1	59	26.11 %	85	37.61 %
	V^0>N^1	26	11.50 %		
Consistent direction (N)	N^0>V^1	34	15.04 %	50	22.12 %
	V^0>N^1	16	7.08 %		
Inconsistent direction	SD (direction) vs RR (unclear)	11	4.87 %	88	38.94 %
	SD (unclear) vs RR (direction)	30	13.27 %		
	Opposite direction (Y)	18	7.96 %		
	Opposite direction (N)	29	12.83 %		
Unresolved direction	SD/RR (unclear)	3	1.33 %	3	1.33 %

				Total	
SD vs RR (D2)	**Direction**	**nPairs**	**%**	**nPairs**	**%**
Consistent direction (Y)	V^1>N^2	12	26.09 %	19	41.30 %
	N^1>V^2	7	15.22 %		
Consistent direction (N)	V^1>N^2	7	15.22 %	14	30.43 %
	N^1>V^2	6	13.04 %		
Inconsistent direction	RR (Y/N) vs SD (unclear)	5	10.87 %	12	26.09 %
	RR (unclear) vs SD (V^1>N^2)	2	4.35 %		
	Opposite direction (Y)	2	4.35 %		
	Opposite direction (N)	3	6.52 %		
Unresolved	RR/SD (unclear)	1	2.17 %	1	2.17 %

An analysis of the consistency of SD and RR (Y) in D2 reveals that:

i. The criteria indicate the same direction in 19 pairs (41.61 %), where the results of RR prove significant (Y). They are also consistent in another 14 (30.43 %) pairs where RR does not prove applicable, according to Fisher's exact test.
ii. The criteria indicate opposite directions in 5 pairs (10.87 %). Only one of the criteria indicates directionality for 7 other pairs (15.22 %).
iii. None of the criteria give a direction for the remaining pair (2.17 %).

The table also shows that, whereas in most cases where an inconsistent direction is signalled by these two criteria, the difference in register usage is not statistically significant, still a quite large number in D1 (18 pairs, 7.96 %) is for cases where the difference in register usage is significant (Y). This is the case even when significance was established for RR only for 159 of the pairs of senses (39.85 %, cf. Table 32).

4.2.6 Consistency between SP and SR

The results of the consistency between the criteria of SP and SR are shown in Table 43.

Table 43: Consistency between SP and SR by sense

				Total	
SP (D1) vs SR	**Direction**	**nPairs**	**%**	**nPairs**	**%**
Consistent direction (SR Y)	$N^0>V^1$	53	23.45 %	84	37.17 %
	$V^0>N^1$	31	13.72 %		
Consistent direction (SR N)	$N^0>V^1$	12	5.31 %	18	7.96 %
	$V^0>N^1$	6	2.56 %		
Inconsistent direction	SP (direction) vs SR (unclear)	68	30.09 %	112	49.56 %
	SP (unclear) vs SR (direction)	24	10.62 %		
	Opposite direction (Y)	14	6.19 %		
	Opposite direction (N)	6	2.65 %		
Unresolved direction	SP (unclear) and SR (unclear)	12	5.31 %	12	5.31 %

The criteria indicate the same direction in 102 pairs (45.13 %), specifically, a Noun-to-Verb direction in 65 pairs (28.76 %), and a Verb-to-Noun direction in 37 pairs (16.37 %). However, as represented in the table, if only the cases where the SR can be taken as indicating a direction with a higher degree of confidence (Y), it can be observed that:

i. The criteria signal the same direction for 84 pairs (37.17 %), specifically, a Noun-to-Verb direction in 53 pairs (23.45 %) and a Verb-to-Noun direction in 31 pairs (13.72 %).
ii. The directionality results of the criteria of SP and SR disagree in 112 pairs (49.56 %). When this is the case:
   a. both criteria indicate opposite directions in 20 pairs (8.85 %),
   b. SP indicates a direction, but the analysis of SR is unclear in 68 pairs (30.09 %); and
   c. the direction based on SP is unclear, but SR indicates a direction in 24 pairs (10.62 %).
iii. None of the criteria can be confidently analysed as indicating a direction for the remaining twelve pairs (5.31 %).

Note that, as in the comparison between SR and SD too, cases for which the criteria of SR and SP indicate opposite directions is not as expected: SR may be expected to disagree with SP especially when the semantic range covered by the senses of the lexemes is marked as close to similar (N), however, the results show that, for a higher number of cases (14 pairs, 6.19 %), an opposite direction is found where SR is applicable (Y).

4.2.7 Consistency between SP and RU

The results of the consistency between the criteria of SP and RU are shown in Table 44. As regards the results in D1, it can be observed that:

i. The criteria indicate the same direction in 45 pairs (19.91 %), specifically, a Noun-to-Verb direction in 28 pairs (12.39 %), and a Verb-to-Noun direction in 17 pairs (7.52 %).
ii. The directionality results of the criteria of SP and RU disagree in 157 pairs (69.47 %). When this is the case:
    a. both criteria indicate an opposite direction in twelve pairs (5.31 %),
    b. SP indicates a direction, but the analysis of RU is unclear in 133 pairs (58.41 %), and
    c. the direction based on SP is unclear, but RU indicates a direction in twelve pairs (5.31 %).
iii. None of the criteria can be confidently analysed as indicating a direction for the remaining 24 pairs (10.62 %).

An analysis of the consistency of SP and RU in D2 reveals the following:

iv. The criteria indicate the same direction in 15 pairs (32.61 %),
v. In the remaining 31 pairs (67.39 %), either one or both criteria cannot be confidently analysed as indicating a direction. Among these, most pairs can be assigned a direction by SP while the direction by RU is unclear (26 pairs, 56.52 %).
vi. Opposite directions by SP and RU are found in two pairs (4.35 %)

Table 44: Consistency between SP and RU by sense

				Total	
SP vs RU (D1)	**Direction**	**nPairs**	**%**	**nPairs**	**%**
Consistent direction	$N^0>V^1$	28	12.39 %	45	19.91 %
	$V^0>N^1$	17	7.52 %		
Inconsistent direction	SP (direction) vs RU (unclear)	133	58.85 %	157	69.47 %
	SP (unclear) vs RU (direction)	12	5.31 %		
	Opposite directions	12	5.31 %		
Unresolved direction	SP (unclear) and RU (unclear)	24	10.62 %	24	10.62 %
				Total	
SP vs RU (D2)	**Direction**	**nPairs**	**%**	**nPairs**	**%**
Consistent direction	$V^1>N^2$	9	13.04 %	15	32.61 %
	$N^1>V^2$	6	21.74 %		
Inconsistent direction	SP (direction) vs RU (unclear)	26	56.52 %	29	63.04 %
	SP (unclear) vs RU (direction)	1	2.17 %		
	Opposite directions	2	4.35 %		
Unresolved direction	SP/RU (Unclear)	2	4.35 %	2	4.35 %

4.2.8 Consistency between SP and FO

The results of the consistency between the criteria of SP and FO are shown in Table 45, by order of derivation. The following results are obtained for the pairs in D1:

i. The criteria initially seem to indicate the same direction for 145 pairs (64.16 %). However, a Chi-squared test confirms the applicability of FO for 120 of those pairs (55.31 %). Specifically, a Noun-to-Verb direction is found by both criteria in 91 pairs (40.27 %), and a Verb-to-Noun direction in 34 pairs (15.04 %).
ii. The directionality results of the criteria of SP and FO disagree for 80 pairs (35.4 %). When this is the case:
    a. both criteria indicate opposite directions in 43 pairs (19.03 %), however the frequency differences between senses are significant and thus serve to identify a direction in 33 pairs (14.60 %),

b. SP indicates a direction, but the analysis of FO is unclear in three pairs (1.33 %), and
c. the direction based on SP is unclear, but FO indicates a direction in 34 other pairs (15.04 %).

iii. None of the criteria give a direction for one remaining pair (0.44 %).

Table 45: Consistency between SP and FO by sense. Significance is indicated for FO (Y/N)

				Total	
SP vs FO (D1)	**Direction**	**nPairs**	**%**	**nPairs**	**%**
Consistent direction (Y)	$N^0>V^1$	91	40.27 %	120	55.31 %
	$V^0>N^1$	34	15.04 %		
Consistent direction (N)	$N^0>V^1$	9	3.98 %	20	8.85 %
	$V^0>N^1$	11	4.87 %		
Inconsistent direction	SP (direction) vs FO (unclear)	3	1.33 %	80	35.4 %
	SP (unclear) vs FO (direction)	34	15.04 %		
	Opposite direction (Y)	33	14.60 %		
	Opposite direction (N)	10	4.42 %		
Unresolved direction	SP/FO (unclear)	1	0.44 %	1	0.44 %
				Total	
SP vs FO (D2)	**Direction**	**nPairs**	**%**	**nPairs**	**%**
Consistent direction (Y)	$V^1>N^2$	20	43.48 %	30	65.22 %
	$N^1>V^2$	10	21.74 %		
Consistent direction (N)	$V^1>N^2$	1	2.17 %	4	8.70 %
	$N^1>V^2$	3	6.52 %		
Inconsistent direction	Opposite direction (Y)	7	15.22 %	9	19.57 %
	Opposite direction (N)	2	4.35 %		
Unresolved direction	FO (Y direction) SP ($V^1>N^2$?)	2	4.35 %	3	6.52 %
	Opposite FO (UND Y) SP ($V^1>N^2$?)	1	2.17 %		

Results of a consistency analysis of SP and FO in D2 are as follows:

i. If significance levels are considered, the criteria show consistent results for 30 pairs (65.22 %), specifically, the direction identified is Verb-to-Noun ($V^1>N^2$) for 20 pairs (43.48 %) and Noun-to-Verb ($N^1>V^2$) for ten pairs (21.74 %).

ii. The criteria indicate opposite directions in 9 pairs (19.57 %), although for two such cases FO is not applicable because the differences between the senses are not statistically significant.
iii. For the remaining three pairs in D2 (6.52 %) no consistency is found as the direction by SP is unclear.

It was expected that cases where the criteria indicate opposite directions would correspond to instances where the difference in frequency of occurrence is not statistically significant (N). However, a quite large number of pairs in D1 and D2 for which the criteria of FO and SP signal opposite directions is for cases where FO proves statistically significant (Y). Again, the results cast doubts on the applicability of the criteria.

4.2.9 Consistency between SP and RR

The results of the consistency between the criteria of SP and RR are shown in Table 46 by order of derivation.

The comparison of SP and RR according to the BNC's retrieval classification into 71 registers yields the following results:

i. If significance levels are considered according to a Fisher's exact test, the criteria indicate the same direction in 83 pairs (36.72 %): a Noun-to-Verb direction in 58 pairs (25.66 %), and a Verb-to-Noun direction in 25 pairs (11.06 %). RR is not considered applicable (N) for the remaining 49 pairs (21.68 %) in which it initially seems to signal the same direction.
ii. The directionality results disagree in 92 pairs (40.71 %) in that:
   a. both criteria indicate opposite directions in 46 pairs (20.35 %), and RR is considered applicable, that is, there is a significant difference between the range of registers covered by the senses, in 29 pairs (12.83 %),
   b. SP indicates a direction, but the analysis of RR is unclear in twelve pairs (5.31 %), and
   c. the direction based on SP is unclear, but RR indicates a direction in 33 pairs (14.6 %).
iii. None of the criteria give a direction for two remaining pairs (0.88 %).

The results of the consistency between the criteria in D2 are as follows:

i. Consistency is found between SP and RR (where RR is applicable) for 21 pairs, 46.65 %), specifically a Verb-to-Noun (V^1>N^2) direction is identified is for 14 pairs (30.43 %) and a Noun-to-Verb (N^1>V^2) direction is found for seven pairs (15.22 %). RR is not applicable based on a Fisher's exact test in other 16 pairs (34.78 %) for which the direction by the criteria seemed consistent at first.
ii. For the remaining nine pairs in D2 (19.57 %), no consistency is found between the direction indicated by SD and RR.

Table 46: Consistency between SP and RR by sense according to BNC's David Lee's classification into 71 registers. Significance is indicated for RR (Y/N)

				Total	
SP vs RR (D1)	**Direction**	**nPairs**	**%**	**nPairs**	**%**
Consistent direction (Y)	$N^0>V^1$	58	25.66 %	83	36.72 %
	$V^0>N^1$	25	11.06 %		
Consistent direction (N)	$N^0>V^1$	33	14.60 %	49	21.68 %
	$V^0>N^1$	16	7.08 %		
Inconsistent direction	SP (direction) vs RR (unclear)	12	5.31 %	92	40.71 %
	SP (unclear) vs RR (direction)	33	14.6 %		
	Opposite direction (Y)	18	7.96 %		
	Opposite direction (N)	29	12.83 %		
Unresolved	SP/RR (unclear)	2	0.88 %	2	0.88 %
				Total	
SP vs RR (D2)	**Direction**	**nPairs**	**%**	**nPairs**	**%**
Consistent direction (Y)	$V^1>N^2$	14	30.43 %	21	45.65 %
	$N^1>V^2$	7	15.22 %		
Consistent direction (N)	$V^1>N^2$	10	21.74 %	16	34.78 %
	$N^1>V^2$	6	13.04 %		
Inconsistent direction	Opposite direction (Y)	2	4.35 %	5	10.87 %
	Opposite direction (N)	3	6.52 %		
Unresolved direction	RR/SP (unclear)	3	6.52 %	4	8.70 %
	RR (unclear) vs SP (direction $V^1>N^2$)	1	2.17 %		

As in the consistency results between SD and RR, the Table shows that SP and RR signal opposite directions in 18 pairs in D1 (7.96 %), where RR is established with confidence too (Y), and two pairs in D2 (4.35 %). These numbers cast serious doubts on the applicability of the criteria.

4.2.10 Consistency between SR and RU

The results of the consistency between the criteria of SR and RU are presented in Table 47.

Table 47: Consistency between SR and RU by sense

				Total	
SR vs RU (D1)	**Direction**	**nPairs**	**%**	**nPairs**	**%**
Consistent direction (SR Y)	N^0>V^1	18	7.96 %	31	13.72 %
	V^0>N^1	13	5.75 %		
Consistent direction (SR N)	N^0>V^1	1	0.44 %	4	1.77 %
	V^0>N^1	3	1.33 %		
Inconsistent direction	SR (direction) vs RU (unclear)	99	43.81 %	134	59.29 %
	SR (unclear) vs RU (direction)	23	10.18 %		
	Opposite directions	12	5.31 %		
Unresolved direction	SR (unclear) and RU (unclear)	57	25.22 %	57	25.22 %

The consistency between the criteria is as follows:

i. SR and RU (D1) indicate the same direction in 31 pairs (13.72 %), specifically, a Noun-to-Verb direction in 18 pairs (7.96 %), and a Verb-to-Noun direction in 13 pairs (5.75 %). The analysis of SR is not as clear for another four pairs which are also consistent with the direction by RU.
ii. The directionality results of SR and RU disagree in 134 pairs (59.29 %). When this is the case:
   a. both criteria indicate an opposite direction for twelve pairs (5.31 %),
   b. SR indicates a direction, but the analysis of RU is unclear in 99 pairs (43.81 %), and
   c. the direction based on SR is unclear, but RU indicates a direction in 23 pairs (10.18 %).
iii. None of the criteria can be confidently analysed as indicating a direction in the remaining 57 pairs (25.22 %).

An analysis of the consistency of the criteria in D2 reveals that a similar consistency level is found between SD and RU:

iv. The criteria indicate the same direction in twelve pairs (26.09 %),
v. In the remaining 34 pairs (73.92 %), either one or both criteria cannot be confidently analysed as indicating a direction. Among these, the major number of pairs correspond to the group that is assigned a direction by SD while the direction by RU is unclear (27 pairs, 58.70 %).

4.2.11 Consistency between SR and FO

The results of the consistency between the criteria of SR and FO are shown in Table 48.

Table 48: Consistency between SR and FO by sense

				Total	
SR vs FO (D1)	**Direction**	**nPairs**	**%**	**nPairs**	**%**
Consistent direction (Y/Y)	Noun-to-Verb	49	21.68 %	78	34.51 %
	Verb-to-Noun	29	12.83 %		
Consistent direct. (N/N; N/Y; Y/N)	Noun-to-Verb or Verb-to-Noun (N/N)	5	2.21 %	31	13.72 %
	Noun-to-Verb or Verb-to-Noun (N/Y)	19	8.41 %		
	Noun-to-Verb or Verb-to-Noun (Y/N)	7	3.10 %		
Inconsistent direction	SR (direction) vs FO (unclear)	3	1.33 %	116	51.33 %
	SR (unclear) vs FO (direction)	79	34.96 %		
	Opposite direction (Y/Y)	20	8.85 %		
	Opposite direction (N/Y)	7	3.10 %		
	Opposite direction (Y/N)	6	2.65 %		
	Opposite direction (N/N)	1	0.44 %		
Unresolved direction	SR (unclear) and FO (unclear)	1	0.44 %	1	0.44 %

It can be observed that:

i. SR and FO indicate the same direction in 109 pairs (48.23 %), specifically, a Noun-to-Verb direction in 66 pairs (29.20 %), and a Verb-to-Noun direction in 43 pairs (19.03 %). However, not in all cases the direction signalled by the criteria is deemed relevant. If unclear SR cases and significance levels are considered for FO, it can be seen that the criteria actually signal the same direction for 78 pairs (34.51 %). Specifically, a Noun-to-Verb direction is found for 49 pairs (21.68 %), and a Verb-to-Noun direction for 29 pairs (12.83 %).

ii. The directionality results of the criteria of SR and FO disagree in 116 pairs (51.33 %). When this is the case:
   a. both criteria indicate opposite directions in 34 pairs (15.04 %),
   b. SR indicates a direction, but the analysis of FO is unclear in three pairs (1.33 %), and

   c. the direction based on SR is unclear, but FO indicates a direction in 79 pairs (34.96 %).
iii. None of the criteria give a direction in one pair (0.44 %).

The low consistency level between SR and FO results partly from a higher inapplicability of SR. It is also relevant that, where SR and FO indicate opposite directions, a quite large number of pairs are found for which both criteria signal a direction with certainty too (Y) (20 pairs, 8.85 %). Again, this casts doubt on the applicability of the criteria.

4.2.12 Consistency between SR and RR

Table 49. presents the results of the consistency of SR with RR according to the BNC's David Lee's classification into 71 registers. The results are as follows:

i. The criteria seem to indicate the same direction in 101 pairs (44.69 %): a Noun-to-Verb direction in 60 pairs (26.55 %), and a Verb-to-Noun direction in 41 pairs (18.14 %). However, the table shows that, if the data where the directionality by an analysis of SR by senses is questionable are left out, and, if the significance levels of RR are considered, the consistency across criteria decreases to 50 pairs (22.12 %). Specifically, a Noun-to-Verb direction is found for 33 pairs (14.6 %), and a Verb-to-Noun direction for 17 pairs (7.52 %).
ii. The directionality results disagree in 117 pairs (51.77 %) in that:
   a. both criteria indicate opposite directions in 39 pairs (17.26 %),
   b. SR indicates a direction, but the analysis of RR is unclear in six pairs (2.65 %), and
   c. the direction based on SR is unclear, but RR indicates a direction in 72 pairs (31.86 %).
iii. None of the criteria give a direction in the remaining eight pairs (3.54 %).

Table 49: Consistency between SR and RR by sense according to BNC's David Lee's classification into 71 registers

				Total	
SR vs RR (D1)	**Direction**	**nPairs**	**%**	**nPairs**	**%**
Consistent direction (Y/Y)	Noun-to-Verb	33	14.60 %	50	22.12 %
	Verb-to-Noun	17	7.52 %		
Consistent direction (N/N; N/Y; Y/N)	Noun-to-Verb or Verb-to-Noun (N/N)	14	6.19 %	51	22.57 %
	Noun-to-Verb or Verb-to-Noun (N/Y)	8	3.54 %		
	Noun-to-Verb or Verb-to-Noun (Y/N)	29	12.83 %		

(Continued)

Table 49: *(Continued)*

				Total	
SR vs RR (D1)	**Direction**	**nPairs**	**%**	**nPairs**	**%**
Inconsistent direction	SR (direction) vs RR (unclear)	6	2.65 %	117	51.77 %
	SR (unclear) vs RR (direction)	72	31.86 %		
	Opposite direction (Y/Y)	16	7.08 %		
	Opposite direction (N/Y)	13	5.75 %		
	Opposite direction (Y/N)	4	1.77 %		
	Opposite direction (N/N)	6	2.65 %		
Unresolved direction	SR (unclear) and RR (unclear)	8	3.54 %	8	3.54 %

Also, Table 49 shows that there are 16 pairs (7.08 %), for which both SR and RR signal opposite directions, both with a higher degree of certainty too (Y). For 17 other cases where the criteria signal opposite directions, only one or the other criterion signals a direction with certainty (7.52 %). Again, the criteria signal opposite directions for a considerable number of pairs, which casts doubts on the applicability of the criteria for directionality.

4.2.13 Consistency between RU and FO

Table 50 presents the results of the consistency between the criteria of RU and FO.

Table 50: Consistency between RU and FO by sense. Significance is indicated for FO (Y/N)

				Total	
RU vs FO (D1)	**Direction**	**nPairs**	**%**	**nPairs**	**%**
Consistent direction (Y)	$N^0>V^1$	28	12.39 %	47	20.79 %
	$V^0>N^1$	19	8.41 %		
Consistent direction (N)	$N^0>V^1$	3	1.33 %	4	1.77 %
	$V^0>N^1$	1	0.44 %		
Inconsistent direction	RU (unclear) vs FO (direction)	152	67.26 %	171	75.66 %
	Opposite direction (Y)	17	7.52 %		
	Opposite direction (N)	2	0.88 %		
Unresolved direction	RU (unclear) and FO (unclear)	4	1.77 %	4	1.77 %

				Total	
RU vs FO (D2)	Direction	nPairs	%	nPairs	%
Consistent direction (Y)	V^1>N^2	10	21.74 %	14	30.43 %
	N^1>V^2	4	8.70 %		
Inconsistent direction	RU (unclear) vs FO (direction)	21	45.65 %	25	54.35 %
	RU (direction) vs FO (unclear)	1	2.17 %		
	Opposite direction (N)	3	6.52 %		
Unresolved direction	RU (unclear) and FO (unclear/N)	7	15.22 %	7	15.22 %

The following results can be observed in D1:

i. The criteria indicate the same direction in 47 pairs (20.79 %), specifically, a Noun-to-Verb direction in 28 pairs (12.39 %), and a Verb-to-Noun direction in 19 pairs (8.41 %).
ii. The directionality results of RU and FO disagree in 171 pairs (75.66 %), specifically, they indicate an opposite direction in 19 pairs (8.41 %), otherwise, the direction according to RU is unclear and only FO indicates a direction (152 pairs, 67.26 %).
iii. None of the criteria signal a direction in the remaining four pairs (1.77 %).

The results are as follows for the pairs in D2:

i. The criteria indicate the same direction in 14 pairs (30.43 %), specifically, a Verb-to-Noun (V^1>N^2) direction in ten pairs (21.74 %), and a Noun-to-Verb (N^1>V^2) direction in four pairs (8.7 %).
ii. RU and FO disagree in 25 pairs in D2 (54.35 %), in most cases (21 pairs, 45.65 %) because RU is not applicable.
iii. None of the criteria signal a direction in seven other pairs (15.22 %).

4.2.14 Consistency between RU and RR

Table 51 presents the consistency results of the criteria of RU and RR.

Table 51: Consistency between RU and RR by sense according to BNC's David Lee's classification into 71 registers. Significance is indicated for RR (Y/N)

				Total	
RU vs RR (D1)	**Direction**	**nPairs**	**%**	**nPairs**	**%**
Consistent direction (Y)	N^0>V^1	21	9.29 %	34	15.04 %
	V^0>N^1	13	5.75 %		
Consistent direction (N)	N^0>V^1	8	3.54 %	16	7.08 %
	V^0>N^1	8	3.54 %		
Inconsistent direction	RU (direction) vs RR (unclear)	3	1.33 %	165	73.01 %
	RU (unclear) vs RR (direction)	145	64.16 %		
	Opposite direction (Y)	7	3.10 %		
	Opposite direction (N)	10	4.42 %		
Unresolved direction	RU (unclear) and RR (unclear)	29	12.83 %	29	12.83 %
				Total	
RU vs RR (D2)	**Direction**	**nPairs**	**%**	**nPairs**	**%**
Consistent direction (Y)	V^1>N^2	10	21.74 %	15	32.61 %
	N^1>V^2	5	10.87 %		
Inconsistent direction	RU (unclear) vs RR (Y)	12	26.09 %	15	32.61 %
	Opposite direction (Y)	2	4.35 %		
	Opposite direction (N)	1	2.17 %		
Unresolved direction	RU (unclear) and RR (unclear/N)	16	34.78 %	16	34.78 %

Specifically, the comparison of RU with RR shows that in D1:

i. The criteria indicate the same direction in 50 pairs in D1 (22.12 %), but when significance levels are considered for RU, consistency can only be claimed for 34 pairs (15.04 %). Specifically, a Noun-to-Verb direction is found in 21 pairs (9.29 %), and a Verb-to-Noun direction in 13 pairs (5.75 %).
ii. The directionality results disagree in 165 pairs in D1 (73.01 %) in that:
   a. both criteria indicate opposite directions in 17 pairs (7.52 %),
   b. RU indicates a direction, but the analysis of RR is unclear in three pairs (1.33 %), and
   c. the direction based on RU is unclear, but RR indicates a direction in 145 pairs (64.16 %).
iii. None of the criteria give a direction in the remaining 29 pairs in D1 (12.83 %).

The results are as follows for the pairs in D2:

i. The criteria indicate the same direction in 14 pairs (30.43 %) specifically, a Noun-to-Verb (N^1>V^2) direction in ten pairs (21.74 %), and a Verb-to-Noun (V^1>N^2) direction in five pairs (10.87 %).
ii. RU and RR disagree in 15 pairs in D2 (32.61 %), in most cases (12 pairs, 26.09 %) because RU is not applicable.
iii. None of the criteria indicate a direction in the remaining 16 pairs in D2 (34.78 %).

Not only do the criteria show consistency for few pairs, but also cases are found where they signal opposite directions, RR being applicable in some of the pairs too (D1: seven pairs, 3.1 %; D2: two pairs, 4.35 %).

As Table 51 shows, the overall consistency across RR and RU is very low. This is partly as a result of the lower applicability of the criteria:

i. in the case of RU because, as described in the results (cf. Table 23), restrictions of usage are often present either in both senses involved in conversion or in none of the senses. Thus, RU only proves applicable for a small number of senses, and
ii. in the case of RR, because a statistical test proves significant differences between a low number of pairs of senses. This is partly because the statistical test may not work well with a low number of registers (including up to 71 categories).

4.2.15 Consistency between FO and RR

Last, the consistency results between the criteria of FO and RR are presented in Table 52.

Table 52: Consistency between FO and RR by sense according to BNC's David Lee's classification into 71 registers. Significance is indicated for FO and RR (Y/N)

				Total	
FO vs RR (D1)	**Direction**	**nPairs**	**%**	**nPairs**	**%**
Consistent direction (Y/Y)	N^0>V^1	72	31.86 %	107	47.35 %
	V^0>N^1	35	15.49 %		
Consistent direction (Y/N)	N^0>V^1	39	17.26 %	62	27.43 %
	V^0>N^1	23	10.18 %		
Consistent direction (N/N)	N^0>V^1	10	4.42 %	25	11.06 %
	V^0>N^1	15	6.64 %		

(Continued)

Table 52: *(Continued)*

				Total	
FO vs RR (D1)	**Direction**	**nPairs**	**%**	**nPairs**	**%**
Inconsistent direction	RR (direction) vs FO (unclear)	1	0.44 %	29	12.83 %
	RR (unclear) vs FO (N)	12	5.31 %		
	Opposite direction (Y/Y)	8	3.54 %		
	Opposite direction (Y/N: 6; N/N: 2)	8	3.54 %		
Unresolved direction	RR (unclear) and FO (unclear)	3	1.33 %	3	1.33 %

				Total	
FO vs RR (D2)	**Direction**	**nPairs**	**%**	**nPairs**	**%**
Consistent direction (Y/Y)	$V^1>N^2$	16	34.78 %	23	50 %
	$N^1>V^2$	7	15.22 %		
Consistent direction (Y/N)	$V^1>N^2$	10	21.74 %	15	32.61 %
	$N^1>V^2$	5	10.87 %		
Consistent direction (N/N)	$V^1>N^2$	2	4.35 %	5	10.87 %
	$N^1>V^2$	3	6.52 %		
Inconsistent direction	RR (unclear) vs FO (N)	1	2.17 %	2	4.35 %
	Opposite direction (Y/Y)	1	2.17 %		
Unresolved direction	RR (unclear) and FO (unclear)	1	2.17 %	1	2.17 %

The results are as follows for the pairs in D1:

i. If every instance where a sense is more frequent or appears in a higher nReg than its counterpart is counted as signalling a direction, the criteria indicate the same direction in 194 pairs (85.84 %): a Noun-to-Verb direction in 121 pairs (53.54 %), and a Verb-to-Noun direction in 73 pairs (32.30 %). A high degree of agreement between the criteria was anticipated because, the more frequent a sense is, the more likely it is to occur in a higher number of registers. However, after significance levels based on two statistical tests (a Chi-squared test for FO and Fisher's exact test for RR) are set, the consistency across FO and RR is considerably lower: they indicate the same direction in 107 pairs (47.35 %): a Noun-to-Verb direction in 72 pairs (31.86 %), and a Verb-to-Noun direction in 35 pairs (15.49 %). For the rest of the pairs, either only FO proves applicable, or none do.

ii. The directionality results disagree in 29 pairs (12.83 %) in that:

   a. both criteria indicate opposite directions in 16 pairs (7.08 %),
   b. FO indicates a direction, but the analysis of RR is unclear in twelve pairs (5.31 %), and
   c. the direction based on FO is unclear, but RR indicates a direction in one pair (0.44 %).

iii. None of the criteria give a direction in the remaining three pairs (1.33 %).

The results are as follows for the pairs in D2:

i. When significance levels are established, the criteria indicate the same direction in 23 pairs (50 %): a Verb-to-Noun (V^1>N^2) direction in 16 pairs (34.78 %), and a Noun-to-Verb (N^1>V^2) direction in seven pairs (15.22 %). For the rest of pairs, either only FO proves applicable (32.61 %), or none of them do (10.87 %).
ii. The criteria indicate opposite directions in one pair (2.17 %).
iii. None of the criteria give a direction in two other pairs (4.35 %).

Note that, as shown in Table 52, most pairs where RR and FO indicate a consistent direction in D1 or D2 are pairs where both criteria are applicable (Y/Y). However, a large part in D1 (62 pairs, 27.43 %) and D2 (15 pairs, 32.61 %) are cases where they signal the same direction, except that only FO is validated statistically. These data cast doubts on the applicability of RR, and on the applicability of the statistical test to establish significance levels used for RR, which may not be appropriate to measure differences between such low number of registers. RR results should thus be taken with caution. Also, as both RR and FO seem to give very similar results on the direction they signal, it may not make sense to use both analyses to establish directionality in conversion and, if only one of the tests were to be used (assuming that the results obtained are correct), the use of FO should be given priority over RR, because significant frequency differences (Y) can be found between a larger number of pairs.

4.3 Overview on the cross-criteria consistency

A comparison of results across criteria (cf. Section 4.2) reveals that different directions are sometimes indicated by the criteria. The consistency between the criteria and how it may vary depending on how strictly the criteria are interpreted is further discussed in this section.

Note that the following table header rows are used in this section:

i. *Unclear direction* is used when none of the criteria show a direction.
ii. *Consistent direction* is used when two criteria indicate the same direction.

iii. *Inconsistent direction* is used when they do not indicate the same direction, including cases where one criterion indicates a direction while the other does not.

4.3.1 Semantic dependence (SD)

Section 4.3.1 discusses the results of the consistency of the direction across criteria, specifically SD vs the rest of criteria under study. Table 53[48] shows the consistency levels between SD and SP, RU, SR, FO, and RR for the 226 pairs according to an analysis by sense and by order of derivation.

As can be observed in Table 53, the picture is very similar in D1 and D2. Overall, SD presents a higher consistency with SP (D1: 83.19 %, D2: 86.96 %), that is, both indicate the same direction for the largest number of pairs. After SP, SD presents higher consistency with FO (D1: 57.08 %, D2: 58.70 %), and with RR and SR in D1 (37.61 %) and RR in D2 (41.3 %), even if the consistency decreases. SD presents the lowest consistency levels with RU (D1: 21.24 %, D2: 26.09 %). This can be regarded as a result of the low applicability of the criteria of RU, which is applicable for a low number of pairs of senses, regardless of the order of derivation.

Table 53: Consistency between SD and other criteria by senses in D1 and D2. *(Y)* and *(N)* stand for senses for which SR, FO, and RR signal a direction, even if the difference in the semantic range covered is close to similar (*SR(N)*) or the difference in frequency or register usage is not significant *(FO(N)* or *RR(N))*

Criteria analysis (D1)	Consistent direction		Inconsistent direction		Unclear direction	
	nPairs	%	nPairs	%	nPairs	%
SD/SP	188	83.19 %	6	2.65 %	32	14.16 %
SD/SR(N)	103	45.58 %	112	49.56 %	11	4.87 %
SD/SR(Y)	85	37.61 %				
SD/RU	48	21.24 %	153	67.7 %	25	11.06 %
SD/FO(N)	147	65.04 %	78	34.51 %	1	0.44 %
SD/FO(Y)	127	56.19 %				
SD/RR(N)	135	59.73 %	88	38.94 %	3	1.33 %
SD/RR(Y)	85	37.61 %				

[48] The tables in Section 4.3 present the results for (Y) separately, showing only the numbers for pairs with a consistent direction. A separate row includes all pairs (N). Cases marked as showing direction with uncertainty are omitted when focusing on (Y) results, partly because their inclusion under "Inconsistent direction" or "Unclear direction" would be inaccurate.

Criteria analysis (D2)	Consistent direction		Inconsistent direction		Unclear direction	
	nPairs	%	nPairs	%	nPairs	%
SD/SP	40	86.96 %	3	6.52 %	3	6.52 %
SD/RU	12	26.09 %	32	69.57 %	2	4.35 %
SD/FO(N)	31	67.39 %	9	19.57 %	6	13.04 %
SD/FO(Y)	27	58.70 %				
SD/RR(N)	33	71.74 %	5	10.87 %	8	17.39 %
SD/RR(Y)	19	41.30 %				

Table 53 also shows that the consistency levels across criteria vary according to how strictly the criteria are interpreted. This is specifically so for the criteria of SR, FO, or RR as follows:

i. The three criteria prove applicable in a larger number of cases, if interpreted strictly, for example, if every instance where a sense shows a higher frequency of occurrence than its related pair is counted as showing a direction between senses, regardless of how large or small the difference in frequency is and if it can be taken as indicating a direction. If such analysis is adopted (represented as (N) in the table), the consistency levels between the criteria are higher too.
ii. The criteria prove applicable in a lower number of cases if significance levels are established, for example, if only cases where a significant difference is found between the senses frequency of occurrence are considered (represented as (Y)). Thus, consistency levels between these and other criteria prove lower too.

Differences are identified between the two analyses. In this study, the restrictive method is followed, and significance levels are established. This is because interpreting a direction is questioned where:

i. the pairs cover a fairly similar semantic range (cf. Section 4.1.3),
ii. the frequency of occurrence between senses is either too low for both senses or is close (cf. Section 4.1.5), and
iii. the range of registers covered between senses is either too low for both senses or is close in number (cf. Section 4.1.6).

4.3.2 Semantic pattern (SP)

Table 54 below shows the consistency levels between SP and SD, RU, SR, FO, and RR for the 226 pairs in the study according to an analysis by sense and by order of derivation

Table 54: Consistency between SP and other criteria by senses in D1 and D2. *(Y)* and *(N)* stand for senses for which SR, FO, and RR signal a direction, even if the difference in the semantic range covered is close to similar (*SR(N)*) or the difference in frequency or register usage is not significant *(FO(N)* or *RR(N))*

Criteria analysis (D1)	Consistent direction		Inconsistent direction		Unclear direction	
	nPairs	%	nPairs	%	nPairs	%
SP/SD	188	83.19 %	6	2.65 %	32	14.16 %
SP/SR(N)	102	45.13 %	112	49.56 %	12	5.31 %
SP/SR(Y)	84	37.17 %				
SP/RU	45	19.91 %	157	69.47 %	24	10.62 %
SP/FO(N)	145	64.16 %	80	35.4 %	1	0.44 %
SP/FO(Y)	126	55.75 %				
SP/RR(N)	133	58.85 %	91	40.27 %	2	0.88 %
SP/RR(Y)	83	36.73 %				
Criteria analysis (D2)	**Consistent direction**		**Inconsistent direction**		**Unclear direction**	
	nPairs	**%**	**nPairs**	**%**	**nPairs**	**%**
SP/SD	40	86.96 %	3	6.52 %	3	6.52 %
SP/RU	15	32.61 %	29	63.04 %	2	4.35 %
SP/FO(N)	34	73.91 %	9	19.57 %	3	6.52 %
SP/FO(Y)	30	65.22 %				
SP/RR(N)	37	80.43 %	5	10.87 %	8	17.39 %
SP/RR(Y)	21	45.65 %				

It can be observed that results for the criteria of SD and SP are very similar. Specifically, SP presents a higher consistency with SD (D1: 83.19 %, D2: 86.96 %), followed by consistency with FO (D1: 55.75 %, D2: 65.22 %, when significance is considered (Y)). The consistency with SR (D1: 37.17 %) and RR (D1: 36.73 %, D2: 45.65 %) is lower, and SP presents the lowest consistency level with RU (D1: 20.35 %, D2: 32.61 %).

Overall, the consistency between the directions by the criteria of SP (or SD) and SR, RR and RU is low because:

i. SR has a lower applicability in the sample than other criteria. Thus, an inconsistent direction is found for a higher number of pairs, especially if a direction is interpreted only when there is a difference in the semantic range covered by the lexemes (cf. the results in Section 4.1.3),
ii. RU proves applicable only for 90 pairs of senses out of 399 in D1 (22.56 %) and 22 pairs of senses out of 67 in D2 (32.84 %) (cf. the results in Table 23), thus, an inconsistent direction is found for a higher number of pairs too, or

iii. the difference between the range of registers (*RR*) covered by pairs of senses is interpreted as significant only for 159 of the pairs of senses in D1 (39.85 %) and 27 of the pairs of senses in D2 (40.3 %), according to Fisher's exact test (cf. Table 32). Thus, an inconsistent direction is found for a higher number of pairs when significance levels are established.

For a large part of the data, the inconsistent results represent cases in which one of the criteria (SP, or also SD) indicates a direction, but the analysis of RU, SR, or RR does not prove applicable to decide on a direction.

4.3.3 Semantic range (SR)

Section 4.3.3 discusses the results of the consistency of the direction across criteria, specifically SR vs the rest of criteria under study (cf. Table 55 below). Note again that the criterion of SR was assessed by considering the range of senses covered by the lexemes, thus a comparison with other criteria is only established for SR and the directions by other criteria in D1.

Overall, the table shows that the results for the consistency levels between SR and any of the criteria are always below 50 %. Furthermore, consistency levels vary according to whether the criterion of SR is interpreted in an inclusive (N) or in a restrictive way (Y). Under the later approach, as in this study, the consistency levels between SR and other criteria are below 40 %, the highest consistency obtained between SR and SD (37.61 %) and the lowest between SR and RU (13.72). These results casts doubt on the applicability of the criterion.4.2.5

Table 55: Consistency between SR and other criteria by senses in D1. *(Y)* and *(N)* stand for senses for which SR, FO, and RR signal a direction, even if the difference in the semantic range covered is close to similar (*SR(N)*) or the difference in frequency or register usage is not significant *(FO(N)* or *RR(N))*

	Consistent direction		Inconsistent direction		Unclear direction	
Criteria	nPairs	%	nPairs	%	nPairs	%
SR(N)/SD	103	45.58 %	112	49.56 %	11	4.87 %
SR(Y)/SD	85	37.61 %				
SR(N)/SP	102	45.13 %	112	49.56 %	12	5.31 %
SR(Y)/SP	84	37.17 %				
SR(N)/RU	35	15.49 %	134	59.29 %	57	25.22 %
SR(Y)/RU	31	13.72 %				
SR(N)/FO(N)	109	48.23 %	116	51.33 %	1	0.44 %
SR(Y)/FO(Y)	78	34.51 %				
SR(N)/RR(N)	101	44.69 %	117	51.77 %	8	3.54 %
SR(Y)/RR(Y)	50	22.12 %				

4.3.4 Restrictions of usage (RU)

Section 4.3.4 discusses the results of the consistency of the direction across criteria, specifically RU vs the rest of the criteria under study.

Table 56 summarizes the results. Specifically, the table shows that consistency levels across criteria, wherever both RU and other criteria give a direction, are always lower than 25 % in D1, while the applicability slightly increases for the analysis of the pairs by sense in D2. If one goes back to the specific results in Section 4.2, it can be observed that the largest percentage of pairs listed as indicating an "inconsistent direction" are pairs for which other criteria indicate a direction while RU does not, for example, in D1, SD or SP (SD (direction) vs RU (unclear): 57.96 %; SP (direction) vs RU (unclear): 58.41 %). The low consistency across criteria in this case, thus, results from the low individual applicability of the criterion of RU. Moreover, the results highlight once again the low applicability of a unified analysis.

Table 56: Consistency between RU and other criteria by senses in D1 and D2. *(Y)* and *(N)* stand for senses for which SR, FO, and RR signal a direction, even if the difference in the semantic range covered is close to similar (*SR(N)*) or the difference in frequency or register usage is not significant *(FO(N)* or *RR(N))*

Criteria analysis (D1)	Consistent direction		Inconsistent direction		Unclear direction	
	nPairs	%	nPairs	%	nPairs	%
RU/SD	48	21.24 %	153	67.7 %	25	11.06 %
RU/SP	45	19.91 %	157	69.47 %	24	10.62 %
RU/SR(N)	35	15.49 %	134	59.29 %	57	25.22 %
RU/SR(Y)	31	13.72 %				
RU/FO(N)	51	22.57 %	171	75.66 %	4	1.77 %
RU/FO(Y)	47	20.79 %				
RU/RR(N)	50	22.12 %	165	73.01 %	29	12.83 %
RU/RR(Y)	34	15.04 %				
Criteria analysis (D2)	**Consistent direction**		**Inconsistent direction**		**Unclear direction**	
	nPairs	**%**	**nPairs**	**%**	**nPairs**	**%**
RU/SD	12	26.09 %	32	69.57 %	2	4.35 %
RU/SP	15	32.61 %	29	63.04 %	2	4.35 %
RU/FO(N)	14	30.43 %	25	54.35 %	7	15.22 %
RU/FO(Y)	14	30.43 %				
RU/RR(N)	15	32.61 %	15	32.61 %	16	34.78 %
RU/RR(Y)	15	32.61 %				

4.3.5 Frequency of occurrence (FO)

Section 4.3.5 discusses the results of the consistency of the direction across criteria, specifically FO vs the rest of criteria under study. Table 57 shows the consistency levels between FO and SD, SP, RU, SR, and RR for the pairs according to an analysis by sense in D1 and D2. The results are according to the two interpretations of FO, SR and RR, specifically:

i. (N) includes cases for which a direction is identified according to the criteria but is questionable, that is, cases for which the semantic range covered by one of the pairs is slightly wider, or where the difference in the frequency of occurrence of the senses or the range of registers that they cover in the BNC is not significant, and
ii. (Y) counts the cases described in (i.) as *unclear*.

Table 57: Consistency between FO and other criteria by senses in D1 and D2. *(Y)* and *(N)* stand for senses for which SR, FO, and RR signal a direction, even if the difference in the semantic range covered is close to similar (*SR(N)*) or the difference in frequency or register usage is not significant *(FO(N)* or *RR(N))*

	Consistent direction		Inconsistent direction		Unclear direction	
Criteria analysis (D1)	**nPairs**	**%**	**nPairs**	**%**	**nPairs**	**%**
FO(N)/SD	147	65.04 %	78	34.51 %	1	0.44 %
FO(Y)/SD	129	57.08 %				
FO(N)/SP	145	64.16 %	80	35.4 %	29	12.83 %
FO(Y)/SP	126	55.75 %				
FO(N)/SR(N)	109	48.23 %	116	51.33 %	1	0.44 %
FO(Y)/SR(Y)	78	37.17 %				
FO(N)/RU	51	22.57 %	171	75.66 %	4	1.77 %
FO(Y)/RU	47	20.8 %				
FO(N)/RR(N)	195	86.28 %	28	12.83 %	3	1.33 %
FO(Y)/RR(Y)	107	47.35 %				
	Consistent direction		**Inconsistent direction**		**Unclear direction**	
Criteria analysis (D2)	**nPairs**	**%**	**nPairs**	**%**	**nPairs**	**%**
FO(N)/SD	31	67.39 %	9	19.57 %	6	13.04 %
FO(Y)/SD	27	58.70 %				
FO(N)/SP	34	73.91 %	9	19.57 %	3	6.52 %
FO(Y)/SP	30	65.22 %				
FO(N)/RU	14	30.43 %	25	54.35 %	7	15.22 %
FO(Y)/RU	14	30.43 %				
FO(N)/RR(N)	43	93.48 %	2	4.35 %	1	2.17 %
FO(Y)/RR(Y)	23	50 %				

As in previous sections, the results for the consistency levels across criteria vary according to how restrictive the analysis of the criteria is: a lower consistency across criteria is found when the analysis of the criteria is restrictive (Y) vs inclusive (N). Overall, according to the results of a restrictive analysis, FO seems to present higher consistency levels with SD followed by SP in D1 (FO(Y)/SD: 57.08 %, FO(Y)/SP: 55.75 %), or the other way around in D2 (FO(Y)/SD: 58.7 %, FO(Y)/SP: 65.22 %). The consistency levels are lower with RU, because of the low applicability that RU has shown in the study.

4.3.6 Range of registers (RR)

Section 4.3.6 discusses the results of the consistency of the direction across criteria, specifically RR vs the rest of criteria under study.

Table 58 shows the consistency levels between for the pairs according to a sense analysis in both D1 and D2. As in previous tables, results are presented according to two interpretations of RR, SR and FO.

Table 58: Consistency between RR and other criteria by senses in D1 and D2. *(Y)* and *(N)* stand for senses for which SR, FO, and RR signal a direction, even if the difference in the semantic range covered is close to similar (*SR(N)*) or the difference in frequency or register usage is not significant *(FO(N)* or *RR(N))*

Criteria analysis (D1)	Consistent direction		Inconsistent direction		Unclear direction	
	nPairs	%	nPairs	%	nPairs	%
RR(N)/SD	135	59.73 %	88	38.94 %	3	1.33 %
RR(Y)/SD	85	37.61 %				
RR(N)/SP	133	58.85 %	91	40.27 %	2	0.88 %
RR(Y)/SP	83	36.73 %				
RR(N)/SR(N)	101	44.69 %	117	51.77 %	8	3.54 %
RR(Y)/SR(Y)	50	22.12 %				
RR(N)/RU	50	22.12 %	165	73.01 %	29	12.83 %
RR(Y)/RU	34	15.04 %				
RR(N)/FO(N)	194	85.84 %	29	12.83 %	3	1.33 %
RR(Y)/FO(Y)	107	47.35 %				
Criteria analysis (D2)	**Consistent direction**		**Inconsistent direction**		**Unclear direction**	
	nPairs	%	nPairs	%	nPairs	%
RR(N)/SD	33	71.74 %	5	10.87 %	8	17.39 %
RR(Y)/SD	19	41.30 %				
RR(N)/SP	37	80.43 %	5	10.87 %	8	17.39 %
RR(Y)/SP	21	45.65 %				

Criteria analysis (D2)	Consistent direction		Inconsistent direction		Unclear direction	
	nPairs	%	nPairs	%	nPairs	%
RR(N)/RU	15	32.61 %	15	32.61 %	16	34.78 %
RR(Y)/RU	15	32.61 %				
RR(N)/FO(N)	43	93.48 %	2	4.35 %	1	2.17 %
RR(Y)/FO(Y)	23	50 %				

If a restrictive analysis is adopted (Y), RR presents higher consistency levels with SD and SP both in D1 (RR(Y)/SD: 37.61 %, RR(Y)/SP: 36.73 %) and D2 (RR(Y)/SD: 41.3 %, RR(Y)/SP: 45.65 %). Again, the table shows that the consistency levels across criteria vary according to whether the analysis is inclusive (N) or restrictive (Y). Overall, higher consistency levels were anticipated between FO and RR because these criteria are based on the same corpus data and typically go together, that is, a higher range of register coverage is expected for senses attested more frequently in the corpus. However, the difference between the consistency levels by the two methods differs greatly, partly as a side effect of the low percentage of significant differences by senses identified by Fisher's exact test when the applicability of RR is analysed. Specifically, the consistency between RR and FO (N) decreases from 194 of the pairs in D1 (85.84 %) or 43 pairs in D2 (93.48 %) to around 50 % in both orders (D1: 107 pairs, 47.35 %; D2: 23 pairs, 50 %) where the criteria identify the same direction as confirmed by two statistical tests (Y). The results thus should be interpreted with caution, especially as regards the applicability of RR where significant differences are found for a lower number of pairs.

CHAPTER 5

On the issues and relevance of the criteria

5.1 Introduction

Chapter 4 presented and discussed the results of the applicability and consistency across the criteria tested in this study. Further discussion on general aspects, exemplification of issues, and on the relevance of the criteria is provided in Section 5.1, as follows:

i. Section 5.2 focuses on the criterion of semantic dependence (SD),
ii. Section 5.3 on semantic pattern (SP),
iii. Section 5.4 on semantic range (SR),
iv. Section 5.5 on restrictions of usage (RU), and
v. Section 5.6 on distributional criteria, frequency of occurrence (FO) and range of registers (RR), discussed together for the similar issues they present.

5.2 Semantic dependence (SD)

Within Marchand's semantic criteria, SD is described as "[...] often sufficient in itself to solve the question of directionality, while other criteria are more or less concomitant in character" (1964: 10). As described in Chapter 2, similar claims are available elsewhere in the literature (cf. Section 2.5.6, and references therein). More importantly, when other criteria are given priority and appear to fail, SD is given priority to decide on directionality (cf. Sanders 1988: 173–174 or Cetnarowska 1993: 32).

This is partly supported by the analysis of SD in this study, which seems to indicate a direction between senses for a large number of pairs (around 80 %). Specifically, SD seems to solve the direction for 193 pairs (85.4 %, cf. Table 15) if senses in the first order of derivation (D1) are considered, and for 40 pairs (86.96 %, cf. Table 16) considering senses in the second order of derivation (D2). Still, the direction between some senses remains unclear (cf. the examples in Section 4.1.1), either because:

i. none of the pair of related senses shows SD strongly, or
ii. because the senses, to some extent, are analysed as showing SD towards the other (cf. also the discussion for example, in Sanders 1988: 173–174).

It must be noted, however, that, not even in affixation, where directionality is initially not an issue, does this criterion prove valid for all cases (cf. Ruz & Cetnarowska 2023).

One of the issues regarding the applicability of SD is that a different degree of applicability (or a different degree of consistency of SD with AD) is reported in previous studies. This may partly be as a result of:

i. different samples of conversion being used,
ii. different resources used to test the criteria, and
iii. partly also because the criterion may be interpreted differently.

Regarding point iii., the interpretation of SD is not always described in detail in previous studies, and interpretations which are substantially different may be found in the literature. For instance, the criterion may be taken to strictly require the counterpart lexeme in the definition, for example, as in Bram (2011) who claims that SD "[…] involves the inclusion or use of the base form in the core meaning or definition of the converted counterpart" (2011: 153), while another may consider it enough for a sense to be defined without using the counterpart term, for example, when it is defined using synonyms which are also used to describe the counterpart lexeme. The latter is the approach adopted in this study, for example, in *dapple*$^{N/V}$ the senses are defined using synonyms, and yet a semantic dependence can be established between them:

(67) *dapple*^{N} (QUALITY)
sense 1 "One of many roundish spots or small blotches of colouring by which a surface is diversified." (OED), for example, "*When they are patterned, their designs tend to be simple spots and* **dapples**. *Bony fish, on the other hand, are strikingly different.*"

(68) *dapple*^{V} (ORNATIVE)
sense 1a "1. a. transitive. To mark or variegate with rounded spots or cloudy patches of different colour or shade. / b. figurative." (OED), for example, "*[…] a large garden, which was protected from the heat by the umbrella of a huge and ancient vine, the shadow of whose leaves* **dappled** *the paved floor.*"

It remains unclear whether the use of parallel definitions to decide on a direction in conversion is enough to establish SD, that is, senses defined using synonymous pairs related by affixation, or whether this may lead to an incorrect analysis in some cases. An instance of this is, for instance:

(69) *piss*^{N} (SUBSTANCE (OR RESULT))
sense 1 "1. Urine, esp. evacuated urine." (OED), for example, "*Some of the lights in the tunnel are busted, and it smells of* **piss**." (BNC)

(70) *piss*^{V} (SUBSTANCE EMISSION (OR EFFECTIVE))
sense 1 "1. a. intransitive. To urinate." (OED), for example, "*I* **pissed** *in a test-tube, had four injections and did twenty press-ups to get my heart going.*" (BNC)

In this study, the decision was to mark the direction by SD as unclear for this pair of senses, although one could rather feel inclined to decide on a Noun-to-Verb direction based on a parallelism with *urine*^{N} and *urinate*^{V}. Note that this decision influences the analysis of the pair and its sense classification into orders of derivation. This example illustrates difficulties in the analysis of SD, and how various interpretations may lead to various analyses: If the nominal sense is taken as the base, the analysis into orders of derivation produces model A, whereas if the verbal sense is interpreted as the base, model B obtains:[49]

piss$^{N(1)}$(SUBSTANCE) → *piss*$^{V(1)}$ (EFFECTIVE) → *piss*$^{N(2)}$ (ACTION)
piss$^{N(1)}$(SUBSTANCE) → *piss*$^{V(3)}$ (EFFECTIVE + INVOLUNTARY)
piss$^{N(1)}$(SUBSTANCE) → *piss*$^{V(2)}$ (SIMILATIVE_EFFECTIVE)
piss$^{N(7)}$(EXT_PHR. ACTION) → *piss*$^{V(11)}$ (EXT_INSTRUMENTAL_INGESTING)
piss$^{V(11)}$ → *piss*$^{N(3)}$ (EXT_PHR.EVENT)

Figure 9: Model A: Directionality for related senses of the pair *piss*$^{N/V}$.

piss$^{V(1/3)}$(SUBSTANCE EMISSION) → *piss*$^{N(1)}$ (RESULT)
piss$^{V(1/3)}$(SUBSTANCE EMISSION) → *piss*$^{N(2)}$ (ACTION)
piss$^{V(2)}$ (EXT_SUBSTANCE EMISSION) ?
piss$^{V(11)}$(EXT_SUBST. INGESTING) → *piss*$^{N(3)}$ (EXT_PHR.EVENT)
piss$^{V(11)}$(EXT_SUBST. INGESTING) → *piss*$^{N(7)}$ (EXT_PHR.ACTION)

Figure 10: Model B: Directionality for related senses of the pair *piss*$^{N/V}$.

The senses in the figures together with examples of use in the BNC are provided in examples (71) and (72):

---

[49] The senses are given as super index and between brackets, following the word-class category specification. Note that further senses are possible, even if most are phrasal expressions which seem to emerge within lexemes, making the picture in *piss*$^{N/V}$ quite complex, for example, *piss and wind* or *get piss* wet, for the noun, or *to piss away* for the verb.

(71) *piss*[N]
sense 1 (SUBSTANCE (OR RESULT))
"1. Urine, esp. evacuated urine." (OED), for example, "*Some of the lights in the tunnel are busted, and it smells of* **piss**." (BNC)
sense 3 (analysed in context) (EXT_PHR_EVENT)
"Piss-up N: an occasion when a lot of alcohol is drunk" related to "3. Alcoholic drink; esp. drink which is regarded as weak or unpalatable alcohol. Cf. on the piss at Phrases 3 and gnat's piss n. at gnat n.1 Compounds, panther piss n. at panther n. Compounds 2." (OED), for example, "*[...] its fucking well out of order* **piss** up *games oh that's right I think we played in, I think we played, you know that British bull dog thing?, we managed to clear.*" (BNC)
sense 7 (P3) (EXT_PHR_ACTION)
related to 3 above "P3. Chiefly British, Australian, and New Zealand. on the piss: out drinking; engaged in a bout or bouts of heavy drinking. Conversely off the piss." (OED), for example, "*'Gawd help us all, look at the state of you! No need to ask who's been on the* **piss** *all weekend, and not for the first time.*" (BNC)

(72) *piss*[V] (EFFECTIVE (OR SUBSTANCE EMISSION))
sense 1 "1. a. intransitive. To urinate." (OED), for example, "*I* **pissed** *in a test-tube, had four injections and did twenty press-ups to get my heart going.*" (BNC)
sense 2 (SIMILATIVE_EFFECTIVE)
"2. a. transitive. To discharge (something, esp. blood) as or with urine. Also with out." (OED), for example, "*Purple and black bruises abounded. 'I've been* **pissing** *blood all night, Tony.*" (BNC)
sense 3 (EFFECTIVE + INVOLUNTARY (OR SUBSTANCE EMISSION))
"3. transitive. To urinate in or on (one's clothing, bed, etc.), esp. involuntarily, as through fear, excitement, or amusement. Frequently reflexive in same sense. Also used hyperbolically, to suggest intense fear, excitement, amusement, etc." (OED), for example, "*Maybe it was best this way, he thought, no time to consider, no time to get scared and* **piss** *down your pants leg.*" (BNC)
sense 11 (EXT_INSTRUMENTAL_INGESTING)
analysed in context: "to drink alcohol, to get drunk" (my definition), for example, "*[...] greeted the bands with abuse and bottles of cider which they had feverishly* **pissed** *in.*" (BNC)

Figures 9 (model A) and 10 (model B) illustrate how the organization of senses and their connection may fit different analyses, as is sometimes the case with semantic categorization. Still, there are few cases where the criterion of SD is unclear regarding senses in the first order of derivation, and even less so in the second order of derivation.[50]

[50] Admittedly, the analysis in this study may be considered too conservative in that SD is marked as *unclear* when considered ambiguous but where one may perceive a directionality (cf. the examples marked as unclear (?) in Sections 3.2.4.1 and 4.1.1). If anything, this may lead to a higher applicability of the criterion by a different linguist.

In model B, however, one of the senses (sense 2, with SD towards a counterpart sense in the noun) would need to be interpreted as extended from the verb, even if it uses the noun in its definition too. Thus, even if the analysis may be ambiguous, model A seems more fitting. Model A also shows recursive patterns, typically found in cases of conversion where the analysis of SD is clearer too. Thus, the analysis of senses defined using affixation should be carefully examined and further research is needed in this regard.

These aspects of SD should be clearly defined, at least with regard to whether a restrictive or an inclusive interpretation of SD is taken, for example, if it allows the interpretation as showing SD or not for senses which are defined based on synonyms (also by affixation). This research argues for an inclusive interpretation, as senses in other word-formation processes are not always defined using the counterpart term, and synonyms play a role too, to cite one such case (cf. Ruz & Cetnarowska 2023).

Last, as has been mentioned throughout, the analysis in this study differs from previous studies in that it is applied at the level of sense (following Plank 2010, and as opposed to considering core senses by lexemes, for instance as in Bram 2011). The approaches differ mainly in that a sense analysis identifies multiple recursive derivation or multiple directions within pairs of lexemes, as illustrated in this chapter, whereas an analysis of core senses will identify unidirectional solutions as a tendency.

5.3 Semantic pattern (SP)

SD and SP are separate criteria, and they do not necessarily always show together, that is, a sense may show SD towards its counterpart sense, but not a SP typical of a derivative, and vice versa. However, the results in this study show that they typically go together in conversion. Ruz & Cetnarowska (2023) showed very similar results for the two criteria in affixation.

Even if the application of SP is, in principle, simpler than that of SD, given that various references on the typical semantic patterns used in conversion or other word-formation process can be found in the literature (Marchand 1969; Clark & Clark 1979; Plag 1999, among many others), directionality remains an issue in some cases, for instance:

(73) *whoop*^{N} (INSTANCE/RESULT (OR SOUND))
sense 1 "1. A cry of 'whoop', or a shout or call resembling this, used to attract attention, as a summons, or to express derision, defiance, support or encouragement, etc., or (now usually) exuberant excitement; spec. (Hunting) a cry of encouragement or celebration, esp. at the kill (cf. whoo-whoop int. and n.); a cry or yell

on rushing into battle, esp. one used by (or said to be used by) North American Indians (cf. war-whoop n.)." (OED), for example, "*Chaka Khan has been around forever, and recently her trademark* **whoops** *and screams have sounded a little forced.*"

(74) *whoop*^V (EFFECTIVE_MANNER OF SPEAKING (OR SOUND EMISSION /MANNER OF SPEAKING))
sense 1 "1. a. intransitive. To utter a 'whoop!' or a cry or shout resembling this, typically in order to attract attention, as a summons, or to express derision, defiance, support or encouragement, etc., or (now usually) exuberant excitement. / c. transitive. With direct speech as object: to say or utter (something) with a whoop; to call out or yell excitedly." (OED), for example, "*A sense of adventure invaded the group, everyone* **whooping** *and yelling as they were flung between towers on their way to Athena Gardens, [...]*".

Regardless of subjective intuitions, the direction between the pairs of senses based on SP remains unclear in this study, because both noun sense 1 and verb sense 1 show a SP typical of a derivative (at the same time both senses are analysed as showing SD). Interestingly, here, as with other cases which are also interjections, the direction seems more difficult to establish, for instance:

(75) "*Most eventually got honorary Lifetime Achievement Awards – alias the '***Whoops***, sorry, we forgot you' Oscars, or even '***Whoops***, sorry, we didn't know you were still around*'" (BNC)

This and other examples where the direction seems to be unclear according to SD or SP, fuel the discussion on the notion of bidirectionality.

Furthermore, while the aim is always an unbiased analysis, for example, by using OED definitions, it must be noted that the OED is constantly under revision. As entries may vary, so too may the results of the analysis of the criteria, for example, as in *anagram*^N/V, here cited as a clear example of Noun-to-Verb conversion (following the OED2; note that senses in grey are not attested in the BNC):

(76) *anagram*^N (ABSTRACT_LANGUAGE TERM)
sense 1 "1. A transposition of the letters of a word, name, or phrase, whereby a new word or phrase is formed." (OED), for example, "*Adam loved words, was fascinated by them, their meanings and what you could do with them, with* **anagrams** *and palindromes and rhetorical terms and etymology.*"
sense 1 "†2. loosely or fig. A transposition, a mutation. Obs." (OED) (not attested in the BNC)

(77) *anagram*^V (EFFECTIVE)
sense 1 "1. trans. To anagrammatize v." (OED) (no transitive use attested in the BNC)
sense 2 "2. intr. To make anagrams." (OED), for example, "*He began* **anagramming***, twisting letters round, keeping in mind where they had been going, where Mary was still going [...]*"

By contrast, the dictionary entries revised as OED3 cause major changes:

(78) *anagram*ᴺ (OED3)
sense 1 "1. A word, phrase, or name formed by rearranging the letters of another word, phrase, or name."
sense 2 "2. figurative. A rearranged or encoded version of something; a transposition."
sense 3 "3. In plural. Any of various games in which players rearrange the letters of a word, phrase, or name to make another word, phrase, or name."

(79) *anagram*ᴺ (OED3)
sense 1 "1. transitive. To rearrange the letters of (a word, phrase, or name) to form another word, phrase, or name."
sense 2 "2. intransitive. To compose or solve anagrams. Also with †upon. rare before late 20th cent."

Thus, even if the same direction is identified based on senses in use, the analysis is not straightforward, for the more complex description of sense 1 for the verb in (79). Changes may influence the analysis of other criteria based on OED data too. For *anagram*, the analysis of RU would differ because OED2 marked the verb senses as rare or obsolete (thus, based on RU a Noun-to-Verb direction was identified), while the OED3 entries do not. An analysis based on the OED3 would thus show no direction based on RU, because none of the senses attested is marked as restricted in use. This example is intended to show that dictionary makers' decisions may affect the analysis, and that this is a major methodological issue, even if identified in few cases.

5.4 Semantic range (SR)

Section 5.4 discusses the reasons why a qualitative analysis of SR was carried out in this study and then delves into the difficulties of the analysis of SR and their implications for the relevance SR to identify directionality in conversion.

Results of a qualitative analysis of SR are not provided because comparison of paronymous lexemes, by counting the number of senses that each lexeme can take, for example, as in a dictionary, corpora, etc., is not always reliable, for various reasons:

i. Differences in sense representation in dictionaries, or similar language resources, for example, in *brood*ᴺ/ⱽ, may be found.
ii. Even if one lexeme presents indeed a larger number of senses, its range may be similar or even narrower than that of its counterpart, for example, *beep*ᴺ/ⱽ the verb with two senses, which are for transitive and intransitive use (CAUSATIVE/EFFECTIVE) related to the noun sense (ABSTRACT_SOUND).

iii. Some pairs may present the same number of senses, but a difference in the SR covered may be easily identified, for example, where restrictions in use are identified, or as in *slob*$^{N/V}$ where both noun and verb present three senses, but two of the verb senses relate to a different lexeme *slobber*^{V}; thus, the SR, according to the semanticallyrelated senses in the pair terms, is Noun-to-Verb.
iv. When many extended or figurative senses are available, they do not necessarily follow similar paths, and it may be unclear which pair member has a wider SR, for example, *snuff*$^{N/V}$.

Partly for these reasons, and because a comparison of the number of senses between lexemes did not prove useful in identifying directionality in a pilot study on affixation (cf. Ruz & Cetnarowska 2023), a qualitative analysis of the SR covered by the pairs was carried out. However, several other issues, partly related to the flexibility in its interpretation, emerged in the qualitative application of the criterion.

One obvious methodological issue of this study, especially in the analysis of SR, is that results may differ substantially according to various approaches (for instance, diachronic vs synchronic). This is because use of all senses (for example in the OED) vs only the senses in use (for example in the BNC) may signal different directions for the same pairs. For instance, for the pair *swipe*$^{N/V}$, based on the senses in the OED, the noun is the base lexeme, but if only senses in use are considered, the lexemes cover a very similar SR (as the senses in use for the pair seem to be in both the noun and the verb). In addition to the senses shared by both lexemes, a slang sense is recorded for the verb "4. transitive. To steal, 'appropriate'; to loot. slang (originally U.S.)" (OED, 22 occurrences in the BNC), but no counterpart is available in the noun. The analysis according to SR differs substantially in this example because some of the senses in the pair are obsolete or have a restricted use.

SR proved difficult to interpret in some cases precisely because the lexemes may develop senses that are not related to any of the senses in the counterpart member (whether in use or not), or because one of the pairs may derive senses by influence from other lexemes, for example, *slob*$^{N/V}$ (because the verb presents senses related to another lexeme *slobber*^{V}). These issues become problematic in polysemous items.

Also, the interpretation of the direction according to SR was sometimes found to be misleading, even when established with certainty (Y), that is, when one of the pairs clearly shows a wider sense coverage than its counterpart, for example, in *bombard*$^{N/V}$, *curtsy*$^{N/V}$ or *dragoon*$^{N/V}$. For instance, for the pair *bombard*$^{N/V}$, SR signals Verb-to-Noun direction as the verb presents a wider SR, but a closer look at the senses shows that the noun refers to the ARTEFACT while the verb's related sense is SIMILATIVE_INSTRUMENTAL. The additional senses in the verb are extended and figurative senses, also expressing the category SIMILATIVE. Thus, based on the pairs' semantics (for instance by SD), the direction is the opposite (Noun-to-Verb).

If the results of the application of SR are considered, the criterion shows limited applicability. The semantic range of one of the pairs is marked as covering a wider semantic range than its counterpart in 49.56% of the pairs, but this percentage is not large enough to consider SR a reliable test for directionality. Based on the sample analysed, a fairly large number of pairs with a similar SR is anticipated in English noun/verb conversion, especially within new formations, the lexemes typically presenting just one sense each. As applied in this study, SR only serves to identify a single direction between a pair of lexemes, while the possibility of multidirectionality does initially have no place. Even if SR was interpreted as a property between pairs of senses, a low applicability is expected too. This is on the assumption that related senses in conversion often show the same meaning, except that with the differences concomitant to the change in word-class category, or as Sweet (1891–1898, I: 39, cited in Valera 2017: 4) puts it: "[...] although conversion does not involve any alteration in the meaning of a word, yet the use of a word as a different part of speech naturally leads to divergence in meaning." (cf. the discussion in Valera 2017, and references therein). It is here believed that applying SR by sense would result in a low applicability, as with RU, because one of the restrictions includes general vs specific/restricted senses.

SR is thus seen as a criterion that is best applied by considering the range of senses covered by conversion-related lexemes, but one which would not allow for the identification of directionality by senses. All in all, it can be noted that the semantic range of the base is not necessarily wider than that of the derivative. This is in line with previous studies arguing that the direction cannot be established just on the basis of lexical growth (see, for instance, Umbreit 2010: 306–307). The low applicability of SR, the fact that it identifies a single direction (as interpreted in this study), and the identification of misleading cases cast doubts on the applicability of SR to decide on directionality.

5.5 Restrictions of usage (RU)

This study first tried to compare the total number of restricted senses that a pair of lexemes shows. However, such method did not prove useful for directionality because a number of misleading analyses (cf. for example *barrack*[N/V] in Section 4.1.4) were easily identified by comparing either:

i. the number of restricted senses by pair, or
ii. the percentage of restricted senses out of the total number of senses that a lexeme takes by contrast with its pair member.

RU was thus considered between pairs of senses related by an arrangement into orders of derivation. Still, the results show that the criterion has a low applicability: It signals a direction only in few pairs of senses (22.56 % in D1 and 32.84 % in D2) and, consequently, in few lexeme pairs when senses are considered (30.53 % in D1 and 34.78 % in D2). As described in Section 4.1.4 (cf. Table 23), the low applicability of the criteria results from:

i. Both senses in a pair showing RU, for example, in *graft*$^{N4/V3}$ both the nominal sense "a. Work, esp. hard work." (RESULT)[51] and the verbal one "intransitive. To work." (ACTION) are marked as slang in the OED.
ii. None of the senses showing RU, for example, in *cloister*$^{N/V}$ neither the nominal sense "2. a. A place of religious seclusion; a monastery or nunnery; a convent." (ABSTRACT_LOCATION/PLACE) nor the counterpart verbal sense "1. transitive. To shut up, enclose, or place in a cloister or monastic house." (LOCATIVE) are marked as restricted.

Overall, RU seems to identify directionality in few cases, and sometimes the analysis is complex, as in the following BNC occurrence of *wax*^{N}:

(80) "*The Seven would be the agents of their own destruction. For the boy carried within him not a ball of* **wax**, *but an idea. One single, all-transforming idea.*" (BNC)

This concordance was classified as part of *wax*^{N3} "*colloquial or slang.* Angry feeling; a fit of anger; chiefly **to be in a wax.**" and interpreted as sense 9b in *wax*^{V1} (81), but it is also analysed based on a separate entry in the OED for the phrase *ball of wax* (82). The criterion of RU is useful for this specific pair of senses, because the nominal use is restricted to the phrasal expression and because it is a slang sense, while the verb seems of general use. However, if the sense is considered as related to the phrase "to wax angry" an unclear analysis of the direction of the pair according to RU would obtain. This is because the later sense is marked as archaic in the OED, as part of the etymological information provided for *wax*^{N3}

[51] Note that these were classified as ACTION and RESULT. However, their direction is left as *unclear* for the criterion RU, but also for semantic criteria (SD, SP, and SR). Admittedly, this analysis may be biased by the relation of the senses with two other lexemes (following the information in the OED): *graft*^{V2} "dialect. intransitive. To dig. [see grafting-tool n. *Grafting Tool, a kind of curved spade made very strong for the purpose of digging canals.*]" and *graft*^{N3} "2. A kind of spade, used in digging drains".

described as "Of doubtful origin; possibly evolved from some phrase like to wax angry (archaic), to wax warm (now dialect): see wax v.1 II.9a.ii."

(81) "II. With complement: to change by growth or increase, to become. (Cf. grow v. 12) 9. a. With adjective complement:(a) With more or less of the idea of growth or increase: to become gradually, grow./(b) Without the idea of growth or increase: To become, turn. (Sometimes used with reference to a sudden or immediate change.) [...]",

(82) "[...] (b) slang (originally and chiefly U.S.) a distinct matter, affair, concern, or situation, (one's) interest; the whole ball of wax: everything relating to a particular situation, the entire matter, the whole thing".

Even when RU seems applicable, it might be misleading and clash with other criteria. For instance, two sense pairs are related for *varnish*$^{N/V}$:[52]

(83) *varnish*^{N}

Sense 1a (SUBSTANCE/MATERIAL) "1. a. Resinous matter dissolved in some liquid and used for spreading over a surface in order to give this a hard, shining, transparent coat, by which it is made more durable or ornamental. In early use, dry resinous matter for making a solution of this kind." (OED), for example, "*The whole hood is then varnished with several coats of 'tinted'* **varnish** *(at least one inside) or to save money your choice of leftover paint.*" (BNC)

Sense 2 (FIG_QUALITY) "2. figurative. a. A specious gloss or outward show; a pretence." (OED), for example, "*[...] were a celebration of Seventies flamboyance, late Eighties neurosis and Nineties positivism. Their high-kitsch* **varnish** *was offset by an overwhelming urge to educate.*" (BNC)

(84) *varnish*^{V}

Sense 1a (INSTRUMENTAL/ORNATIVE) "1. a. transitive. To paint over, to coat, with varnish; to overlay with a thin coating composed of varnish." (OED), for example, "*Whilst we were at it, we thought we'd strip the floor and* **varnish** *it.*" (BNC)

Sense 3 (FIG_ORNATIVE) "3. To cover or overlay with a specious or deceptive appearance; to gloss over, disguise." (OED), for example, "*I was pleased to see his grin* **varnish** *when Mala gave him the vicious edge of her tongue for ignoring the Ardakkean request for discretion* [...]" (BNC)

For the analysis of *varnish* in D1, then, the criteria were compared between:

i. the nominal sense 1a and the verbal sense 1a, and
ii. the nominal sense 2 vs the verbal sense 3.

[52] Although both lexemes present further senses, those are analysed as extended within one or the other word class, or as senses derived recursively or in subsequent orders of derivation, for example, the ACTION/INSTANCE deverbal sense "An act of varnishing; an application of varnish." (cf. the discussion in Section 5.4.6).

The analysis of RU reveals that none of the senses in i. exhibit RU, while only the nominal sense in ii. is marked as figurative.[53] Thus, RU based on the OED's sense descriptions suggests a Verb-to-Noun direction, which contrasts with the direction identified based on other criteria, for example, SD or SP. Even though the OED holds authority to identify restrictions in the use of senses, caution is warranted, particularly when considering figurative senses.

Additionally, the application of RU in this study may be misleading too, that is, although it serves to identify a direction between senses (granted for a low number of pairs), a direction was decided based on a computation of all the pairs of senses. However, for some examples, various senses are identified as unrestricted while only one or few of the senses in one of the various pairs may be restricted. While RU may identify differences between senses or a direction between specific senses, it is unclear to what extent it identifies a direction between a pair, that is, whether the identification of a single or few senses showing RU is enough to decide on a direction in a polysemous pair. It is argued that the search for a single direction may not make sense.

The low applicability of the criterion and the complexities in its application lead to the conclusion that RU should be regarded as a secondary criterion, especially because it is applicable only for very specific cases. Also, the analysis of RU makes sense only at the level of sense.

5.6 Quantitative-distributional criteria: FO and RR

Section 5.6 discusses the issues found in the analysis of quantitative-distributional criteria, namely frequency of occurrence (FO) and the range of registers covered by the pairs (RR), here presented together because these are analysed based on the same source, and their application raises similar issues.

Quantitative-distributional criteria (FO and RR) stand out as objective, empirical, and measurable criteria, but their results may differ according to the source used for their study, specifically according to:

i. the size of the corpus, and
ii. the varieties of English or the registers represented by corpora.

Issues regarding the use of FO are highlighted elsewhere (cf. among others, Štekauer 1996: 129, or Umbreit 2010: 309). Regarding point i., note, for example,

[53] Note, however, that the verb sense is also interpreted as figurative in the semantic categorization in this study as indicated by the semantic category provided among brackets (FIG_ORNATIVE).

that Balteiro (2007) used a rather small corpus (ICE corpus, ca. one million words) and admits that the frequency of use of the lexemes should be studied using a larger corpus. Use of a data source that is not representative enough for research on directionality in conversion may become a methodological issue, for example, many of the terms have a low frequency of use and, more relevantly, many do not occur in the corpus (Balteiro 2007: 126–129). This becomes even more problematic if directionality is studied by senses, as a larger number of senses would not be attested. By contrast, Bram (2011) uses three corpora to test FO across lexemes, and a higher number of pairs were reported to be found in the larger corpus (the BNC) (Bram 2011: 240, 261).

In this study, the BNC was selected as a data source because it is a large corpus which includes texts from various registers. It is considered a representative source to include the lexemes and the senses of the polysemous lexemes in our sample. Admittedly, different results might be found if a different corpus is used, for example, a corpus of a different variety of English such as American English, especially regarding the criterion of RR. Also, the BNC represents the usage of British English in the late 90s, and recent senses may not be represented.[54] However, FO and RR results are expected to vary only for a limited number of senses, like slang or dialectal senses, while the usage of more general senses is not expected to vary much across corpora.

5.6.1 Level of application: lexeme vs sense

A crucial difference between this study and previous research on directionality is the level of application of the criteria: lexeme vs sense. Previous studies compared the frequency by lexeme pairs. More recently, Ševčíková (2021: 107, on directionality in Czech conversion) mentioned that the criterion of FO was not used in her study because the corpus used is not disambiguated for senses, arguing that an adequate analysis of the criterion is therefore impossible. This study agrees with Ševčíková's (2021) claim and argues, in line with Plank (2010), that an analysis of directionality should be carried out by senses and not by lexemes.

Thus, FO and RR are researched by senses in this study. As the BNC is not disambiguated by sense, senses were manually identified by a classification of the BNC's concordances into the senses of the OED for each term. It must be noted

[54] Note that recent senses may not be included in the dictionary used too, even if the OED is under constant revision. In fact, examples of senses in the BNC not represented in the OED were identified, and definitions were provided ad hoc (e.g. sense 5b for *soak*^{N} in Section 4.3.1).

that a sense classification of the concordances is considered relevant even in an analysis which does not considers senses, because it involves:

i. the concordances' reclassification as the correct word class (where mistakes in the word class indicated by the corpus were found), and
ii. the identification and separation of senses of homonymous lexemes.

I argue that these two steps are necessary because the inclusion of unrelated instances and of instances of homonymous lexemes could have a considerable effect on the overall frequency of occurrence of lexemes, and ultimately, on the directionality indicated by FO.

To highlight the relevance of this point, examples from Tables 8 and 9 are recalled here (Table 59 below) to illustrate the variation in the frequency of occurrence of some pairs after concordance reclassification and the separation of senses into homonymous lexemes:

Table 59: Exemplification of the variation of the raw frequency of some sample terms and the variation of the directionality signalled by FO after concordance reclassification [examples originally from Tables 8 and 9]

	Initial frequencies		Direction	Revised frequencies		Direction
Pairs	Noun	Verb	By FO	Noun	Verb	by FO
barter	83	109	Verb-to-Noun	121	71	Noun-to-Verb
pinion	29	19	Noun-to-Verb	21	27	Verb-to-Noun
graft	185	187	Verb-to-Noun	210	162	–
graft$^{N1/V1}$				122	147	Verb-to-Noun
graft$^{N3/V2}$				11	1	Noun-to-Verb
graft$^{N4/V3}$				52	9	Noun-to-Verb
graft$^{N5/V4}$				25	5	Noun-to-Verb

Since the proposed steps, that is, the reclassification of concordances as their correct word class and the identification and separation of homonymous lexemes cf. also Sections 3.2.2 and 3.2.4.5), are time-consuming, perhaps future research could benefit from using corpora or data sources that incorporate sense information alongside word class, potentially simplifying the process.

5.6.2 FO and RR: issues in their applicability

Several issues concerning the applicability of the two criteria are identified. First, it is here argued that the criteria are not applicable to identify a directionality when the values in terms of FO or RR are too close or too low. In this sense, deciding from which point a difference in FO or RR is relevant or not is a necessary step for the correct interpretation of the criteria.[55] Specifically, this study used a Chi-squared test to identify significance levels between the differences in the frequency of occurrence of the senses. For RR, Fisher's exact test was used to identify significance levels between the differences in the range of registers covered by the senses. However, the applicability of the statistical test in RR remains controversial because the categorical values (that is, the number of registers in which a sense can appear in the BNC) are low.

As anticipated, if significance levels are established, the applicability of the criteria decreases. Also, the consistency levels with other criteria are naturally lower too. This is a relevant point sometimes disregarded in previous studies on directionality in conversion, for example, in Bram (2011) or Kisselew et al. (2016), or doubtfully established by using different methods. For instance, Balteiro (2007: 127–129) proposed to establish the average difference between conversion pair types and to interpret the direction as unclear if the difference between a pair of lexemes is lower than 25 % of the average for each direction. However, she acknowledges the limitations of this method, as it cannot be generalized because it is based on calculations from her sample, which is barely representative.

Regarding the applicability of RR, it should be noted that in Ruz (2025) two register classifications were tested, one consisting of twelve categories and the other of 71 categories. The results show that a more fine-grained classification gives better results for the directionality of the pairs. This is because the registers covered by a pair of senses will most likely differ for a higher number of pairs if the number of registers into which they are annotated is higher too. Similarly, the consistency of RR with other criteria is higher. Thus, this study presents results using the BNC's classification into 71 registers.

For the same reasons, FO solves directionality between senses for a higher number of pairs, that is, because lexemes with frequency up to 1,000 are included in the study, there is a greater chance that the frequency of occurrence of senses will significantly differ for a higher number of pairs.

As for their results, consistency levels between FO and RR reveal that both criteria suggest similar tendencies. To which extent they do signal the same direction or not varies greatly according to whether significance levels are considered for RR, because the statistical test proved a significant difference only for a limited number of pairs of senses in RR (D1: 159 pairs, 39.85 %, D2: 27 pairs, 40.3 %; cf. Table 32). I argue that the point from which a difference in frequency or the range of registers covered by senses needs to be established. However, while for

[55] This is noted in previous references too (among others, Umbreit 2010: 309).

FO the statistical test applied seems to provide reliable results, further research is needed to establish significance levels regarding RR between pairs of senses.

If significance is omitted, the results are in line with those of FO, although some cases in which the direction by these two criteria differ are found too. If significance levels are considered, RR does not seem to be as applicable and should thus be given secondary importance. More generally, the consistency levels of FO and RR with other criteria reveal similar tendencies too (RR being less consistent because of its lower applicability). Overall, the consistency of these criteria seems to be higher with SD or SP. However, consistency levels are not as high as expected. This is because it was presumed that the criteria would point to the correct directions and thus align for the same pairs, but a closer look reveals that the criteria signal opposite directions for a rather large number of pairs. As discussed in previous sections, these numbers cast doubt on the applicability of the criteria.

Even if it is expected for the base to be more frequent than the derived counterpart sense, or to appear in a wider range of registers, this is not necessarily the case. Previous research has pointed out this fact, highlighting the limited reliability of FO between lexeme pairs (cf. Umbreit 2010: 309; also Bram 2011: 234 or Kisselew et al. 2016: 97, as regards Verb-to-Noun conversion, when FO is contrasted with AD). Specifically, Kisselew et al. (2016: 97) mentions that "[…] frequency is a poor predictor of the direction of derivation […] possibly because semantic regularity allows usages to become entrenched".

Examples of misleading cases are found in our sample too, that is, where FO or RR seem to give a wrong interpretation of directionality. For instance, for *bombard*$^{N/V}$, senses identified as derived are more frequent than base senses:

(85) *bombard*^{V}

sense 1 (ARTEFACT; five occurrences in the BNC)
"1. a. The earliest kind of cannon, usually throwing a stone ball or a very large shot. †b. transferred. The ball or stone thrown by a bombard. Obsolete. rare—1." (OED), for example, "*[…] and the big hooped* **bombards** *and mortars, repositioned, were firing their three-hundred pounders as frequently as* **bombards** *were ever able to do, with a hundred balls beside each to do it with.*" (BNC)
Sense 2 (ARTEFACT; two occurrences in the BNC)
"2. A bomb-vessel or bomb-ketch; = bomb n. 4." (OED), for example, "*There was no softening in his stare. He said, 'Niccolò vander Poele. I am told there are* **bombards**. *Did you plant them?'*" (BNC)

(86) *bombard*^{V}

sense 1/2 (SIMILATIVE_INSTRUMENTAL; 60 occurrences in the BNC)
"†1. intransitive. To fire off bombards or heavy guns. Obsolete (except as absolute use of 2). / 2. transitive. a. To batter with shot and shell; to assault with ordnance so as to destroy, disable, or reduce to submission." (OED), for example, "*Witnesses describe how the army initially* **bombards** *an area of marshes to drive away the population.*" (BNC)

Additionally, the verb presents further extended and figurative senses. In fact, the most frequent sense in the pair is its figurative use (FIG_SIMILATIVE) "2. b. figurative. To assail with persistent force or violence." (OED), for example, "[...] we are actually **bombarded** by an increasingly heterogeneous mix of musical methods and messages [...]" (BNC).

Indeed, a higher frequency of occurrence is quite often observed for figurative senses within pairs, which in this study are many times classified in D2. If senses were not classified into orders of derivation, FO results would differ for some pairs, for example, in *pillory*$^{N/V}$, because the figurative sense of the verb is more frequent than the related figurative sense of the noun, or the sense pairs in D1 (sense 1 for the noun and verb). Thus, if the direction is considered between lexemes, it would be Verb-to-Noun because the figurative use of the verb shows a higher frequency, whereas an analysis by senses into orders of derivation signals an unclear direction based on FO in D1 (because the frequency of the senses related in the first order is too low), and a Verb-to-Noun direction in the D2:[56]

(87) *pillory*^{N}

sense 1 (INSTRUMENT; nine occurrences in the BNC)

"1. A device for punishment, usually consisting of a wooden framework mounted on a post, with holes or rings for trapping the head and hands, in which an offender was confined so as to be subjected to public ridicule, abuse, assault, etc.; punishment of this kind. Now historical. (In Great Britain the punishment of the pillory was abolished, except for perjury, in 1815, and totally in 1837. In Delaware, U.S., it was not abolished till 1905. In quot. c1390: Christ's cross.)" (OED), for example, "*had followed the King's army from London to Coventry was 'taken by the soldiers, and first led about the city then set in a* **pillory**, *after in a cage then ducked in a river, and at last banished the city*'" (BNC)

Sense 2 (EVENT/INSTANCE/RESULT; one occurrence in the BNC)

"2. figurative. Public abuse, ridicule, or defamation; subjection to abuse, humiliation; a place in which a person or thing is subjected to abuse; (also) a person subjected to abuse." (OED), for example, "*was frankly un désastre and that I was amazed she had walked the streets to my apartment in broad daylight and escaped* **pillory**." (BNC)

(88) *pillory*^{V}

sense 1 (INSTRUMENTAL; five occurrences in the BNC)

"1. a. transitive. To put (a person) in a pillory; to punish by means of a pillory. Now historical. / †b. transitive. In extended use: to constrict (a person) as though in a pillory. Obsolete." (OED), for example, "*Samuel Butler and others have* **pilloried** *the Victorian paterfamilias, and there were indeed families that suffered the tyranny of fathers using religion as [...]*" (BNC)

sense 2 (FIG_SIMILATIVE; 48 occurrences in the BNC)

56 The analysis of FO gives closer results to that of the criteria of SD or SP, where the direction identified is Noun-to-Verb in the first order and Verb-to-Noun in the second order.

"2. transitive. figurative. To abuse, ridicule, or defame (a person or thing); to expose to public abuse or ridicule; to reproach." (OED), for example, "*Within days of the episode, vicious rumours had spread throughout Ayrshire, Rough's children were* **pilloried** *at school and his wife was humiliated on future shopping trips.*" (BNC)

Additionally, as described in Section 3.3, the classification in this study allows to identify related pairs of senses, and senses extended within lexemes but for which no counterpart sense is found in the derivative. If this difference is overlooked, dissimilar results are obtained for some pairs, for example, *twit*$^{N/V}$:

(89) *twit*^{N1}
sense 1 (INSTANCE/RESULT; one occurrence in the BNC)
"1. a. A criticism or reproach, esp. one made in a good-humoured or teasing way; a taunt, a jibe. Cf. twit v. 1a." (OED), for example, "*[...] that's concise enough to be published whilst covering all the points you want to raise – especially in reply to* **twits** *like. Still, I'll work on it.*" (BNC)
sense 2 (EXT_HUMAN+CHARACTERISTICS; 65 occurrences in the BNC)
"2. b. colloquial (originally and chiefly British). A stupid, silly, or annoying person; a fool, an idiot." (OED), for example, "*[...] laid out into seven levels, each offering a choice of two to move on to once completed. Confused? Look at the screenshot,* **twit**!." (BNC)
(90) *twit*^{V}
sense 1 (NEGATIVE JUDGMENT; five occurrences in the BNC)
"1. a. To censure, reproach, or upbraid (a person), esp. in a good-humoured or teasing way; to find fault with, to blame; to taunt." (OED), for example, "*The good lady thought that he was shy, and constantly* **twitted** *him to bring him into the talk; Paul hoped that she would get over it as the days passed, and this proved to be the case.*" (BNC)

In the pair *twit*$^{N/V}$, the first sense in the OED for both the noun and verb entries is related. However, sense 2 for the noun is analysed as an extended use for which no counterpart verb sense is attested in the BNC. Thus, a comparison by lexemes would signal a Noun-to-Verb direction, while a sense analysis signals a Verb-to-Noun direction (N).

Overall, even though the criteria of FO and RR may signal a direction, their reliability remains uncertain, even in cases where they show significant differences between senses and thus suggest a clear direction, assuming that the identified direction signals directionality correctly. It is here argued that distributional criteria may not be as reliable for the study of directionality in conversion as previously thought. While they may provide insights into the current usage of senses within lexeme pairs, and often align with the correct direction for a number of senses, their role in directionality is secondary. Their results should always be considered alongside semantic criteria, which play a more decisive role in establishing directionality.

CHAPTER 6

Conclusions

6.1 Introduction

The issue of directionality in conversion has received considerable attention in the literature (cf. the review in Chapter 2). Within the approaches which view directionality as a relevant issue in conversion, several criteria have been proposed for its identification. The criteria discussed or applied in the literature, presented in Section 2.5, have often been transmitted uncritically. Their application, as in Bram's (2011) thesis, as the largest study on directionality in English conversion, reveals a degree of indeterminacy that remains unresolved to this day. The hypothesis is that directionality in conversion remains a difficult issue:

i. for the difficulty inherent in the process of conversion,
ii. for the criteria used in the identification of directionality, and
iii. for the scale (lexeme vs sense) at which these criteria have been applied in previous references.

Regarding the latter point, as described in Section 2.4.3.3, although the role of senses has been emphasized in the literature, directionality has often been studied at the level of lexeme. A key contribution of this study is that it considers the sense as the scale for the identification of conversion, following Plank (2010: 87). Specifically, the focus is on testing several semantic and quantitative-distributional criteria for directionality in a sample of presentday English noun/verb conversion, to find out:

i. how feasible it is to apply the criteria at the level of sense (following Plank 2010), and
ii. how true Marchand's (1964) criteria for directionality are when applied by senses.

6.2 Findings

6.2.1 The influence of methodological decisions

This study has shown how various methodological decisions may affect the analysis of directionality. Not only does the use of criteria of dissimilar nature yield dissimilar results, but other methodological aspects may have an impact on the conclusions on the directionality between English noun/verb conversion pairs, among others:

i. the sources selected for the analysis of the criteria (lexicographic and corpus),
ii. the level of analysis, that is, lexeme vs sense, and
iii. an analysis of senses in use vs one that examines all senses, including those no longer in use.

Regarding i., lexicographic decisions may affect the analysis too. This is a major methodological issue, even if it has been identified only in a few cases (cf. *anagram*$^{N/V}$ in Section 5.3).

This study has also shown how different results are obtained according to the interpretation of the criteria. This calls for the need of a more precise description of the criteria, and whether a restrictive or an inclusive interpretation is adopted, for example, whether SD applies only when the counterpart sense is mentioned in the definition of a sense, or if it applies also to senses defined based on synonyms (or parallel senses by affixation; cf. Section 5.2). Emphasis is also laid on the need to establish significance levels when quantitative-distributional criteria are tested. This applies not only to the study of directionality but also more generally to any study on differences in the frequency or register usage of senses.

6.2.2 Relevance of the criteria

Previous studies on directionality compared the results of semantic or distributional criteria with that by other criteria too. Notably in previous references, the direction indicated by semantic criteria is often contrasted with the direction indicated by etymology or dates of first attestation (cf. Balteiro 2007; Bram 2011; Kisselew et al. 2016). However, as noted in the literature, an approach to conversion from these two perspectives (diachronic vs synchronic) often gives contradictory results (Marchand 1963a: 180; Adams 1973: 40; Cetnarowska 1993: 37–39; Bauer & Valera 2005: 11; Bram 2011: 90, among others; cf. also the description in Section 2.4.3.2). This is because the two approaches focus on different aspects of conversion.

The approach in this study is synchronic and the focus is on the directions that can be found in conversion according to the sense relations between pairs in present-day English. Consequently, only semantic and quantitative-distributional criteria (cf. Marchand 1964) are tested.

In this sense, a higher consistency between the results of the criteria tested was anticipated. The results were not as expected in that:

i. a low applicability was found for some of the criteria (SR, RR, and RU) for various reasons and, consequently, also a low consistency between these and other criteria, and
ii. even if the criteria are tested with a focus on the use of the pairs synchronically, the results across criteria point to opposite directions in some cases, which casts doubts on the overall applicability of the criteria.

At a general level, it has been shown that:

i. SD and SP give the best results in a sense-based analysis of directionality, even though their applicability presents issues and the results are not always conclusive. Notably, the criteria do not prove to be conclusive in all cases even in overt affixation (cf. Ruz & Cetnarowska 2023).
ii. Distributional criteria (FO and RR) may not be as reliable for the study of directionality in conversion as previously thought. While FO or RR may give an account of the current usage of senses within pairs of lexemes, and even if they tend to signal a direction for a number of senses, the direction by these criteria is not always correct, that is, the derived sense is not necessarily always the most widely used one.
iii. The applicability of SR to study directionality is questioned, partly because it is a criterion which is best applied by lexemes, thus not allowing the identification of multiple directions at the sense level, and partly also because it is argued that a wider semantic range does not necessarily point to a consistent derivational direction, even between monosemous pairs.
iv. RU is highlighted as a secondary criterion, and one which is applicable for very specific cases and only at the level of sense.
v. Overall, the criteria demonstrate a higher level of applicability and consistency for the senses in D2 compared to those in D1, although the difference is not particularly striking.

Regarding the aims of the study, it has been demonstrated that:

i. The criteria can be applied at the level of sense (with the exception of SR as interpreted in this study) and the results obtained by a sense analysis are undoubtedly closer to how the derivational process may have operated in each case. However, the applicability of the criteria differs, and some of the criteria prove applicable only in specific cases (for instance RU).
ii. The relevance of the criteria when applied by senses varies too and, while the semantic criteria of SD or SP seem to give the best results, a number of misleading cases are found in the application of other criteria, revealing,

for example, that it is not necessarily the case that the derivative sense is used less frequently than the base sense, or that the semantic range of the derivative is narrower.

Overall, the results show that directionality in conversion can hardly be ascertained according to Marchand's (1964) criteria viewed as a unitary set of criteria, even less when run according to senses instead of by lexemes. Directionality in English noun/verb conversion cannot be identified consistently by the set of criteria, if a perfect match across criteria is aimed at. Instead, a frequent profile is one where some criteria clearly signal one direction whereas others signal the opposite.

6.2.3 Theoretical implications

In the previous literature, conversion has sometimes been claimed to be simply unpredictable (in terms of bidirectionality or multidirectionality) for the difficulties it poses, or it has been described as unidirectional too. In this study, several patterns are found for conversion pairs:

i. Sometimes conversion is unidirectional, that is, a single direction can be found between some pairs: This is when lexemes present a single sense, or when only one of the senses of a lexeme undergoes conversion. However, as new senses may emerge for the lexemes and these may be converted in one or the other direction, the possibility for multiple conversion remains open.
ii. In other pairs, directionality is multiple, in that various directions may be found between pairs of lexemes, according to specific senses. The results of the sense analysis in this study prove that several directions can be found between polysemous lexemes. In contrast to approaches that consider directionality as unpredictable, this study proves that, for most cases, a direction can be found between senses, and that this is best decided according to SD or SP.
iii. The criteria tested in this study do not always prove applicable to decide on the direction between some pairs. Ambiguous cases, where both directions are plausible based on semantic analysis, may need to be described as bidirectional, with the implications that this may have for the treatment of conversion in related studies, for example, for the semantic relations between conversion pairs. Bidirectionality is understood as the possibility that both directions may be processed simultaneously. Perhaps certain lexemes with a root origin may best fit this description.

Overall, the picture here presented shows that the description of the direction in conversion is better established between related senses and not between lexemes. The identification of recursive sense derivation in conversion as in subsequent orders of derivation is here argued to be an effective method for the identification of directionality in conversion between polysemous pairs. The proposal here is thus, in line with Plank (2010), that directionality is a property of related senses between lexeme pairs and that it should be studied at the sense level.

6.3 Limitations and future research

This study is on the directions between the senses of noun/verb conversion pairs by order of derivation. It remains for future research:

i. To see if the criteria show a similar applicability when in pairs with a frequency higher than 1000.
ii. To identify the more frequent directional patterns in English noun/verb conversion.
iii. To determine the applicability of directionality criteria at a sense level, as well as the most frequent patterns, when other word classes are involved, for example, adjectives.

Other limitations are mainly methodological:

i. This study involves a great deal of manual analysis, especially as regards sense classification of concordances.
ii. Because all the concordances of the pairs of lexemes in the sample were manually classified into the OED senses, the sample was restricted to the frequency ranges 0–1,000. The sample in this study is considered representative in that polysemous lexemes are included too, but such a sample may not be representative of all the directional patterns or controversial issues in conversion in English.
iii. As in any semantic analysis, some degree of subjectivity may be involved, but this was prevented as far as possible by conducting an analysis according to the senses in the OED.

Regarding these limitations, it may be interesting to explore AI models to automatize sense categorization for future work, which may be useful for the classification of high-frequency lexemes.

Bibliography

Adams, Valerie. 1973. *An Introduction to Modern English Word-Formation*. London: Longman. <https://doi.org/10.4324/9781315504254>.

Alexiadou, Artemis & Jane Grimshaw. 2008. Verbs, nouns, and affixation. In Florian Schäfer (ed.), *Working Papers of the SFB 732 Incremental Specification in Context. Vol. 1*, 1–16. Universität Stuttgart. <http://dx.doi.org/10.18419/opus-5695>.

Aronoff, Mark. 1976. *Word Formation in Generative Grammar*. Cambridge, MA: MIT Press.

Balteiro, Isabel. 2007. *The Directionality of Conversion in English: A Dia-Synchronic Study*. Bern: Peter Lang.

Bauer, Laurie. 1983. *English Word-Formation*. Cambridge: Cambridge University Press. <https://doi.org/10.1017/CBO9781139165846>.

Bauer, Laurie. 1997. Derivational paradigms. In Geert E. Booij & Jaap van Marle (eds.), *Yearbook of Morphology 1996*, 243–256. Dordrecht: Kluwer. <https://doi.org/10.1007/978-94-017-3718-0_13>.

Bauer, Laurie. 2019. *Rethinking Morphology*, Edinburgh: Edinburgh University Press. <https://doi.org/10.1515/9781474436175>.

Bauer, Laurie & Rodney Huddleston. 2002. Lexical word-formation. In Rodney Huddleston & Geoffrey K. Pullum (eds.), *The Cambridge Grammar of the English Language*, 1621–1722. Cambridge: Cambridge University Press. <https://doi.org/10.1017/9781316423530.020>.

Bauer, Laurie & Salvador Valera. 2005. *Approaches to Conversion / Zero-Derivation*. Münster: Waxmann.

Bauer, Laurie, Rochelle Lieber & Ingo Plag. 2013. *The Oxford Reference Guide to English Morphology*. Oxford: Oxford University Press. <https://doi.org/10.1093/acprof:oso/9780198747062.001.0001>.

Bauer, Laurie & Salvador Valera. 2015. Sense inheritance in English word-formation. In Laurie Bauer, Lívia Körtvélyessy & Pavol Štekauer (eds.), *Semantics of Complex Words*, 67–84. Dordrecht: Springer. <https://doi.org/10.1007/978-3-319-14102-2_5>.

Bauer, Laurie & Salvador Valera. Forthcoming. Conversion: A position paper. In Laurie Bauer & Salvador Valera (eds.), Conversion in Morphology: Theory, Typology. Oxford: Oxford University Press.

Beard, Robert. 1995. *Lexeme-Morpheme Base Morphology. A General Theory of Inflection and Word-Formation*, SUNY Series in Linguistics. New York: State University of New York Press.

Beard, Robert. 1998. Derivation. In Andrew Spencer & Arnold M. Zwicky (eds.), *The Handboook of Morphology*, 44–65. Oxford: Blackwell.

Beard, Robert & Mark Volpe. 2005. Lexeme-morpheme base morphology. In Pavol Štekauer & Rochelle Lieber (eds.), *Handbook of word-formation*. Dordrecht: Springer, 189–205.

Beecher, Henry. 2004. Derivational paradigm in word formation. <https://es.scribd.com/document/305704929/Derivational-Paradigm-in-Word-Formation>. (last accessed 10 December 2024)

Bisong, Ekaba. 2019. Google Colaboratory. In Ekaba Bisong (ed.), *Building Machine Learning and Deep Learning Models on Google Cloud Platform*, 59–64. Berkeley, CA: Apress. <https://doi.org/10.1007/978-1-4842-4470-8_7>.

Bergenholtz, Henning & Joachim Mugdan. 1979. *Einführung in die Morphologie*. Stuttgart: Kohlhammer Verlag.

Biese, Yrjoe. 1941. Origin and development of conversion in English. *Annales Academiae Scientiarum Fennicae* B XLV/2.

Bladin, Vilhelm. 1911. *Studies on denominative verbs in English*. Uppsala: Almqvist & Wiksells boktryckerei-a.-b. (Doctoral dissertation.)

Bram, Barli. 2011. *Major total conversion in English: The question of directionality*. Wellington: Victoria University of Wellington. (Doctoral dissertation.)

Brezina, Vaclav. 2018. *Statistics in corpus linguistics: A practical guide*. Cambridge: Cambridge University Press. <https://doi.org/10.1017/9781316410899>.

Bybee, Joan L. 1985. *Morphology. A Study of the Relation between Meaning and Form*. Amsterdam: John Benjamins.

Bybee, Joan L. 1988. Morphology as lexical organization. In Michael Hammond & Michael Noonan (eds.), *Theoretical Morphology: Approaches in Modern Linguistics*, 119–141. San Diego, CA: Academic Press.

Cetnarowska, Bożena. 1993. *The Syntax, Semantics and Derivation of Bare Nominalisations in English*. Katowice: Wydawnictwo Uniwersytetu Śląskiego.

Cetnarowska, Bożena. 2011. Conversion as metonymy and the problem of recursiveness. In Bogusław Bierwiaczonek, Bożena Cetnarowska & Anna Turula (eds.), *Syntax in Cognitive Grammar*, 13–26. Częstochowa: WSL.

Cetnarowska, Bożena. 2017. Where is conversion in Slavonic languages? *Word Structure* 10(1), 121–138.

Clark, Eve V. & Herbert H. Clark. 1979. When nouns surface as verbs. *Language* 55(4), 767–811. <https://doi.org/10.2307/412745>.

Crocco Galèas, Grazia. 1990. Conversion as a morphological metaphor. In: Julián Méndez-Dosuna & Carmen Pensado (eds.), *Naturalists at Krems: Papers from the Workshop on Natural Phonology and Natural Morphology (Krems/Austria, July, 1–7, 1988)*, 23–32. Salamanca: Ediciones de la Universidad de Salamanca.

Cruse, Alan. 1986. *Lexical Semantics*. Cambridge: Cambridge University Press.

Davies, Mark. 2004. *British National Corpus* (from Oxford University Press). Available at <https://www.englishcorpora.org/bnc/> (last accessed 30 October 2021).

Dearmond, Richard C. 1969. The concept of word-derivation. *Lingua* 22, 329–361.

Díaz-Negrillo, Ana & Cristina Fernández-Alcaina. 2023. A corpus-based study of the semantic distribution of denominal verb formation in English. *SKASE Journal of Theoretical Linguistics* 20(4), 2–19. <http://www.skase.sk/Volumes/JTL55/01.pdf>.

Dirven, René. 1999. Conversion as a conceptual metonymy of event schemata. In Klaus-Uwe Panther & Günter Radden (eds.), *Metonymy in Language and Thought*, 275–288. Amsterdam/Philadelphia: John Benjamins.

Dixon, Robert M. W. [1991] 2005. *A Semantic Approack to English Grammar.* 2nd edn. Oxford: Oxford University Press.

Don, Jan. 1993. *Morphological Conversion*. OTS Dissertation series. Utrecht: Research Institute for Language and Speech. (Doctoral dissertation.)

Don, Jan. 2004. Categories in the lexicon. *Linguistics* 42(5), 931–956.

Don, Jan. 2005. On conversion, relisting and zero-derivation. *SKASE Journal of Theoretical Linguistics* 2(2), 2–16.

Don, Jan. 2023. Category change without overt marking. In Peter Ackema, Sabrina Bendjaballah, Eulàlia Bonet & Antonio Fábregas (eds.), *The Wiley Blackwell Companion to Morphology*, 1–32. Wiley Online Library. <https://doi.org/10.1002/9781119693604.morphcom015>.

Fábregas, Antonio. 2005. *The definition of the grammatical category in a syntactically-oriented morphology*. Universidad Autónoma de Madrid. (Doctoral dissertation.)

Farrell, Patrick. 2001. Functional shift as category underspecification. *English Language and Linguistics* 5(1), 109–130. <https://doi.org/10.1017/S1360674301000156>.

Fernández-Alcaina, Cristina & Salvador Valera. 2022. Conversion/Zero-affixation: Theories, Data. Workshop at the *Word-Formation Theories VI & Typology and Universals in Word-Formation V Conference*, University Pavol Jozef Safarík, Košice, 23–26 June 2022.

Fernández-Alcaina, Cristina & Salvador Valera. 2024. Conversion/Zero-derivation: Aspects of the theory. Workshop at the *Biennial of Czech Linguistics*, Charles University, Prague, 18–20 September 2024.

Fernández-Domínguez, Jesús, Alexandra Bagasheva & Cristina Lara-Clares. 2020. What paradigms and what for? In Jesús Fernández-Domínguez, Jesús, Alexandra Bagasheva & Cristina Lara-Clares (eds.), *Paradigmatic Relations in Word Formation*, 1–20. Leiden: Brill; <https://doi.org/10.1163/9789004433410_002>.

Giegerich, Heinz J. 1999. *Lexical Strata in English: Morphological Causes, Phonological Effects*. Cambridge: Cambridge University Press.

Ginzburg, R. S., S. S. Khidekel, G. Y. Knyazeva & A. A. Sankin. [1966] 1979. A course in modern English lexicology. 2nd edn. Moscow: Vyssaja Škola.

Grimshaw, Jane. 1990. *Argument Structure*. Cambridge, MA: MIT Press.

Grzega, Joachim. 2004. *Bezeichnungswandel: Wie, Warum, Wozu? Ein Beitrag zur englischen und allgemeinen Onomasiologie*. Heidelberg: Winter.

Haselow, Alexander. 2011. *Typological changes in the lexicon. Analytic tendencies in English noun formation*. Berlin: de Gruyter Mouton. <https://doi.org/10.1515/9783110238211>.

Hardie, Andrew. 2012. CQPweb – combining power, flexibility and usability in a corpus analysis tool. *International Journal of Corpus Linguistics* 17(3), 380–409.

Hayes, Bruce. 1981. *A Metrical Theory of Stress Rules*. Indiana University Linguistics Club. (Doctoral dissertation.)

Hertrampf, Alfons. 1932. *Die Entstehung von Substantiven aus Verben im Neuenglischen*. Beslau: Breslau Dissertations. (Doctoral dissertation.)

Hledíková, Hana & Magda Ševčíková. 2024. Conversion in languages with different morphological structures: A semantic comparison of English and Czech. *Morphology* 34, 73–102. <https://doi.org/10.1007/s11525-024-09422-1>.

Iacobini, Claudio. 2000. Base and direction of derivation. In Geert E. Booij, Christian Lehmann & Joachim Mugdan (eds.), *Morphologie. Morphology.*

Ein internationales Handbuch zur Flexion und Wortbildung. An International Handbook on Inflection and Word-Formation. 1. Halband. Volume 1. In collaboration with Wolfgang Kesselheim & Stavros Skopeteas, 865–876. Berlin: W. de Gruyter.

Iordăchioaia, Gianina. 2019. Event structure and argument realization in English zero-derived nominals with particles. *Nordlyd* 44(1): 35–51. <https://doi.org/10.7557/12.5205>.

Iordăchioaia, Gianina. 2022. Paradigmatic aspects of deverbal noun conversion in English. In Alba E. Ruz, Cristina Fernández-Alcaina & Cristina Lara-Clares (eds.), *Paradigms in Word Formation: Theory and Applications*, 155–180. Amsterdam: John Benjamins.

Iordăchioaia, Gianina & Chiara Melloni. 2020. Derivational zero affixes. Workshop at the *53rd Annual Meeting of the Societas Linguistica Europaea*, 26 August–1 September 2020.

Iordăchioaia, Gianina, Susanne Schweitzer, Yaryna Svyryda & María Camila Buitrago Cabrera. 2020. Deverbal zero-nominalization and verb classes: Insights from a database. *Zeitschrift für Wortbildung/Journal of Word Formation* 4(2): 120–142.

Iordăchioaia, Gianina & Chiara Melloni. 2023. The zero suffix in English and Italian deverbal nouns. *Zeitschrift für Sprachwissenschaft* 42(1), 109–132.

Ivanová, Martina. 2016. Variation and variants in the dictionary of multiword expressions (focussing on complex nominals/noun compounds). *SKASE Journal of Theoretical Linguistics* 13(3), 14–28.

Ivanová, Martina & Martin Ološtiak. 2015. Slovak. In Peter O. Müller, Ingeborg Ohnheiser, Susan Olsen & Franz Rainer (eds.), *Word-formation: An international handbook of the languages of Europe, Vol. 4*, 2892–2912. Berlin: De Gruyter Mouton. <https://doi.org/10.1515/9783110379082-026>.

Jackendoff, Ray S. 1974. *Semantic Interpretation in Generative Grammar.* Cambridge, MA: The MIT Press.

Jespersen, Otto. 1909–49. *A Modern English Grammar on Historical Principles. Vol. VII.* Copenhagen: Ejnar Munksgaard.

Josefsson, Gunlög. 1997. *On the Principles of Word Formation in Swedish.* Lund: Lund University Press.

Kastovsky, Dieter. 1969. Wortbildung und Nullmorphem. *Linguistische Berichte* 2, 1–13.

Kastovsky, Dieter. 1976. *Word-formation, or: At the crossroads of morphology, syntax, semantics, and the lexicon*. L.A.U.T. (Linguistic Agency, University of Trier).

Kastovsky, Dieter. 1989. Typological changes in the history of English word-formation. In Heinz-Joachim Müllenbrock & Renate Noll-Wiemann (eds.), *Anglistentag 1988, Göttingen: Vorträge*, 281–293. Tübingen: Max Niemeyer.

Kastovsky, Dieter. 1994. Verbal derivation in English: A historical survey or much ado about nothing. In Derek Britton (ed.), *English Historical Linguistics 1994. Papers from the 8th International Conference on English Historical Linguistics (8. ICEHL, Edinburgh, 19–23 September 1994)*, 93–117. Amsterdam: John Benjamins.

Kastovsky, Dieter. 1997. Sign-oriented vs. form-oriented linguistics and word-formation. *Studia Anglica Posnaniensia* XXXI, 79–90.

Kastovsky, Dieter. 2005. Conversion and/or zero: Word-formation theory, historical linguistics, and typology. In Laurie Bauer & Salvador Valera (eds.), *Approaches to Conversion/Zero-Derivation*, 31–49. Münster: Waxmann.

Katamba, Francis. 1993. *Morphology*. Basingstoke/Hampshire: Macmillan.

Kerleroux, Françoise. 1999. Identification d'un procédé morphologique: La conversion. *Faits de Langues: Revue de Linguistique* 14, 89–100.

Kilby, David. 1984. *Descriptive Syntax and the English Verb*. London: Croom Helm.

Kilgarriff, Adam, Vít Baisa, Jan Bušta, Miloš Jakubíček, Vojtěch Kovář, Jan Michelfeit, Pavel Rychlý & Vít Suchomel. 2014. The Sketch Engine: ten years on. *Lexicography* 1, 7–36.

Kiparsky, Paul. 1982. Word formation and the lexicon. In Frances Ingemann (ed.), *Proceedings of the 1982 Mid-America Linguistics Conference*, 3–29. Lawrence, KS: University of Kansas.

Kiparsky, Paul. 1997. Remarks on denominal verbs. *Complex Predicates* 64, 473–499.

Kisselew, Max, Laura Rimell, Alexis Palmer & Sebastian Padó. 2016. Predicting the direction of derivation in English conversion. In *Proceedings of the ACL SIG-MORPHON workshop, Berlin, 93–98*. Association for Computational Linguistics. <https://doi.org/10.18653/v1/W16-2015>.

Kopecka, Beata. 2013. Whatever the weather – on semantic change and word-formation processes. In Jacek Fisiak & Magdalena Bator (eds.), *Historical English Word-Formation and Semantics*, 353–366. Frankfurt am Main/New York: Peter Lang.

Körtvélyessy, Lívia, Alexandra Bagasheva & Pavol Štekauer. 2020. *Derivational Networks Across Languages*. Berlin: De Gruyter Mouton. <https://doi.org/10.1515/9783110686630>.

Kövecses, Zoltán & Günter Radden. 1998. Metonymy: Developing a cognitive linguistic view. *Cognitive Linguistics* 9–1, 37–77. <https://doi.org/10.1515/cogl.1998.9.1.37>.

Koziol, Herbert. 1937. *Handbuch der englischen Wortbildungslehre*. Heidelberg: Carl Winter.

Kruisinga, Etsko. 1927. Contributions to English syntax. XVII: On the history of conversions in English. *English Studies* IX, 103–108.

Kruisinga, Etsko. [1911] 1931–32. *A Handbook of PresentDay English*. 5th edn. Groningen: P. Noordhoff.

Langenfelt, Gosta. 1933. *Select Studies in Colloquial English of the Late Middle Ages*. Lund: Gleerupska Univ. Bokhandeln.

Lara-Clares, Cristina. 2023. *Morphological Competition in PresentDay English Nominalisation*. Granada: University of Granada. (Doctoral dissertation.)

Lara-Clares, Cristina & Paul Thompson. 2019. Nominal competition in present-day English affixation: Zero-affixation vs. *-ness* with the semantic category STATIVE. *SKASE Journal of Theoretical Linguistics* 16(2), 25–49. <http://www.skase.sk/Volumes/JTL40/pdf_doc/02.pdf>.

Lee, David. 2001. Genres, registers, text types, domain, and styles: Clarifying the concepts and navigating a path through the BNC jungle. *Language Learning & Technology* 5(3), 37–72. <https://dx.doi.org/10125/44565>.

Leech, Geoffrey N. [1974] 1981. *Semantics: The Study of Meaning*. 2nd edn. Harmondsworth: Penguin.

Lieber, Rochelle. 1980. *On the Organization of the Lexicon*. Cambridge, MA: Massachusetts Institute of Technology. (Doctoral dissertation.)

Lieber, Rochelle. 1992. *Deconstructing Morphology: Word Formation in Syntactic Theory*. Chicago: University of Chicago Press.

Lieber, Rochelle. 2004. *Morphology and Lexical Semantics*. Cambridge: Cambridge University Press. <https://doi.org/10.1017/CBO9780511486296>.

Lieber, Rochelle. 2005. Word formation processes in English. In Pavol Štekauer & Rochelle Lieber (eds.), *Handbook of Word Formation*, 375–422. Dordrecht: Springer.

Lipka, Leonhard. 1971. Grammatical categories, lexical items and word-formation. *Foundations of Language* 7, 211–238.

Lipka, Leonhard. 1990. *An Outline of English Lexicology: Lexical Structure, Word Semantics, and Word-Formation*. Tübingen: Max Niemeyer.

Ljung, Magnus, 1977. Problems in the derivation of instrumental verbs. In Herbert E. Brekle & Dieter Kastovsky (eds.), *Perspektiven der Wortbildungsforschung: Beiträge zum Wuppertaler Wortbildungskolloquium vom 9.–10. Juli 1976, anlässlich des 70. Geburtstags von Hans Marchand am 1. Oktober 1977*, 165–179. Bonn: Bouvier.

Lohmann, Arne. 2017. Phonological properties of word classes and directionality in conversion. *Word Structure* 10(2), 204–234. <https://doi.org/10.3366/word.2017.0108>.

Lyons, John. 1977. *Semantics, Vol. II.* Cambridge: Cambridge University Press.

Manova, Stela. 2011. *Understanding Morphological Rules with Special Emphasis on Conversion and Subtraction in Bulgarian, Russian and Serbo-Croatian.* Dordrecht: Springer. <https://doi.org/10.1007/978-90-481-9547-3>.

Marchand, Hans. 1963a. On a question of contrary analysis with derivationally connected but morphologically uncharacterized words. *English Studies* 44, 176–187.

Marchand, Hans. 1963b. On content as a criterion of derivational relationship with back-derived words. *Indogermanische Forschungen* 68, 170–175. <https://doi.org/10.1515/9783110243109.170>.

Marchand, Hans. 1964. A set of criteria for the establishing of derivational relationship between words unmarked by derivational morphemes. *Indogermanische Forschungen* 69, 10–19. <https://doi.org/10.1515/9783110243116.10>.

Marchand, Hans, 1969. *The Categories and Types of Present-Day English Word-Formation: A Synchronic-Diachronic Approach.* Munich: Carl Beck.

Martsa, Sándor. 2014. Rule or analogy? *Argumentum* 10, 449–471.

Mîrzea Vasile, Carmen, Christian Moroianu & Salvador Valera. 2022. Conversion/Zero-Derivation. Workshop at the *22nd International Conference of the Department of Linguistics: Synchronic, Diachronic and Typological Linguistics.* University of Bucharest, Bucharest, 18–19 November, 2022.

Mititelu, Verginica, Gianina Iordăchioaia, Svetlozara Leseva & Ivelina Stoyanova. 2023. The meaning of zero nouns and zero verbs. In Sven Kotowski & Ingo Plag (eds.), *The Semantics of Derivational Morphology*, 63–102. De Gruyter, Berlin. <https://doi.org/10.1515/9783111074917-004>.

Murphy, M. Lynne. 2010. *Lexical Meaning.* Cambridge: Cambridge University Press. <https://doi.org/10.1017/CBO9780511780684>.

Myers, Scott. 1984. Zero-derivation and inflection. In Margaret Speas & Richard Sproat (eds.), *MIT Working Papers in Linguistics* 7, 53–69.

McGregor, William B. 2003. The nothing that is, the zero that isn't. *Studia Linguistica* 57, 75–119.

Nagórko, Alicja. 2016. Polish. In Peter O. Müller, Ingeborg Ohnheiser, Susan Olsen & Franz Rainer (eds), *Word-Formation: An International Handbook of the Languages of Europe, Vol. 4*, 2831–2852. Berlin: De Gruyter Mouton. <https://doi.org/10.1515/9783110379082-023>.

Nida, Eugene A. [1946] 1949. *Morphology. The Descriptive Analysis of Words*. 2nd edn. Ann Arbor, MI: The University of Michigan Press.

Nida, Eugene A. 1975. *Exploring Semantic Structures*. Munich: Wilhelm Fink.

Oxford English Dictionary (OED). Oxford: Oxford University Press. Available at <https://oed.com/> (last accessed 30 October 2023).

Payne, Thomas E. 1997. *Describing Morphosyntax. A Guide for Field Linguists*. Cambridge: Cambridge University Press. <https://doi.org/10.1017/CBO9780511805066>.

Pennanen, Esko V. 1984. What happens in conversion? In Håken Ringbom & Matti Rissanen (eds.), *Proceedings from the Second Nordic Conference for English Studies, Hanasaari/Hanaholmen, 19th–21st May 1983*, 79–93. Åbo: Åbo Akademi.

Plag, Ingo. 1999. *Morphological Productivity*. Cambridge: Cambridge University Press.

Plag, Ingo. 2003. *Word-Formation in English*. Cambridge: Cambridge University Press. <https://doi.org/10.1017/CBO9780511841323>.

Plag, Ingo, Maria Braun, Sabine Lappe & Mareile Schramm. [2007] 2009. *Introduction to English Linguistics*. 2nd edn. Berlin: Walter de Gruyter.

Plank, Frans. 2010. Variable direction in zero-derivation and the unity of polysemous lexical items. *Word Structure* 3(1), 82–97. <https://doi.org/10.3366/E1750124510000498>.

Popova, Gergana. 2020. Derivational networks in English. In Lívia Körtvélyessy, Alexandra Bagasheva & Pavol Štekauer (eds.), *Derivational Networks Across Languages*, 147–156. Berlin: De Gruyter Mouton. <https://doi.org/10.1515/9783110686630-015>.

Quirk, Randolph & Sidney Greenbaum. 1973. *A University Grammar of English*. London: Longman.

Quirk, Randolph, Sydney Greenbaum, Geoffrey N. Leech & Jan Svartvik. 1985. *A Comprehensive Grammar of the English Language*. London: Longman.

Radden, Günter & Zoltán Kövecses. 1999. Towards a theory of metonymy. In Klaus-Uwe Panther & Günter Radden (eds.), *Metonymy in Language and Thought*, 17–60. Amsterdam/Philadelphia: John Benjamins. <https://doi.org/10.1075/hcp.4.03rad>.

Rainer, Franz. 1993. *Spanische Wortbildungslehre*. Berlin: de Gruyter. <https://doi.org/10.1515/9783110956054>.

Rainer, Franz. 2014. Polysemy in derivation. In Rochelle Lieber & Pavol Štekauer (eds.), *The Oxford Handbook of Derivational Morphology*,

338–353. Oxford: Oxford University Press. <https://doi.org/10.1093/oxfordhb/9780199641642.013.0019>.

Rappaport Hovav, Malka & Beth Levin. 1998. Building verb meanings. In Miriam Butt & Wilhelm Geuder (eds.), *The Projection of Arguments: Lexical and Compositional Factors*, 97–134. Stanford, CA: CSLI Publications.

Riese, Timothy. 2016. Mari. In Peter O. Müller, Ingeborg Ohnheiser, Susan Olsen & Franz Rainer (eds.), *Word-Formation: An International Handbook of the Languages of Europe, Vol. 5*, 3275–3288. Berlin: De Gruyter Mouton. <https://doi.org/10.1515/9783110424942-011>.

Robins, Robert H. 1987. Polysemy and the lexicographer. In Robert W. Burchfield (ed.), *Studies in Lexicography*, 52–75. Oxford: Clarendon Press.

Ruz, Alba E. 2025. *Directionality in conversion: The influence of criteria and senses*. Granada: University of Granada. (Doctoral dissertation.)

Ruz, Alba E. & Bożena Cetnarowska. 2023. Directionality in affixation: the applicability of Marchand's (1964) semantic criteria. *Linguistica Pragensia* 33(1): 7–44. <https://doi.org/10.14712/18059635.2023.1.1>.

Sanders, Gerald. 1988. Zero derivation and the overt analogue criterion. In Michael Hammond & Michael Noonan (eds.), *Theoretical Morphology: Approaches in Modern Linguistics*, 155–175. San Diego, CA: Academic Press.

Schönefeld, Doris. 2005. Zero-derivation – functional change – metonymy. In Laurie Bauer & Salvador Valera (eds.), *Approaches to Conversion/Zero-Derivation*, 131–159. Münster: Waxmann.

Schulte, Marion. 2015. *The Semantics of Derivational Morphology. A Synchronic and Diachronic Investigation of the suffixes -age and -ery in English*. Narr.

Segel, Esben. 2008. Re-evaluating zero: When nothing makes sense. *SKASE Journal of Theoretical Linguistics* 5(2), 1–20. <http://www.skase.sk/Volumes/JTL12/pdf_doc/Segel.pdf>.

Ševčíková, Magda. 2021. Action nouns vs. nouns as bases for denominal verbs in Czech: A case study on directionality in derivation. *Word Structure* 3, 97–128. <https://doi.org/10.3366/word.2021.0181>.

Ševčíková, Magda & Hana Hledíková. 2022. Paradigms in English and Czech noun/verb conversion: A contrastive study of corresponding lexemes. In Alba E. Ruz, Cristina Fernández-Alcaina & Cristina Lara-Clares (eds.), *Paradigms in Word Formation: Theory and Applications*, 181–214. Amsterdam: John Benjamins. <https://doi.org/10.1075/slcs.225.08sev>.

Soares Rodrigues, Alexandra. 2009. Portuguese converted deverbal nouns: constraints on their bases. *Word Structure* 2(1), 69–107. <https://doi.org/10.3366/E1750124509000300>.

Štekauer, Pavol. 1996. *A Theory of Conversion in English*. Frankfurt am Main: Peter Lang.

Stockwell, Robert & Donka Minkova. 2001. *English Words: History and Structure*. Cambridge: Cambridge University Press. <https://doi.org/10.1017/CBO9780511791161>.

Strang, Barbara M. H. [1962] 1968. *Modern English Structure*. 2nd edn. London: Edward Arnold.

Strauss, Steven. 1982. On 'relatedness paradoxes' and related paradoxes. *Linguistic Inquiry* 13, 694–700. <https://www.jstor.org/stable/4178306>.

Sundby, Bertil. 1995. *English Word-Formation as Described by English Grammarians 1600–1800*. Oslo: Novus. <https://doi.org/10.1075/sl.21.2.19dal>.

Sweet, Henry. 1891–1898. *A New English Grammar. Logical and historical*. Oxford: Clarendon Press.

Szymanek, Bogdan. 1988. *Categories and Categorization in Morphology*. Lublin: Redakcja Wydawnictw Katolickiego Uniwersytetu Lubelskiego.

Tournier, Jean. [1985] 2007. *Introduction descriptive à la lexicogénétique de l'anglais contemporain*. 2nd edn. Paris/Geneva: Champion-Slatkine.

Tribout, Delphine. 2020. Nominalization, verbalization or both? Insights from the directionality of noun-verb conversion in French. *Zeitschrift für Wortbildung / Journal of Word Formation* 4, 187–207. <https://doi.org/10.3726/zwjw.2020.02.10>.

Trnka, Bohumil. 1954. *Rozbor Nynějsi Spisovné Angličtiny, II: Morfologie, Slovnich Druhů a Tvoření Slov*. Prague: SPN.

Trnka, Bohumil. 1969. Conversion in English. *Brno Studies in English* 8, 183–187.

Twardzisz, Piotr. 1997. *Zero Derivation in English: A Cognitive Grammar Approach*. Lublin: Uniwersytetu Marii Curie Skłodowskiej.

Umbreit, Birgit. 2010. Does *love* come from *to love* or *to love* from *love*? Why lexical motivation has to be regarded as bidirectional. In Alexander Onysko & Sasha Michel (eds.), *Cognitive Perspectives on Word Formation*, 301–333. Mouton de Gruyter. <https://doi.org/10.1515/9783110223606.301>.

Ungerer, Friedrich. 2003. The conceptual function of derivational word-formation in English. *Anglia* 120(4), 534–567. <https://doi.org/10.1515/ANGL.2002.534>.

Valera, Salvador 1999. Many questions and few answers: on conversion in English. *Revista Alicantina de Estudios Ingleses* 12: 181–198. <https://doi.org/10.14198/raei.1999.12.14>.

Valera, Salvador 2014. Conversion. In Rochelle Lieber & Pavol Štekauer (eds.), *The Oxford Handbook of Derivational Morphology* 154–168. Oxford: Oxford University Press. <https://doi.org/10.1093/oxfordhb/9780199641642.013.0010>.

Valera, Salvador. 2015. Conversion. In Peter O. Müller & Ingeborg Ohnheiser, Susan Olsen & Franz Rainer (eds.), *Word-Formation: An International Handbook of the Languages of Europe, Vol. 1*, 322–339. Berlin: De Gruyter Mouton. <https://doi.org/10.1515/9783110246254-019>.

Valera, Salvador 2017. Conversion and figurative extension of meaning. *SKASE Journal of Theoretical Linguistics* 14(2), 2–17. <http://www.skase.sk/Volumes/JTL35/pdf_doc/01.pdf>.

Valera, Salvador. 2020. Semantic patterns in noun-to-verb conversion in English. In Lívia Körtvélyessy & Pavol Štekauer (eds.), *Complex Words*, 311–334. Cambridge: Cambridge University Press. <https://doi.org/10.1017/9781108780643.017>.

Valera, Salvador. 2023. The semantics of noun-to-verb zero-derivation in English and Spanish. *Zeitschrift für Sprachwissenschaft* 42(1), 153–180. <https://doi.org/10.1515/zfs-2022-2016>.

Valera, Salvador & Alba E. Ruz. 2021. Conversion in English: Homonymy, polysemy and paronymy. *English Language and Linguistics* 25(1), 181–204. <https://doi.org/10.1017/S1360674319000546>.

Vogel, Petra M. 1996. *Wortarten und Wortartenweschel: Zu Konversion und verwandten Erscheinungen im Deutschen und in anderen Sprachen*. Berlin/New York: de Gruyter.

Whorf, Benjamin L. 1945. Grammatical categories. *Language* 21, 1–11. <https://doi.org/10.2307/410199>.

Zandvoort, Reinard W. [1957] 1975. *A Handbook of English Grammar.* 7th edn. London: Longman.

Appendix

A.3. OED raw frequencies as verb (V_FREQ) and noun (N_FREQ) for the pairs analysed, with representation of homonymy, and after exclusion of mistakes, unrelated concordances, and reclassification of concordances as their correct category.

An asterisk "*" following any of the pair's category information (N/V) in the column *Pair* indicates that no corresponding entry is found in the OED as the word class that precedes the asterisk but one is interpreted based on context analysis. The word-class category N/V is followed by a number when various entries are found in the OED, thus, the specific entries are so specified. To avoid repetition and miscalculations, an asterisk in columns *N_FREQ* or *V_FREQ* is used when the frequency values for a specific lexeme are already provided in the previous row in the table. INT/S (in grey) refers to uses of the terms as interjections, representing sounds and are excluded from the total frequencies for the nouns and verbs.

Sample pairs after concordance recategorization and OED sense classification in alphabetical order				**Sample pairs after concordance recategorization and OED sense classification in alphabetical order**			
Pair		N_FREQ	V_FREQ	Pair		N_FREQ	V_FREQ
1	*aggregate*$^{N/V}$	481	147	116	*nosh*$^{N/V}$	21	3
2	*anagram*$^{N/V}$	51	1	117	*pander*$^{N/V}$	4	106
3	*arse*$^{N/V}$	473	15	118	*parody*$^{N/V}$	302	83
4	*assart*$^{N/V}$	16	2	119	*paste*$^{N/V}$	439	152
5	*baffle*$^{N/V}$	43	130	120	*pauper*$^{N/V}$	191	1
6	*bale*$^{N3/V2}$	194	18	121	*paw*$^{N/V}$	344	83
7	*barrack*$^{N1/V1}$	78	2	122	*perfume*$^{N/V}$	633	33
8	*barter*$^{N/V}$	117	71	123	*picket*$^{N/V}$	421	93

(Continued)

(*Continued*)

Sample pairs after concordance recategorization and OED sense classification in alphabetical order				Sample pairs after concordance recategorization and OED sense classification in alphabetical order			
Pair		**N_FREQ**	**V_FREQ**	**Pair**		**N_FREQ**	**V_FREQ**
9	*bayonet*$^{\text{N/V}}$	145	11	124	*pillory*$^{\text{N/V}}$	10	53
10	*beep*$^{\text{N/V}}$	69	15	125	*pinion*$^{\text{N2/V}}$	21	27
–	*beep*$^{\text{INT/S}}$	71		126	*piss*$^{\text{N/V}}$	238	550
11	*belch*$^{\text{N/V}}$	27	142	127	*piston*$^{\text{N/V}}$	236	6
12	*blab*$^{\text{N/V}}$	2	11	128	*plague*$^{\text{N/V}}$	516	347
13	*blank*$^{\text{N/V}}$	350	102	129	*plume*$^{\text{N/V}}$	292	12
14	*blather*$^{\text{N/V}}$	6	9	130	*ponce*$^{\text{N/V}}$	23	8
15	*blazon*$^{\text{N/V}}$	12	21	131	*prick*$^{\text{N/V}}$	164	273
16	*blind*$^{\text{N/V}}$	630	369	132	*prostitute*$^{\text{N/V}}$	693	25
17	*blossom*$^{\text{N/V}}$	333	271	133	*puff*$^{\text{N/V}}$	296	279
18	*bluster*$^{\text{N/V}}$	35	47	–	*puff*$^{\text{INT/S}}$	17	
19	*bombard*$^{\text{N/V}}$	7	260	134	*punt*$^{\text{N1/V2}}$	96	22
20	*bonk*$^{\text{N/V}}$	11	27	135	*punt*$^{\text{N4/V3}}$	11	3
–	*bonk*$^{\text{INT/S}}$	7		136	*punt*$^{\text{N5/V1}}$	18	8
21	*boomerang*$^{\text{N/V}}$	21	6	137	*purl*$^{\text{N1/V2}}$	26	11
22	*botch*$^{\text{N2/V1}}$	14	35	138	*puzzle*$^{\text{N/V}}$	704	321
23	*bray*$^{\text{N1/V1}}$	12	46	139	*quack*$^{\text{N2/V2}}$	69	2
24	*bribe*$^{\text{N/V}}$	325	256	140	*quack*$^{\text{N3/V1}}$	35	33
25	*brig*$^{\text{N1/V*}}$	32	2	–	*quack*^{INT}	10	
26	*bristle*$^{\text{N/V}}$	151	185	141	*rebuke*$^{\text{N/V}}$	136	205
27	*brood*$^{\text{N/V}}$	249	188	142	*reel*$^{\text{N1/V2}}$	262	110
28	*burlesque*$^{\text{N/V}}$	28	4	143	*reel*$^{\text{N2/V1}}$	6	265
29	*cartoon*$^{\text{N/V}}$	742	2	144	*reel*$^{\text{N3/V3}}$	30	3
30	*chalk*$^{\text{N/V}}$	826	108	145	*retail*$^{\text{N/V}}$	34	220
31	*chaperon(e)*$^{\text{N/V}}$	63	30	146	*reverence*$^{\text{N/V}}$	245	14
32	*cheep*$^{\text{N/V}}$	19	7	147	*rot*$^{\text{N/V}}$	327	378
33	*chirp*$^{\text{N/V}}$	19	43	148	*rummage*$^{\text{N/V}}$	34	215
34	*chirrup*$^{\text{N/V}}$	9	20	149	*rustle*$^{\text{N/V}}$	117	195
35	*clamp*$^{\text{N1/V1}}$	176	394	150	*saddle*$^{\text{N/V}}$	699	235
36	*clamp*$^{\text{N3/V2}}$	26	6	151	*scaffold*$^{\text{N/V}}$	72	1
37	*click*$^{\text{N1/V1}}$	328	714	152	*scar*$^{\text{N2/V}}$	594	145
–	*click*^{INT}	61		153	*scoff*$^{\text{N1/V1}}$	3	149
38	*cloister*$^{\text{N/V}}$	173	6	154	*scoff*$^{\text{N2/V2}}$	1	37
39	*clot*$^{\text{N/V}}$	127	37	155	*scowl*$^{\text{N/V}}$	113	293
40	*coppice*$^{\text{N/V}}$	56	8	156	*scum*$^{\text{N/V}}$	550	2
41	*cork*$^{\text{N/V}}$	322	10	157	*scythe*$^{\text{N/V}}$	94	53
42	*crampon*$^{\text{N/V}}$	97	2	158	*serenade*$^{\text{N/V}}$	94	24

Pair		N_FREQ	V_FREQ
	Sample pairs after concordance recategorization and OED sense classification in alphabetical order		
43	*crank*$^{N1/V1}$	51	70
44	*crank*$^{N2/V1}$	78	*
45	*crest*$^{N/V}$	592	21
46	*crimson*$^{N/V}$	65	5
47	*crochet*$^{N/V}$	60	22
48	*curtsy*$^{N/V}$	41	26
49	*dapple*$^{N/V}$	3	23
50	*dial*$^{N/V}$	269	510
51	*doom*$^{N/V}$	290	326
52	*doze*$^{N/V}$	36	260
53	*dragoon*$^{N/V}$	182	24
54	*dupe*$^{N1/V1}$	69	96
55	*dupe*$^{N2/V2}$	5	1
56	*dwarf*$^{N/V}$	632	163
57	*dybbuk*$^{N/V}$	46	3
58	*dye*$^{N/V}$	520	183
59	*excerpt*$^{N/V}$	151	10
60	*fathom*$^{N/V}$	94	137
61	*fatigue*$^{N/V}$	530	4
62	*fission*$^{N/V}$	91	1
63	*flea*$^{N/V}$	312	3
64	*floss*$^{N/V}$	50	6
65	*flounce*$^{N1/V1}$	3	57
66	*flounce*$^{N2/V2}$	21	1
67	*flounder*$^{N2/V}$	2	189
68	*fluff*$^{N1/V1}$	94	55
69	*frisbee*$^{N/V*}$	25	1
70	*frizz*$^{N/V}$	16	8
71	*furl*$^{N/V}$	1	8
72	*fuss*$^{N/V}$	782	234
73	*garrison*$^{N/V}$	600	23
74	*glissade*$^{N/V}$	7	3
75	*gorge*$^{N/V}$	384	74
76	*graft*$^{N1/V1}$	122	147
77	*graft*$^{N3/V2}$	11	1
78	*graft*$^{N4/V3\ (<TRANSF.\ V2)}$	52	9
79	*graft*$^{N5/V4}$	25	5
80	*grub*$^{N/V}$	193	53
81	*hank*$^{N/V}$	31	1
	Sample pairs after concordance recategorization and OED sense classification in alphabetical order		
159	*shark*$^{N/V}$	512	2
160	*shudder*$^{N/V}$	215	654
161	*shush*$^{N/V}$	2	19
162	*sire*$^{N/V}$	125	71
163	*skid*$^{N/V}$	119	200
164	*skive*$^{N/V}$	2	38
165	*skulk*$^{N/V}$	1	68
166	*slack*$^{N3/V}$	92	22
167	*slaver*$^{N1/V}$	2	27
168	*sledge*$^{N1/V1}$	18	1
169	*sledge*$^{N2/V2}$	179	11
170	*sleet*$^{N/V}$	72	7
171	*slit*$^{N/V}$	372	110
172	*slob*$^{N/V}$	62	4
173	*sloosh*$^{N/V}$	1	2
174	*sludge*$^{N/V}$	216	5
175	*slurp*$^{N/V}$	22	48
–	*slurp*$^{INT/S}$	6	
176	*smirk*$^{N/V}$	82	127
177	*snarl*$^{N1/V1}$	12	17
178	*snarl*$^{N2/V2}$	90	352
179	*snuff*$^{N1/V1}$	15	102
180	*snuff*$^{N2/V2}$	2	12
181	*snuff*$^{N3/V2}$	93	*
182	*soak*$^{N/V}$	59	765
183	*spasm*$^{N/V}$	275	14
184	*spire*$^{N3/V3}$	8	1
185	*sprain*$^{N/V}$	49	31
186	*squawk*$^{N/V}$	38	95
187	*stammer*$^{N/V}$	49	167
188	*stew*$^{N2/V2}$	324	68
189	*stilt*$^{N/V}$	91	9
190	*swerve*$^{N/V}$	21	225
191	*swipe*$^{N/V}$	80	56
192	*swoon*$^{N/V}$	18	55
193	*swot*$^{N/V}$	34	17
194	*tack*$^{N1/V1}$	305	245
195	*tack*$^{N7/V5}$	84	9
196	*tar*$^{N/V}$	216	57

(Continued)

(*Continued*)

Sample pairs after concordance recategorization and OED sense classification in alphabetical order			Sample pairs after concordance recategorization and OED sense classification in alphabetical order		
Pair	**N_FREQ**	**V_FREQ**	**Pair**	**N_FREQ**	**V_FREQ**
82 *helm*$^{N2/V2}$	179	8	197 *tattle*$^{N/V}$	9	3
83 *hex*$^{N1/V}$	12	1	198 *thud*$^{N/V}$	191	152
84 *hoax*$^{N/V}$	164	5	199 *thwack*$^{N/V}$	9	4
85 *holler*$^{N/V}$	10	54	– *thwack*$^{INT/S}$	3	
86 *hoover*$^{N/V}$	146	83	200 *torment*$^{N/V}$	274	235
87 *huddle*$^{N/V}$	72	222	201 *torture*$^{N/V}$	799	490
88 *hug*$^{N/V}$	243	752	202 *trammel*$^{N/V}$	3	7
89 *hymn*$^{N/V}$	677	8	203 *transect*$^{N/V}$	7	5
90 *jab*$^{N/V}$	127	217	204 *trash*$^{N/V}$	195	35
91 *jangle*$^{N/V}$	31	97	205 *trump*$^{N2/V3}$	142	39
92 *jaunt*$^{N/V}$	96	1	206 *trumpet*$^{N/V}$	473	89
93 *jog*$^{N1/V}$	80	381	207 *tumble*$^{N/V}$	190	798
94 *jolt*$^{N/V}$	163	170	208 *tup*$^{N/V}$	10	2
95 *jot*$^{N/V}$	69	150	209 *twit*$^{N1/V}$	66	5
96 *joust*$^{N/V}$	21	16	210 *umpire*$^{N/V}$	471	20
97 *jumble*$^{N1/V}$	399	36	211 *varnish*$^{N/V}$	358	75
98 *keek*$^{N/V}$	1	4	212 *vow*$^{N/V1}$	326	525
99 *kerf*$^{N/V}$	3	2	213 *vow*$^{N/V2}$	*	98
100 *knob*$^{N/V}$	400	5	214 *wanton*$^{N/V2}$	7	1
101 *lapse*$^{N/V}$	331	396	215 *wax*$^{N1/V2}$	631	38
102 *latch*$^{N1/V1}$	200	141	216 *wax*$^{N2/V1}$	7	91
103 *latch*$^{N1/V3}$	*	18	217 *wax*$^{N3/V1}$	4	*
104 *leer*$^{N/V}$	53	112	218 *welsh*$^{N/V}$	107	3
105 *lesion*$^{N/V}$	790	2	219 *whap*$^{N/V}$	1	1
106 *levy*$^{N1/V}$	675	604	220 *whimper*$^{N/V}$	72	165
107 *libel*$^{N/V}$	816	30	221 *whomp*$^{N/V}$	1	1
108 *lisp*$^{N/V}$	53	19	222 *whoop*$^{N/V}$	31	90
109 *louse*$^{N/V}$	205	7	– *whoop*$^{INT/S}$	12	
110 *mace*$^{N5/V3}$	5	2	223 *witch*$^{N/V}$	776	4
111 *manacle*$^{N/V}$	24	9	224 *wrangle*$^{N/V}$	108	19
112 *mash*$^{N1/V1}$	122	95	225 *wuff*$^{N/V}$	1	2
113 *mash*$^{N2/V1}$	*	1	– *wuff*$^{INT/S}$	3	
114 *massacre*$^{N/V}$	682	134	226 *yawn*$^{N/V}$	134	387
115 *nibble*$^{N/V}$	53	245			
Total number of concordances (excluding INT/S uses, in grey)					
Nouns		38,906	**Total (N+V)**	**61,652**	
Verbs		22,746			

Index

Linguistic Insights

Studies in Language and Communication

This series aims to promote specialist language studies in the fields of linguistic theory and applied linguistics, by publishing volumes that focus on specific aspects of language use in one or several languages and provide valuable insights into language and communication research. A cross-disciplinary approach is favoured and most European languages are accepted.

The series includes two types of books:

- Monographs – featuring in-depth studies on special aspects of language theory, language analysis or language teaching.
- Collected papers – assembling papers from workshops, conferences or symposia.

Each volume of the series is subjected to a double peer-reviewing process.

Vol. 1 Maurizio Gotti & Marina Dossena (eds)
Modality in Specialized Texts. Selected Papers of the 1st CERLIS Conference.
421 pages. 2001. ISBN 3-906767-10-8 · US-ISBN 0-8204-5340-4

Vol. 2 Giuseppina Cortese & Philip Riley (eds)
Domain-specific English. Textual Practices across Communities and Classrooms.
420 pages. 2002. ISBN 3-906768-98-8 · US-ISBN 0-8204-5884-8

Vol. 3 Maurizio Gotti, Dorothee Heller & Marina Dossena (eds)
Conflict and Negotiation in Specialized Texts. Selected Papers of the 2nd CERLIS Conference.
470 pages. 2002. ISBN 3-906769-12-7 · US-ISBN 0-8204-5887-2

Vol. 4 Maurizio Gotti, Marina Dossena, Richard Dury, Roberta Facchinetti & Maria Lima
Variation in Central Modals. A Repertoire of Forms and Types of Usage in Middle English and Early Modern English.
364 pages. 2002. ISBN 3-906769-84-4 · US-ISBN 0-8204-5898-8

Editorial address:
Prof. Maurizio Gotti Università di Bergamo, Dipartimento di Lingue, Letterature e Culture Straniere Piazza Rosate 2, 24129 Bergamo, Italy. Fax: + 39 035 2052789,
E-Mail: m.gotti@unibg.it

Vol. 5 Stefania Nuccorini (ed.)
Phrases and Phraseology. Data and Descriptions.
187 pages. 2002. ISBN 3-906770-08-7 · US-ISBN 0-8204-5933-X

Vol. 6 Vijay Bhatia, Christopher N. Candlin & Maurizio Gotti (eds)
Legal Discourse in Multilingual and Multicultural Contexts. Arbitration Texts in Europe.
385 pages. 2003. ISBN 3-906770-85-0 · US-ISBN 0-8204-6254-3

Vol. 7 Marina Dossena & Charles Jones (eds)
Insights into Late Modern English.
2nd edition. 378 pages. 2003, 2007. ISBN 978-3-03911-257-9 · US-ISBN 978-0-8204-8927-8

Vol. 8 Maurizio Gotti
Specialized Discourse. Linguistic Features and Changing Conventions.
351 pages. 2003, 2005.ISBN 3-03910-606-6 · US-ISBN 0-8204-7000-7

Vol. 9 Alan Partington, John Morley & Louann Haarman (eds)
Corpora and Discourse.
420 pages. 2004. ISBN 3-03910-026-2 · US-ISBN 0-8204-6262-4

Vol. 10 Martina Möllering
The Acquisition of German Modal Particles. A Corpus-Based Approach.
290 pages. 2004. ISBN 3-03910-043-2 · US-ISBN 0-8204-6273-X

Vol. 11 David Hart (ed.)
English Modality in Context. Diachronic Perspectives.
261 pages. 2003. ISBN 3-03910-046-7 · US-ISBN 0-8204-6852-5

Vol. 12 Wendy Swanson
Modes of Co-reference as an Indicator of Genre.
430 pages. 2003. ISBN 3-03910-052-1 · US-ISBN 0-8204-6855-X

Vol. 13 Gina Poncini
Discursive Strategies in Multicultural Business Meetings.
2nd edition. 338 pages. 2004, 2007. ISBN 978-3-03911-296-8 · US-ISBN 978-0-8204-8937-7

Vol. 14 Christopher N. Candlin & Maurizio Gotti (eds)
Intercultural Aspects of Specialized Communication.
2nd edition. 369 pages. 2004, 2007. ISBN 978-3-03911-258-6 · US-ISBN 978-0-8204-8926-1

Vol. 15 Gabriella Del Lungo Camiciotti & Elena Tognini Bonelli (eds)
Academic Discourse. New Insights into Evaluation.
234 pages. 2004. ISBN 3-03910-353-9 · US-ISBN 0-8204-7016-3

Vol. 16 Marina Dossena & Roger Lass (eds)
Methods and Data in English Historical Dialectology.
405 pages. 2004. ISBN 3-03910-362-8 · US-ISBN 0-8204-7018-X

Vol. 17 Judy Noguchi
The Science Review Article. An Opportune Genre in the Construction of Science.
274 pages. 2006. ISBN 3-03910-426-8 · US-ISBN 0-8204-7034-1

Vol. 18 Giuseppina Cortese & Anna Duszak (eds)
Identity, Community, Discourse. English in Intercultural Settings.
495 pages. 2005. ISBN 3-03910-632-5 · US-ISBN 0-8204-7163-1

Vol. 19 Anna Trosborg & Poul Erik Flyvholm Jørgensen (eds)
Business Discourse. Texts and Contexts.
250 pages. 2005. ISBN 3-03910-606-6 · US-ISBN 0-8204-7000-7

Vol. 20 Christopher Williams
Tradition and Change in Legal English. Verbal Constructions in Prescriptive Texts.
2nd revised edition. 216 pages. 2005, 2007. ISBN 978-3-03911-444-3.

Vol. 21 Katarzyna Dziubalska-Kolaczyk & Joanna Przedlacka (eds)
English Pronunciation Models: A Changing Scene.
2nd edition. 476 pages. 2005, 2008. ISBN 978-3-03911-682-9.

Vol. 22 Christián Abello-Contesse, Rubén Chacón-Beltrán, M. Dolores López-J iménez & M. Mar Torreblanca-López (eds)
Age in L2 Acquisition and Teaching.
214 pages. 2006. ISBN 3-03910-668-6 · US-ISBN 0-8204-7174-7

Vol. 23 Vijay K. Bhatia, Maurizio Gotti, Jan Engberg & Dorothee Heller (eds)
Vagueness in Normative Texts.
474 pages. 2005. ISBN 3-03910-653-8 · US-ISBN 0-8204-7169-0

Vol. 24 Paul Gillaerts & Maurizio Gotti (eds)
Genre Variation in Business Letters.
2nd printing. 407 pages. 2008. ISBN 978-3-03911-681-2.

Vol. 25 Ana María Hornero, María José Luzón & Silvia Murillo (eds)
Corpus Linguistics. Applications for the Study of English.
2nd printing. 526 pages. 2006, 2008. ISBN 978-3-03911-726-0

Vol. 26 J. Lachlan Mackenzie & María de los Ángeles Gómez-González (eds)
Studies in Functional Discourse Grammar.
259 pages. 2005. ISBN 3-03910-696-1 · US-ISBN 0-8204-7558-0

Vol. 27 Debbie G. E. Ho
Classroom Talk. Exploring the Sociocultural Structure of Formal ESL Learning.
2nd edition. 254 pages. 2006, 2007. ISBN 978-3-03911-434-4

Vol. 28 Javier Pérez-Guerra, Dolores González-Álvarez, Jorge L. Bueno-Alonso & Esperanza Rama-Martínez (eds)
'Of Varying Language and Opposing Creed'. New Insights into Late Modern English.
455 pages. 2007. ISBN 978-3-03910-788-9

Vol. 29 Francesca Bargiela-Chiappini & Maurizio Gotti (eds)
Asian Business Discourse(s).
350 pages. 2005. ISBN 3-03910-804-2 · US-ISBN 0-8204-7574-2

Vol. 30 Nicholas Brownlees (ed.)
News Discourse in Early Modern Britain. Selected Papers of CHINED 2004.
300 pages. 2006. ISBN 3-03910-805-0 · US-ISBN 0-8204-8025-8

Vol. 31 Roberta Facchinetti & Matti Rissanen (eds)
Corpus-based Studies of Diachronic English.
300 pages. 2006. ISBN 3-03910-851-4 · US-ISBN 0-8204-8040-1

Vol. 32 Marina Dossena & Susan M. Fitzmaurice (eds)
Business and Official Correspondence. Historical Investigations.
209 pages. 2006. ISBN 3-03910-880-8 · US-ISBN 0-8204-8352-4

Vol. 33 Giuliana Garzone & Srikant Sarangi (eds)
Discourse, Ideology and Specialized Communication.
494 pages. 2007. ISBN 978-3-03910-888-6

Vol. 34 Giuliana Garzone & Cornelia Ilie (eds)
The Use of English in Institutional and Business Settings. An Intercultural Perspective.
372 pages. 2007. ISBN 978-3-03910-889-3

Vol. 35 Vijay K. Bhatia & Maurizio Gotti (eds)
Explorations in Specialized Genres.
316 pages. 2006. ISBN 3-03910-995-2 · US-ISBN 0-8204-8372-9

Vol. 36 Heribert Picht (ed.)
Modern Approaches to Terminological Theories and Applications.
432 pages. 2006. ISBN 3-03911-156-6 · US-ISBN 0-8204-8380-X

Vol. 37 Anne Wagner & Sophie Cacciaguidi-Fahy (eds)
Legal Language and the Search for Clarity / Le langage juridique et la quête de clarté. Practice and Tools / Pratiques et instruments.
487 pages. 2006. ISBN 3-03911-169-8 · US-ISBN 0-8204-8388-5

Vol. 38 Juan Carlos Palmer-S ilveira, Miguel F. Ruiz-Garrido & Inmaculada Fortanet-Gómez (eds)
Intercultural and International Business Communication. Theory, Research and Teaching.
2nd edition. 343 pages. 2006, 2008. ISBN 978-3-03911-680-5

Vol. 39 Christiane Dalton-Puffer, Dieter Kastovsky, Nikolaus Ritt & Herbert Schendl (eds)
Syntax, Style and Grammatical Norms. English from 1500– 2000.
250 pages. 2006. ISBN 3-03911-181-7 · US-ISBN 0-8204-8394-X

Vol. 40 Marina Dossena & Irma Taavitsainen (eds)
Diachronic Perspectives on Domain-Specific English.
280 pages. 2006. ISBN 3-03910-176-0 · US-ISBN 0-8204-8391-5

Vol. 41 John Flowerdew & Maurizio Gotti (eds)
Studies in Specialized Discourse.
293 pages. 2006. ISBN 3-03911-178-7

Vol. 42 Ken Hyland & Marina Bondi (eds)
Academic Discourse Across Disciplines.
320 pages. 2006. ISBN 3-03911-183-3 · US-ISBN 0-8204-8396-6

Vol. 43 Paul Gillaerts & Philip Shaw (eds)
The Map and the Landscape. Norms and Practices in Genre.
256 pages. 2006. ISBN 3-03911-182-5 · US-ISBN 0-8204-8395-4

Vol. 44 Maurizio Gotti & Davide Giannoni (eds)
New Trends in Specialized Discourse Analysis.
301 pages. 2006. ISBN 3-03911-184-1 · US-ISBN 0-8204-8381-8

Vol. 45 Maurizio Gotti & Françoise Salager-Meyer (eds)
Advances in Medical Discourse Analysis. Oral and Written Contexts.
492 pages. 2006. ISBN 3-03911-185-X · US-ISBN 0-8204-8382-6

Vol. 46 Maurizio Gotti & Susan Šarcevic´ (eds)
Insights into Specialized Translation.
396 pages. 2006. ISBN 3-03911-186-8 · US-ISBN 0-8204-8383-4

Vol. 47 Khurshid Ahmad & Margaret Rogers (eds)
Evidence-based LSP. Translation, Text and Terminology.
584 pages. 2007. ISBN 978-3-03911-187-9

Vol. 48 Hao Sun & Dániel Z. Kádár (eds)
It's the Dragon's Turn. Chinese Institutional Discourses.
262 pages. 2008. ISBN 978-3-03911-175-6

Vol. 49 Cristina Suárez-Gómez
Relativization in Early English (950-1250). the Position of Relative Clauses.
149 pages. 2006. ISBN 3-03911-203-1 · US-ISBN 0-8204-8904-2

Vol. 50 Maria Vittoria Calvi & Luisa Chierichetti (eds)
Nuevas tendencias en el discurso de especialidad.
319 pages. 2006. ISBN 978-3-03911-261-6

Vol. 51 Mari Carmen Campoy & María José Luzón (eds)
Spoken Corpora in Applied Linguistics.
274 pages. 2008. ISBN 978-3-03911-275-3

Vol. 52 Konrad Ehlich & Dorothee Heller (Hrsg.)
Die Wissenschaft und ihre Sprachen.
323 pages. 2006. ISBN 978-3-03911-272-2

Vol. 53 Jingyu Zhang
The Semantic Salience Hierarchy Model. The L2 Acquisition of Psych Predicates
273 pages. 2007. ISBN 978-3-03911-300-2

Vol. 54 Norman Fairclough, Giuseppina Cortese & Patrizia Ardizzone (eds)
Discourse and Contemporary Social Change.
555 pages. 2007. ISBN 978-3-03911-276-0

Vol. 55 Jan Engberg, Marianne Grove Ditlevsen, Peter Kastberg & Martin Stegu (eds)
New Directions in LSP Teaching.
331 pages. 2007. ISBN 978-3-03911-433-7

Vol. 56 Dorothee Heller & Konrad Ehlich (Hrsg.)
Studien zur Rechtskommunikation.
322 pages. 2007. ISBN 978-3-03911-436-8

Vol. 57 Teruhiro Ishiguro & Kang-kwong Luke (eds)
Grammar in Cross-Linguistic Perspective. The Syntax, Semantics, and Pragmatics of Japanese and Chinese.
304 pages. 2012. ISBN 978-3-03911-445-0

Vol. 58 Carmen Frehner
Email – SMS – MMS
294 pages. 2008. ISBN 978-3-03911-451-1

Vol. 59 Isabel Balteiro
The Directionality of Conversion in English. A Dia-Synchronic Study.
276 pages. 2007. ISBN 978-3-03911-241-8

Vol. 60 Maria Milagros Del Saz Rubio
English Discourse Markers of Reformulation.
237 pages. 2007. ISBN 978-3-03911-196-1

Vol. 61 Sally Burgess & Pedro Martín-Martín (eds)
English as an Additional Language in Research Publication and Communication.
259 pages. 2008. ISBN 978-3-03911-462-7

Vol. 62 Sandrine Onillon
Pratiques et représentations de l'écrit.
458 pages. 2008. ISBN 978-3-03911-464-1

Vol. 63 Hugo Bowles & Paul Seedhouse (eds)
Conversation Analysis and Language for Specific Purposes.
2nd edition. 337 pages. 2007, 2009. ISBN 978-3-0343-0045-2

Vol. 64 Vijay K. Bhatia, Christopher N. Candlin & Paola Evangelisti Allori (eds)
Language, Culture and the Law. The Formulation of Legal Concepts across Systems and Cultures.
342 pages. 2008. ISBN 978-3-03911-470-2

Vol. 65 Jonathan Culpeper & Dániel Z. Kádár (eds)
Historical (Im)politeness.
300 pages. 2010. ISBN 978-3-03911-496-2

Vol. 66 Linda Lombardo (ed.)
Using Corpora to Learn about Language and Discourse.
237 pages. 2009. ISBN 978-3-03911-522-8

Vol. 67 Natsumi Wakamoto
Extroversion/ Introversion in Foreign Language Learning. Interactions with Learner Strategy Use.
159 pages. 2009. ISBN 978-3-03911-596-9

Vol. 68 Eva Alcón-Soler (ed.)
Learning How to Request in an Instructed Language Learning Context.
260 pages. 2008. ISBN 978-3-03911-601-0

Vol. 69 Domenico Pezzini
The Translation of Religious Texts in the Middle Ages.
428 pages. 2008. ISBN 978-3-03911-600-3

Vol. 70 Tomoko Tode
Effects of Frequency in Classroom Second Language Learning. Quasi-experiment and stimulated-recall analysis.
195 pages. 2008. ISBN 978-3-03911-602-7

Vol. 71 Egor Tsedryk
Fusion symétrique et alternances ditransitives.
211 pages. 2009. ISBN 978-3-03911-609-6

Vol. 72 Cynthia J. Kellett Bidoli & Elana Ochse (eds)
English in International Deaf Communication.
444 pages. 2008. ISBN 978-3-03911-610-2

Vol. 73 Joan C. Beal, Carmela Nocera & Massimo Sturiale (eds)
Perspectives on Prescriptivism.
269 pages. 2008. ISBN 978-3-03911-632-4

Vol. 74 Carol Taylor Torsello, Katherine Ackerley & Erik Castello (eds)
Corpora for University Language Teachers.
308 pages. 2008. ISBN 978-3-03911-639-3

Vol. 75 María Luisa Pérez Cañado (ed.)
English Language Teaching in the European Credit Transfer System. Facing the Challenge.
251 pages. 2009. ISBN 978-3-03911-654-6

Vol. 76 Marina Dossena & Ingrid Tieken-Boon van Ostade (eds)
Studies in Late Modern English Correspondence. Methodology and Data.
291 pages. 2008. ISBN 978-3-03911-658-4

Vol. 77 Ingrid Tieken-Boon van Ostade & Wim van der Wurff (eds)
Current Issues in Late Modern English.
436 pages. 2009. ISBN 978-3-03911-660-7

Vol. 78 Marta Navarro Coy (ed.)
Practical Approaches to Foreign Language Teaching and Learning.
297 pages. 2009. ISBN 978-3-03911-661-4

Vol. 79 Qing Ma
Second Language Vocabulary Acquisition.
333 pages. 2009. ISBN 978-3-03911-666-9

Vol. 80 Martin Solly, Michelangelo Conoscenti & Sandra Campagna (eds)
Verbal/ Visual Narrative Texts in Higher Education.
384 pages. 2008. ISBN 978-3-03911-672-0

Vol. 81 Meiko Matsumoto
From Simple Verbs to Periphrastic Expressions: The Historical Development of Composite Predicates, Phrasal Verbs, and Related Constructions in English.
235 pages. 2008. ISBN 978-3-03911-675-1

Vol. 82 Melinda Dooly
Doing Diversity. Teachers' Construction of Their Classroom Reality.
180 pages. 2009. ISBN 978-3-03911-687-4

Vol. 83 Victoria Guillén-Nieto, Carmen Marimón-Llorca & Chelo Vargas-Sierra (eds)
Intercultural Business Communication and Simulation and Gaming Methodology.
392 pages. 2009. ISBN 978-3-03911-688-1

Vol. 84 Maria Grazia Guido
English as a Lingua Franca in Cross-cultural Immigration Domains.
285 pages. 2008. ISBN 978-3-03911-689-8

Vol. 85 Erik Castello
Text Complexity and Reading Comprehension Tests.
352 pages. 2008. ISBN 978-3-03911-717-8

Vol. 86 Maria-Lluisa Gea-Valor, Isabel García-Izquierdo & Maria-José Esteve (eds)
Linguistic and Translation Studies in Scientific Communication.
317 pages. 2010. ISBN 978-3-0343-0069-8

Vol. 87 Carmen Navarro, Rosa Ma Rodríguez Abella, Francesca Dalle Pezze & Renzo Miotti (eds)
La comunicación especializada.
355 pages. 2008. ISBN 978-3-03911-733-8

Vol. 88 Kiriko Sato
The Development from Case-Forms to Prepositional Constructions in Old English Prose.
231 pages. 2009. ISBN 978-3-03911-763-5

Vol. 89 Dorothee Heller (Hrsg.)
Formulierungsmuster in deutscher und italienischer Fachkommunikation. Intra-und interlinguale Perspektiven.
315 pages. 2008. ISBN 978-3-03911-778-9

Vol. 90 Henning Bergenholtz, Sandro Nielsen & Sven Tarp (eds)
Lexicography at a Crossroads. Dictionaries and Encyclopedias Today, Lexicographical Tools Tomorrow.
372 pages. 2009. ISBN 978-3-03911-799-4

Vol. 91 Manouchehr Moshtagh Khorasani
The Development of Controversies. From the Early Modern Period to Online Discussion Forums.
317 pages. 2009. ISBN 978-3-3911-711-6

Vol. 92 María Luisa Carrió-Pastor (ed.)
Content and Language Integrated Learning. Cultural Diversity.
178 pages. 2009. ISBN 978-3-3911-818-2

Vol. 93 Roger Berry
Terminology in English Language Teaching. Nature and Use.
262 pages. 2010. ISBN 978-3-0343-0013-1

Vol. 94 Roberto Cagliero & Jennifer Jenkins (eds)
Discourses, Communities, and Global Englishes
240 pages. 2010. ISBN 978-3-0343-0012-4

Vol. 95 Facchinetti Roberta, Crystal David, Seidlhofer Barbara (eds)
From International to Local English – And Back Again.
268 pages. 2010. ISBN 978-3-0343-0011-7

Vol. 96 Cesare Gagliardi & Alan Maley (eds)
EIL, ELF, Global English. Teaching and Learning Issues
376 pages. 2010. ISBN 978-3-0343-0010-0

Vol. 97 Sylvie Hancil (ed.)
The Role of Prosody in Affective Speech.
403 pages. 2009. ISBN 978-3-03911-696-6

Vol. 98 Marina Dossena & Roger Lass (eds)
Studies in English and European Historical Dialectology.
257 pages. 2009. ISBN 978-3-0343-0024-7

Vol. 99 Christine Béal
Les interactions quotidiennes en français et en anglais. De l'approche comparative à l'analyse des situations interculturelles.
424 pages. 2010. ISBN 978-3-0343-0027-8

Vol. 100 Maurizio Gotti (ed.)
Commonality and Individuality in Academic Discourse.
398 pages. 2009. ISBN 978-3-0343-0023-0

Vol. 101 Javier E. Díaz Vera & Rosario Caballero (eds)
Textual Healing. Studies in Medieval English Medical, Scientific and Technical Texts.
213 pages. 2009. ISBN 978-3-03911-822-9

Vol. 102 Nuria Edo Marzá
The Specialised Lexicographical Approach. A Step further in Dictionary-making.
316 pages. 2009. ISBN 978-3-0343-0043-8

Vol. 103 Carlos Prado-Alonso, Lidia Gómez-García, Iria Pastor-Gómez & David Tizón-Couto (eds)
New Trends and Methodologies in Applied English Language Research. Diachronic, Diatopic and Contrastive Studies.
348 pages. 2009. ISBN 978-3-0343-0046-9

Vol. 104 Françoise Salager-Meyer & Beverly A. Lewin
Crossed Words. Criticism in Scholarly Writing?
371 pages. 2011. ISBN 978-3-0343-0049-0.

Vol. 105 Javier Ruano-García
Early Modern Northern English Lexis. A Literary Corpus-Based Study.
611 pages. 2010. ISBN 978-3-0343-0058-2

Vol. 106 Rafael Monroy-Casas
Systems for the Phonetic Transcription of English. Theory and Texts.
280 pages. 2011. ISBN 978-3-0343-0059-9

Vol. 107 Nicola T. Owtram
The Pragmatics of Academic Writing. A Relevance Approach to the Analysis of Research Article Introductions.
311 pages. 2009. ISBN 978-3-0343-0060-5

Vol. 108 Yolanda Ruiz de Zarobe, Juan Manuel Sierra & Francisco Gallardo del Puerto (eds)
Content and Foreign Language Integrated Learning. Contributions to Multilingualism in European Contexts.
343 pages. 2011. ISBN 978-3-0343-0074-2

Vol. 109 Ángeles Linde López & Rosalía Crespo Jiménez (eds)
Professional English in the European context. The EHEA challenge.
374 pages. 2010. ISBN 978-3-0343-0088-9

Vol. 110 Rosalía Rodríguez-Vázquez
The Rhythm of Speech, Verse and Vocal Music. A New Theory.
394 pages. 2010. ISBN 978-3-0343-0309-5

Vol. 111 Anastasios Tsangalidis & Roberta Facchinetti (eds)
Studies on English Modality. In Honour of Frank Palmer.
392 pages. 2009. ISBN 978-3-0343-0310-1

Vol. 112 Jing Huang
Autonomy, Agency and Identity in Foreign Language Learning and Teaching.
400 pages. 2013. ISBN 978-3-0343-0370-5

Vol. 113 Mihhail Lotman & Maria-Kristiina Lotman (eds)
Frontiers in Comparative Prosody. In memoriam: Mikhail Gasparov.
426 pages. 2011. ISBN 978-3-0343-0373-6

Vol. 114 Merja Kytö, John Scahill & Harumi Tanabe (eds)
Language Change and Variation from Old English to Late Modern English. A Festschrift for Minoji Akimoto.
422 pages. 2010. ISBN 978-3-0343-0372-9

Vol. 115 Giuliana Garzone & Paola Catenaccio (eds)
Identities across Media and Modes. Discursive Perspectives.
379 pages. 2009. ISBN 978-3-0343-0386-6

Vol. 116 Elena Landone
Los marcadores del discurso y cortesía verbal en español.
390 pages. 2010. ISBN 978-3-0343-0413-9

Vol. 117 Maurizio Gotti & Christopher Williams (eds)
Legal Discourse across Languages and Cultures.
339 pages. 2010. ISBN 978-3-0343-0425-2

Vol. 118 David Hirsh
Academic Vocabulary in Context.
217 pages. 2010. ISBN 978-3-0343-0426-9

Vol. 119 Yvonne Dröschel
Lingua Franca English. The Role of Simplification and Transfer.
358 pages. 2011. ISBN 978-3-0343-0432-0

Vol. 120 Tengku Sepora Tengku Mahadi, Helia Vaezian & Mahmoud Akbari
Corpora in Translation. A Practical Guide.
135 pages. 2010. ISBN 978-3-0343-0434-4

Vol. 121 Davide Simone Giannoni & Celina Frade (eds)
Researching Language and the Law. Textual Features and Translation Issues.
278 pages. 2010. ISBN 978-3-0343-0443-6

Vol. 122 Daniel Madrid & Stephen Hughes (eds)
Studies in Bilingual Education.
472 pages. 2011. ISBN 978-3-0343-0474-0

Vol. 123 Vijay K. Bhatia, Christopher N. Candlin & Maurizio Gotti (eds)
The Discourses of Dispute Resolution.
290 pages. 2010. ISBN 978-3-0343-0476-4

Vol. 124 Davide Simone Giannoni
Mapping Academic Values in the Disciplines. A Corpus-Based Approach.
288 pages. 2010. ISBN 978-3-0343-0488-7

Vol. 125 Giuliana Garzone & James Archibald (eds)
Discourse, Identities and Roles in Specialized Communication.
419 pages. 2010. ISBN 978-3-0343-0494-8

Vol. 126 Iria Pastor-Gómez
The Status and Development of N+ N Sequences in Contemporary English Noun Phrases.
216 pages. 2011. ISBN 978-3-0343-0534-1

Vol. 127 Carlos Prado-Alonso
Full-verb Inversion in Written and Spoken English.
261 pages. 2011. ISBN 978-3-0343-0535-8

Vol. 128 Tony Harris & María Moreno Jaén (eds)
Corpus Linguistics in Language Teaching.
214 pages. 2010. ISBN 978-3-0343-0524-2

Vol. 129 Tetsuji Oda & Hiroyuki Eto (eds)
Multiple Perspectives on English Philology and History of Linguistics. A Festschrift for Shoichi Watanabe on his 80th Birthday.
378 pages. 2010. ISBN 978-3-0343-0480-1

Vol. 130 Luisa Chierichetti & Giovanni Garofalo (eds)
Lengua y Derecho. líneas de investigación interdisciplinaria.
283 pages. 2010. 978-3-0343-0463-4

Vol. 131 Paola Evangelisti Allori & Giuliana Garzone (eds)
Discourse, Identities and Genres in Corporate Communication. Sponsorship, Advertising and Organizational Communication.
324 pages. 2011. 978-3-0343-0591-4

Vol. 132 Leyre Ruiz de Zarobe & Yolanda Ruiz de Zarobe (eds)
Speech Acts and Politeness across Languages and Cultures.
402 pages. 2012. 978-3-0343-0611-9

Vol. 133 Thomas Christiansen
Cohesion. A Discourse Perspective.
387 pages. 2011. 978-3-0343-0619-5

Vol. 134 Giuliana Garzone & Maurizio Gotti
Discourse, Communication and the Enterprise. Genres and Trends.
451 pages. 2011. ISBN 978-3-0343-0620-1

Vol. 135 Zsuzsa Hoffmann
Ways of the World's Words. Language Contact in the Age of Globalization.
334 pages 2011. ISBN 978-3-0343-0673-7

Vol. 136 Cecilia Varcasia (ed.)
Becoming Multilingual. Language Learning and Language Policy between Attitudes and Identities.
213 pages. 2011. ISBN 978-3-0343-0687-5

Vol. 137 Susy Macqueen
The Emergence of Patterns in Second Language Writing. A Sociocognitive Exploration of Lexical Trails.
325 pages. 2012. ISBN 978-3-0343-1010-9

Vol. 138 Maria Vittoria Calvi & Giovanna Mapelli (eds)
La lengua del turismo. Géneros discursivos y terminología.
365 pages. 2011. ISBN 978-3-0343-1011-6

Vol. 139 Ken Lau
Learning to Become a Professional in a Textually-Mediated World. A Text-Oriented Study of Placement Practices.
261 pages. 2012. ISBN 978-3-0343-1016-1

Vol. 140 Sandra Campagna, Giuliana Garzone, Cornelia Ilie & Elizabeth Rowley-Jolivet (eds)
Evolving Genres in Web-mediated Communication.
337 pages. 2012. ISBN 978-3-0343-1013-0

Vol. 141 Edith Esch & Martin Solly (eds)
The Sociolinguistics of Language Education in International Contexts.
263 pages. 2012. ISBN 978-3-0343-1009-3

Vol. 142 Forthcoming.

Vol. 143 David Tizón-Couto
Left Dislocation in English. A Functional-Discoursal Approach.
416 pages. 2012. ISBN 978-3-0343-1037-6

Vol. 144 Margrethe Petersen & Jan Engberg (eds)
Current Trends in LSP Research. Aims and Methods.
323 pages. 2011. ISBN 978-3-0343-1054-3

Vol. 145 David Tizón-Couto, Beatriz Tizón-Couto, Iria Pastor-Gómez & Paula Rodríguez-Puente (eds)
New Trends and Methodologies in Applied English Language Research II. Studies in Language Variation, Meaning and Learning.
283 pages. 2012. ISBN 978-3-0343-1061-1

Vol. 146 Rita Salvi & Hiromasa Tanaka (eds)
Intercultural Interactions in Business and Management.
306 pages. 2011. ISBN 978-3-0343-1039-0

Vol. 147 Francesco Straniero Sergio & Caterina Falbo (eds)
Breaking Ground in Corpus-based Interpreting Studies.
254 pages. 2012. ISBN 978-3-0343-1071-0

Vol. 148 Forthcoming.

Vol. 149 Vijay K. Bhatia & Paola Evangelisti Allori (eds)
Discourse and Identity in the Professions. Legal, Corporate and Institutional Citizenship.
352 pages. 2011. ISBN 978-3-0343-1079-6

Vol. 150 Maurizio Gotti (ed.)
Academic Identity Traits. A Corpus-Based Investigation.
363 pages. 2012. ISBN 978-3-0343-1141-0

Vol. 151 Priscilla Heynderickx, Sylvain Dieltjens, Geert Jacobs, Paul Gillaerts & Elizabeth de Groot (eds)
The Language Factor in International Business. New Perspectives on Research, Teaching and Practice.
320 pages. 2012. ISBN 978-3-0343-1090-1

Vol. 152 Paul Gillaerts, Elizabeth de Groot, Sylvain Dieltjens, Priscilla Heynderickx & Geert Jacobs (eds)
Researching Discourse in Business Genres. Cases and Corpora.
215 pages. 2012. ISBN 978-3-0343-1092-5

Vol. 153 Yongyan Zheng
Dynamic Vocabulary Development in a Foreign Language.
262 pages. 2012. ISBN 978-3-0343-1106-9

Vol. 154 Carmen Argondizzo (ed.)
Creativity and Innovation in Language Education.
357 pages. 2012. ISBN 978-3-0343-1080-2

Vol. 155 David Hirsh (ed.)
Current Perspectives in Second Language Vocabulary Research.
180 pages. 2012. ISBN 978-3-0343-1108-3

Vol. 156 Seiji Shinkawa
Unhistorical Gender Assignment in Lahamon's *Brut*. A Case Study of a Late Stage in the Development of Grammatical Gender toward its Ultimate Loss.
186 pages. 2012. ISBN 978-3-0343-1124-3

Vol. 157 Yeonkwon Jung
Basics of Organizational Writing: A Critical Reading Approach.
151 pages. 2014. ISBN 978-3-0343-1137-3.

Vol. 158 Bárbara Eizaga Rebollar (ed.)
Studies in Linguistics and Cognition.
301 pages. 2012. ISBN 978-3-0343-1138-0

Vol. 159 Giuliana Garzone, Paola Catenaccio, Chiara Degano (eds)
Genre Change in the Contemporary World. Short-term Diachronic Perspectives.
329 pages. 2012. ISBN 978-3-0343-1214-1

Vol. 160 Carol Berkenkotter, Vijay K. Bhatia & Maurizio Gotti (eds)
Insights into Academic Genres.
468 pages. 2012. ISBN 978-3-0343-1211-0

Vol. 161 Beatriz Tizón-Couto
Clausal Complements in Native and Learner Spoken English. A corpus-based study with Lindsei and Vicolse.
357 pages. 2013. ISBN 978-3-0343-1184-7

Vol. 162 Patrizia Anesa
Jury Trials and the Popularization of Legal Language. A Discourse Analytical Approach.
247 pages. 2012. ISBN 978-3-0343-1231-8

Vol. 163 David Hirsh
Endangered Languages, Knowledge Systems and Belief Systems.
153 pages. 2013. ISBN 978-3-0343-1232-5

Vol. 164 Eugenia Sainz (ed.)
De la estructura de la frase al tejido del discurso. Estudios contrastivos español/italiano.
305 pages. 2014. ISBN 978-3-0343-1253-0

Vol. 165 Julia Bamford, Franca Poppi & Davide Mazzi (eds)
Space, Place and the Discursive Construction of Identity.
367 pages. 2014. ISBN 978-3-0343-1249-3

Vol. 166 Rita Salvi & Janet Bowker (eds)
Space, Time and the Construction of Identity. Discursive Indexicality in Cultural, Institutional and Professional Fields.
324 pages. 2013. ISBN 978-3-0343-1254-7

Vol. 167 Shunji Yamazaki & Robert Sigley (eds)
Approaching Language Variation through Corpora. A Festschrift in Honour of Toshio Saito.
421 pages. 2013. ISBN 978-3-0343-1264-6

Vol. 168 Franca Poppi
Global Interactions in English as a Lingua Franca. How written communication is changing under the influence of electronic media and new contexts of use.
249 pages. 2012. ISBN 978-3-0343-1276-9

Vol. 169 Miguel A. Aijón Oliva & María José Serrano
Style in syntax. Investigating variation in Spanish pronoun subjects.
239 pages. 2013. ISBN 978-3-0343-1244-8

Vol. 170 Inés Olza, Óscar Loureda & Manuel Casado-Velarde (eds)
Language Use in the Public Sphere. Methodological Perspectives and Empirical Applications.
564 pages. 2014. ISBN 978-3-0343-1286-8

Vol. 171 Aleksandra Matulewska
Legilinguistic Translatology. A Parametric Approach to Legal Translation.
279 pages. 2013. ISBN 978-3-0343-1287-5

Vol. 172 Maurizio Gotti & Carmen Sancho Guinda (eds)
Narratives in Academic and Professional Genres.
513 pages. 2013. ISBN 978-3-0343-1371-1

Vol. 173 Madalina Chitez
Learner corpus profiles. The case of Romanian Learner English.
244 pages. 2014. ISBN 978-3-0343-1410-7

Vol. 174 Chihiro Inoue
Task Equivalence in Speaking Tests.
251 pages. 2013. ISBN 978-3-0343-1417-6

Vol. 175 Gabriel Quiroz & Pedro Patiño (eds.)
LSP in Colombia: advances and challenges.
339 pages. 2014. ISBN 978-3-0343-1434-3

Vol. 176 Catherine Resche
Economic Terms and Beyond: Capitalising on the Wealth of Notions. How Researchers in Specialised Varieties of English Can Benefit from Focusing on Terms.
332 pages. 2013. ISBN 978-3-0343-1435-0

Vol. 177 Wei Wang
Media representation of migrant workers in China. Identities and stances
198 pages. 2018. 978-3-0343-1436-7

Vol. 178 Cécile Desoutter & Caroline Mellet (dir.)
Le discours rapporté: approches linguistiques et perspectives didactiques.
270 pages. 2013. ISBN 978-3-0343-1292-9

Vol. 179 Ana Díaz-N egrillo & Francisco Javier Díaz-Pérez (eds)
Specialisation and Variation in Language Corpora.
341 pages. 2014. ISBN 978-3-0343-1316-2

Vol. 180 Pilar Alonso
A Multi-dimensional Approach to Discourse Coherence. From Standardness to Creativity.
247 pages. 2014. ISBN 978-3-0343-1325-4

Vol. 181 Alejandro Alcaraz-Sintes & Salvador Valera-Hernández (eds)
Diachrony and Synchrony in English Corpus Linguistics.
393 pages. 2014. ISBN 978-3-0343-1326-1

Vol. 182 Runhan Zhang
Investigating Linguistic Knowledge of a Second Language.
207 pages. 2015. ISBN 978-3-0343-1330-8

Vol. 183 Hajar Abdul Rahim & Shakila Abdul Manan (eds.)
English in Malaysia. Postcolonial and Beyond.
267 pages. 2014. ISBN 978-3-0343-1341-4

Vol. 184 Virginie Fasel Lauzon
Comprendre et apprendre dans l'interaction. Les séquences d'explication en classe de français langue seconde.
pages. 2014. ISBN 978-3-0343-1451-0

Vol. 185 Forthcoming.

Vol. 186 Wei Ren
L2 Pragmatic Development in Study Abroad Contexts
256 pages. 2015. ISBN 978-3-0343-1358-2

Vol. 187 Marina Bondi & Rosa Lorés Sanz (eds)
Abstracts in Academic Discourse. Variation and Change.
361 pages. 2014. ISBN 978-3-0343-1483-1

Vol. 188 Giuditta Caliendo
Rethinking Community. Discourse, Identity and Citizenship in the European Union.
240 pages. 2017. ISBN 978-3-0343-1561-6

Vol. 189 Paola Evangelisti Allori (ed.)
Identities in and across Cultures.
315 pages. 2014. ISBN 978-3-0343-1458-9

Vol. 190 Erik Castello, Katherine Ackerley & Francesca Coccetta (eds).
Studies in Learner Corpus Linguistics. Research and Applications for Foreign Language Teaching and Assessment.
358 pages. 2015. ISBN 978-3-0343-1506-7

Vol. 191 Ruth Breeze, Maurizio Gotti & Carmen Sancho Guinda (eds)
Interpersonality in Legal Genres.
389 pages. 2014. ISBN 978-3-0343-1524-1

Vol. 192 Paola Evangelisti Allori, John Bateman & Vijay K. Bhatia (eds)
Evolution in Genre. Emergence, Variation, Multimodality.
364 pages. 2014. ISBN 978-3-0343-1533-3

Vol. 193 Jiyeon Kook
Agency in Arzt-Patient-Gesprächen. Zur interaktionistischen Konzeptualisierung von Agency.
271 pages. 2015. ISBN 978-3-0343-1666-8

Vol. 194 Susana Nicolás Román & Juan José Torres Núñez (eds)
Drama and CLIL. A new challenge for the teaching approaches in bilingual education.
170 pages. 2015. ISBN 978-3-0343-1629-3

Vol. 195 Alessandra Molino & Serenella Zanotti (eds)
Observing Norm, Observing Usage. Lexis in Dictionaries and in the Media.
430 pages. 2015. ISBN 978-3-0343-1584-5

Vol. 196 Begoña Soneira
A Lexical Description of English for Architecture. A Corpus-based Approach.
267 pages. 2015. ISBN 978-3-0343-1602-6

Vol. 197 M Luisa Roca-Varela
False Friends in Learner Corpora. A corpus-based study of English false friends in the written and spoken production of Spanish learners.
348 pages. 2015. ISBN 978-3-0343-1620-0

Vol. 198 Rahma Al-Mahrooqi & Christopher Denman
Bridging the Gap between Education and Employment. English Language Instruction in EFL Contexts.
416 pages. 2015. ISBN 978-3-0343-1681-1

Vol. 199 Rita Salvi & Janet Bowker (eds)
The Dissemination of Contemporary Knowledge in English. Genres, discourse strategies and professional practices.
171 pages. 2015. ISBN 978-3-0343-1679-8

Vol. 200 Maurizio Gotti & Davide S. Giannoni (eds)
Corpus Analysis for Descriptive and Pedagogical Purposes. ESP Perspectives.
432 pages. 2014. ISBN 978-3-0343-1516-6

Vol. 201 Ida Ruffolo
The Perception of Nature in Travel Promotion Texts. A Corpus-based Discourse Analysis.
148 pages. 2015. ISBN 978-3-0343-1521-0

Vol. 202 Ives Trevian
English suffixes. Stress-assignment properties, productivity, selection and combinatorial processes.
471 pages. 2015. ISBN 978-3-0343-1576-0

Vol. 203 Maurizio Gotti, Stefania Maci & Michele Sala (eds)
Insights into Medical Communication.
422 pages. 2015. ISBN 978-3-0343-1694-1

Vol. 204 Carmen Argondizzo (ed.)
European Projects in University Language Centres. Creativity, Dynamics, Best Practice.
371 pages. 2015. ISBN 978-3-0343-1696-5

Vol. 205 Aura Luz Duffé Montalván (ed.)
Estudios sobre el léxico. Puntos y contrapuntos.
502 pages. 2016. ISBN 978-3-0343-2011-5

Vol. 206 Maria Pavesi, Maicol Formentelli & Elisa Ghia (eds)
The Languages of Dubbing. Mainstream Audiovisual Translation in Italy.
275 pages. 2014. ISBN 978-3-0343-1646-0

Vol. 207 Ruth Breeze & Inés Olza (eds)
Evaluation in media discourse. European perspectives.
268 pages. 2017. ISBN 978-3-0343-2014-6

Vol. 208 Vijay K. Bhatia & Maurizio Gotti (eds)
Arbitration Discourse in Asia.
331 pages. 2015. ISBN 978-3-0343-2032-0

Vol. 209 Sofía Bemposta-Rivas, Carla Bouzada-Jabois, Yolanda Fernández-Pena, Tamara Bouso, Yolanda J. Calvo-Benzies, Iván Tamaredo (eds)
New trends and methodologies in applied English language research III. Synchronic and diachronic studies on discourse, lexis and grammar processing.
280 pages. 2017. ISBN 978-3-0343-2039-9

Vol. 210 Francisco Alonso Almeida, Laura Cruz García & Víctor González Ruiz (eds)
Corpus-based studies on language varieties.
285 pages. 2016. ISBN 978-3-0343-2044-3

Vol. 211 Juan Pedro Rica Peromingo
Aspectos lingüísticos y técnicos de la traducción audiovisual (TAV).
177 pages. 2016. ISBN 978-3-0343-2055-9

Vol. 212 Maria Vender
Disentangling Dyslexia. VenderPhonological and Processing Deficit in Developmental Dyslexia.
338 pages. 2017. ISBN 978-3-0343-2064-1

Vol. 213 Zhilong Xie
Bilingual Advantages. Contributions of Different Bilingual Experiences to Cognitive Control Differences Among Young-adult Bilinguals.
221 pages. 2016. ISBN 978-3-0343-2081-8

Vol. 214 Larissa D'Angelo
Academic posters. A textual and visual metadiscourse analysis.
367 pages. 2016. ISBN 978-3-0343-2083-2

Vol. 215 Evelyne Berger
Prendre la parole en L2. Regard sur la compétence d'interaction en classe de langue.
246 pages. 2016. ISBN 978-3-0343-2084-9

Vol. 216 David Lasagabaster and Aintzane Doiz (eds)
CLIL experiences in secondary and tertiary education: In search of good practices.
262 pages. 2016. ISBN 978-3-0343-2104-4

Vol. 217 Elena Kkese
Identifying Plosives in L2 English: The Case of L1 Cypriot Greek Speakers.
317 pages. 2016. ISBN 978-3-0343-2060-3

Vol. 218 Sandra Campagna, Elana Ochse, Virginia Pulcini & Martin Solly (eds)
Languaging in and across Communities: New Voices, New Identities. Studies in Honour of Giuseppina Cortese.
507 pages. 2016. ISBN 978-3-0343-2073-3

Vol. 219 Adriana Orlandi & Laura Giacomini (ed.)
Defining collocation for lexicographic purposes. From linguistic theory to lexicographic practice.
328 pages. 2016. ISBN 978-3-0343-2054-2

Vol. 220 Pietro Luigi Iaia
Analysing English as a Lingua Franca in Video Games. Linguistic Features, Experiential and Functional Dimensions of Online and Scripted Interactions.
139 pages. 2016. ISBN 978-3-0343-2138-9

Vol. 221 Dimitrinka G. Níkleva (ed.)
La formación de los docentes de español para inmigrantes en distintos contextos educativos.
390 pages. 2017. ISBN 978-3-0343-2135-8

Vol. 222 Katherine Ackerley, Marta Guarda & Francesca Helm (eds)
Sharing Perspectives on English-Medium Instruction.
308 pages. 2017. ISBN 978-3-0343-2537-0

Vol. 223 Juana I. Marín-Arrese, Julia Lavid-López, Marta Carretero, Elena Domínguez Romero, Ma Victoria Martín de la Rosa & María Pérez Blanco (eds)
Evidentiality and Modality in European Languages. Discourse-pragmatic perspectives.
427 pages. 2017. ISBN 978-3-0343-2437-3

Vol. 224 Gilles Col
Construction du sens : un modèle instructionnel pour la sémantique.
292 pages. 2017. ISBN 978-3-0343-2572-1

Vol. 225 Ana Chiquito & Gabriel Quiroz (eds)
Pobreza, Lenguaje y Medios en América Latina.
362 pages. 2017. ISBN 978-3-0343-2142-6

Vol. 226 Xu Zhang
English Quasi-Numeral Classifiers. A Corpus-Based Cognitive-Typological Study.
360 pages. 2017. ISBN 978-3-0343-2818-0

Vol. 227 María Ángeles Orts, Ruth Breeze & Maurizio Gotti (eds)
Power, Persuasion and Manipulation in Specialised Genres. Providing Keys to the Rhetoric of Professional Communities.
368 pages. 2017. ISBN 978-3-0343-3010-7

Vol. 228 Maurizio Gotti, Stefania Maci & Michele Sala (eds)
Ways of Seeing, Ways of Being: Representing the Voices of Tourism.
453 pages. 2017. ISBN 978-3-0343-3031-2

Vol. 229 Dino Selvaggi
Plurilingual Code-Switching between Standard and Local Varieties. A Socio-Psycholinguistic Approach.
371 pages. 2018. ISBN 978-3-0343-2663-6

Vol. 230 Anca-Cristina Sterie
Interprofessional interactions at the hospital. Nurses' requests and reports of problems in calls with physicians.
371 pages. 2017. ISBN 978-3-0343-2734-3

Vol. 231 Xiaodong Zhang
Understanding Chinese EFL Teachers' Beliefs and Practices in the Textbook-Based Classroom.
189 pages. 2017. ISBN 978-3-0343-3053-4

Vol. 232 Manuela Caterina Moroni & Federica Ricci Garotti (Hrsg.)
Brücken schlagen zwischen Sprachwissenschaft und DaF-Didaktik.
345 pages. 2017. ISBN 978-3-0343-2667-4

Vol. 233 Dimitrinka Georgieva Níkleva
Necesidades y tendencias en la formación del profesorado de español como lengua extranjera.
401 pages. 2017. ISBN 978-3-0343-2946-0

Vol. 234 Juan Santana-Lario & Salvador Valera (Hrsg.) Competing patterns in English affixation.
272 pages. 2017. ISBN 978-3-0343-2701-5

Vol. 235 Francisco Salgado-Robles
Desarrollo de la competencia sociolingüística por aprendices de español en un contexto de inmersión en el extranjero.
241 pages. 2018. ISBN 978-3-0343-2323-9

Vol. 236 Maria Chiara Janner
Sguardi linguistici sulla marca. Analisi morfosintattica dei nomi commerciali in italiano.
345 pages. 2017. ISBN 978-3-0343-2667-4

Vol. 237 Bárbara Herrero Muñoz-Cobo & Otman El Azami Zalachi
La primavera del árabe marroquí.
192 pages. 2017. ISBN 978-3-0343-3104-3

Vol. 238 Consuelo Pascual Escagedo
El papel del oyente en la construcción de la conversación espontánea de estudiantes italianos en su interlengua y en su lengua materna.
295 pages. 2017. ISBN 978-3-0343-3186-9

Vol. 239 Stefania M. Maci
The MS Digby 133 Mary Magdalene. Beyond scribal practices: language, discourse, values and attitudes.
336 pages. 2017. ISBN 978-3-0343-3256-9

Vol. 240 Eliecer Crespo-Fernández
Taboo in Discourse. Studies on Attenuation and Offence in Communication.
326 pages. 2018. ISBN 978-3-0343-3018-3

Vol. 241 Jana Altmanova, Maria Centrella, Katherine E. Russo (eds)
Terminology & Discourse / Terminologie et discours.
424 pages. 2018. ISBN 978-3-0343-2417-5

Vol. 242 Xavier Blanco et Inès Sfar (dir.)
Lexicologie(s) : approches croisées en sémantique lexicale.
442 pages. 2018. ISBN 978-3-0343-3056-5

Vol. 243 Yunfeng Ge
Resolution of Conflict of Interest in Chinese Civil Court Hearings. A Perspective of Discourse Information Theory.
302 pages. 2018. ISBN 978-3-0343-3313-9

Vol. 244 Carla Vergaro
Illocutionary Shell Nouns in English.
322 pages. 2018. ISBN 978-3-0343-3069-5

Vol. 245 Paolo Frassi
L'adjectif en français et sa définition lexicographique.
270 pages. 2018. ISBN 978-3-0343-3394-8

Vol. 246 Suwilai Premsrirat and David Hirsh (eds)
Language Revitalization. Insights from Thailand.
328 pages. 2018. ISBN 978-3-0343-3497-6

Vol. 247 Wei Wang
Researching Learning and Learners in Genre-based Academic Writing Instruction.
282 pages. 2018. ISBN 978-3-0343-3297-2

Vol. 248 Isusi Alabarte, Alberto & Lahuerta Martínez, Ana Cristina (eds)
La comprensión lectora de lengua extranjera Estudio de los factores de familiaridad, interés, género y métodos de evaluación.
336 pages. 2018. ISBN 978-3-0343-3493-8

Vol. 249 Mercedes Eurrutia Cavero
Approche didactique du langage techno-scientifique Terminologie et discours.
374 pages. 2018. ISBN 978-3-0343-3512-6

Vol. 250 Aurora Ruiz Mezcua (ed.)
Approaches to Telephone Interpretation Research, Innovation, Teaching and Transference.
268 pages. 2018. ISBN 978-3-0343-3330-6

Vol. 251 Morini Massimiliano
A Day in the News A Stylistic Analysis of Newsspeak.
188 pages. 2018. ISBN 978-3-0343-3507-2

Vol. 252 Ignacio Guillén-G alve & Ignacio Vázquez-Orta (eds.)
English as a Lingua Franca and Intercultural Communication Implications and Applications in the Field of English Language Teaching.
414 pages. 2018. ISBN 978-3-0343-2763-3

Vol. 253 Bianca Del Villano
Using the Devil with Courtesy. Shakespeare and the Language of (Im)Politeness.
216 pages. 2018. ISBN 978-3-0343-2315-4

Vol. 254 David Hirsh (ed.)
Explorations in Second Language Vocabulary Research.
252 pages. 2018. ISBN 978-3-0343-2940-8

Vol. 255 Tania Baumann (ed.)
Reiseführer - Sprach-und Kulturmittlung im Tourismus / Le guide turistiche - mediazione linguistica e culturale in ambito. turistico 270 pages. 2018. ISBN 978-3-0343-3402-0

Vol. 256 Ariadna Sánchez-Hernández & Ana Herraiz-Martínez (eds)
Learning second language pragmatics beyond traditional contexts.
376 pages. 2018. ISBN 978-3-0343-3437-2

Vol. 257 Albert Bastardas-Boada, Emili Boix-Fuster, Rosa Maria Torrens (eds)
Family Multilingualism in Medium-Sized Linguistic Communities.
336 pages. 2019. ISBN 978-3-0343-2536-3

Vol. 258 Yuyang Cai
Examining the Interaction among Components of English for Specific Purposes Ability in Reading. The Triple-Decker Model.
296 pages. 2020. 978-3-0343-2913-2

Vol. 259 Catia Nannoni
Participe présent et gérondif dans la presse française contemporaine.
176 pages. 2019. ISBN 978-3-0343-3631-4

Vol. 260 Nieves Rodríguez Pérez & Bárbara Heinsch (eds.)
Contextos multilingües. Mediadores interculturales, formación del profesorado de lenguas extranjeras.
289 pages. 2019. ISBN 978-3-0343-3768-7

Vol. 261 Giuliana Elena Garzone, Mara Logaldo, Francesca Santulli (eds.)
Investigating Conflict Discourses in the Periodical Press.
244 pages. 2020. ISBN 978-3-0343-3668-0

Vol. 262 Laura Nadal
Lingüística experimental y contraargumentación.
233 pages. 2019. ISBN 978-3-0343-3791-5

Vol. 263 Claudia Claridge & Merja Kytö (eds.)
Punctuation in Context – Past and Present Perspectives.
288 pages. 2019. ISBN 978-3-0343-3790-8

Vol. 264 Maurizio Gotti, Stefania Maci, Michele Sala (eds.)
Scholarly Pathways.
530 pages. 2020. ISBN 978-3-0343-3860-8

Vol. 265 Ruth Breeze, Ana M. Fernández Vallejo (eds.)
Politics and populism across modes and media.
350 pages. 2020. ISBN 978-3-0343-3707-6

Vol. 266 Jean Marguerite Jimenez
Understanding the Effects of Immediate Electronic Corrective Feedback on Second Language Development.
252 pages. 2020. ISBN 978-3-0343-3815-8

Vol. 267 Sergio Rodríguez-Tapia, Adela González-Fernández (eds)
Lenguas y turismo: estudios en torno al discurso, la didáctica y la divulgación.
380 pages. 2020. ISBN 978-3-0343-3881-3

Vol. 268 Ana Bocanegra-Valle (ed.)
Applied Linguistics and Knowledge Transfer. Employability, Internationalisation and Social Challenges.
344 pages. 2020. ISBN 978-3-0343-3714-4

Vol. 269 Beatrice Garzelli
La traducción audiovisual español-italiano.Películas y cortos entre humor y habla soez.
202 pages. 2020. ISBN 978-3-0343-4013-7

Vol. 270 Iván Tamaredo
Complexity, Efficiency, and Language Contact. Pronoun Omission in World Englishes.
292 pages. 2020. ISBN 978-3-0343-3902-5

Vol. 271 Silvia Domenica Zollo
Origine et histoire du vocabulaire des arts de la table. Analyse lexicale et exploitation de corpus textuels.
239 pages. 2020. ISBN 978-3-0343-3890-5

Vol. 272 Paola Paissa, Michelangelo Conoscenti, Ruggero Druetta, Martin Solly (eds.)
Metaphor and Conflict / Métaphore et conflit.
385 pages. 2021. 978-3-0343-4068-7

Vol. 273 María Martínez-Atienza de Dios
Entre el léxico y la sintaxis: las fases de los eventos.
178 pages. 2021. 978-3-0343-4173-8

Vol. 274 Noelia Castro-Chao
Argument Structure in Flux. The Development of Impersonal Constructions in Middle and Early Modern English, with Special Reference to Verbs of Desire.
300 pages. 2021. 978-3-0343-4189-9

Vol. 275 Gabriella Carobbio, Cécile Desoutter, Aurora Fragonara (eds.)
Macht, Ratio und Emotion: Diskurse im digitalen Zeitalter / Pouvoir, raison et émotion: les discours à l'ère du numérique.
246 pages. 2020. 978-3-0343-4184-4

Vol. 276 Miguel Fuster-Márquez, José Santaemilia, Carmen Gregori-Signes, Paula Rodríguez-Abruñeiras (eds.)
Exploring discourse and ideology through corpora.
pages. 2021. 978-3-0343-3969-8

Vol. 277 Tamara Bouso
Changes in Argument Structure The Transitivizing Reaction Object Construction.
392 pages. 2021. 978-3-0343-4095-3

Vol. 278 Maria Luisa Maggioni, Amanda Murphy (eds.)
Back to the Future. English from Past to Present.
250 pages. 2021. 978-3-0343-4273-5

Vol. 279 Luisa Chierichetti
Diálogos de serie. Una aproximación a la construcción discursiva de personajes basada en corpus.
246 pages. 2021. 978-3-0343-4274-2

Vol. 280 Cristina Lastres-López
From subordination to insubordination. A functional-pragmatic approach to if/s i-constructions in English, French and Spanish spoken discourse.
258 pages. 2021. 978-3-0343-4220-9

Vol. 281 Eleonora Federici, Stefania Maci (eds.)
Gender issues. Translating and mediating languages, cultures and societies.
500 pages. 2021. 978-3-0343-4022-9

Vol. 282 José Mateo, Francisco Yus (eds.)
Metaphor in Economics and specialised Discourse.
354 pages. 2021. 978-3-0343-4048-9

Vol. 283 Nicholas Brownlees (ed.)
The Role of Context in the Production and Reception of Historical News Discourse.
376 pages. 2021. 978-3-0343-4181-3

Vol. 284 Catalina Fuentes Rodriguez, María Ester Brenes Peña, Víctor Pérez Béjar (eds.)
Sintaxis discursiva: construcciones y operadores en español.
396 pages. 2021. 978-3-0343-4306-0

Vol. 285 Dominic Stewart
Frequency in the dictionary. A corpus-assisted contrastive analysis of English and Italian.
178 pages. 2021. 978-3-0343-4368-8

Vol. 286 Carla Bouzada-Jabois
Nonfinite supplements in the recent history of English.
386 pages. 2021. 978-3-0343-4226-1

Vol. 287 Sofía Bemposta Rivas
Verb-governed infinitival complementation in the recent history of English.
340 pages. 2021. 978-3-0343-4227-8

Vol. 288 Mirella Agorni
Translating Italy for the Nineteenth Century. Translators and an Imagined Nation in the Early Romantic Period 1816– 1830s.
182 pages. 2021. 978-3-0343-3612-3

Vol. 289 David Hirsh (ed.)
Research Perspectives in Language and Education.
276 pages. 2021. 978-3-0343-4219-3

Vol. 290 Federica Vezzani
Terminologie numérique : conception, représentation et gestion.
238 pages. 2022. 978-3-0343-4394-7

Vol. 291 Stefania M. Maci
Evidential verbs in the genre of medical posters. A corpus-based analysis.
498 pages. 2022. 978-3-0343-4521-7

Vol. 292 Francisco J. Álvarez-Gil
Stance devices in tourism-related research articles: A corpus-based study.
170 pages. 2022. 978-3-0343-4555-2

Vol. 293 Annalisa Baicchi / Stefania Biscetti (eds.)
The Language of Fashion. Linguistic, Cognitive, and Cultural Insights
192 pages. 2022. 978-3-0343-4428-9

Vol. 294 Ana Maria Piquer-Píriz
E-learning in EMI. Academic language for university students.
228 pages. 2022. 978-3-0343-4589-7

Vol. 295 Geneviève Henrot Sostero (ed.)
Alle radici della fraseologia europea.
638 pages. 2023. 978-3-0343-4645-0

Vol. 296 Klara Dankova
Les fibres textiles entre synchronie et diachronie: études terminologiques.
288 pages. 2023. 978-3-0343-4587-3

Vol. 297 Marta Carretero, Juana I. Marín-Arrese, Elena Domínguez Romero, Mª Victoria Martín de la Rosa (eds.)
Evidentiality and Epistemic Modality. Conceptual and Descriptive issues.
414 pages. 2023. 978-3-0343-3993-3

Vol. 298 Kim Grego, Alessandra Vicentini, Virpi Ylänne (eds.)
Age-Specific Issues. Language, Spaces, Technologies.
280 pages. 2023. 978-3-0343-4411-1

Vol. 299 Giovanni Garofalo (ed.)
Estudios de género asistidos por corpus. Enfoques multidisciplinarios.
290 pages. 2022. 978-3-0343-4548-4

Vol. 300 Giuseppe Palumbo, Katia Peruzzo, Gianluca Pontrandolfo (eds.)
What's Special About Specialised Translation? Essays in Honour of Federica Scarpa.
298 pages. 2023. 978-3-0343-4411-1

Vol. 301 Raquel P. Romasanta
Probabilistic variability in clausal verb complementation in World Englishes.
374 pages. 2023. 978-3-0343-4703-7

Vol. 302 Giulia Adriana Pennisi
A linguistic Insight into Legislative Drafting. Tradition and Change in the UK Legislation.
296 pages. 2023. 978-3-0343-4700-6

Vol. 303 Javier Fernández-Cruz, Antonio Moreno-Ortiz
Economic terms in the news during the Great Recession. A diachronic sentiment and collocational analysis.
192 pages. 2023. 978-3-0343-4778-5

Vol. 304 Stefania Maci, Mark McGlashan (eds.)
(Critical) Discourse Studies and the (new?) normal. Analysing discourse in times of crisis.
400 pages. 2024. 978-3-0343-4767-9

Vol. 305 Ana Elvira Ojanguren López
Predications in competition and the rise of serial verb constructions in English. The verbal and nominal complementation of Old English aspectual and manipulative verbs.
534 pages. 2024. 978-3-0343-4644-3

Vol. 306 Stefania Maci, Giovanni Garofalo (eds.)
Investigating Discourse and Text. Corpus-Assisted Analytical Perspectives.
372 pages. 2023. 978-3-0343-4753-2

Vol. 307 Víctor Pérez Béjar
Las construcciones suspendidas en español. Un paradigma en gramática del discurso.
494 pages. 2024. 978-3-0343-4799-0

Vol. 308 Javier Calle Martín / Jesús Romero Barranco (eds.)
Corpora and Language Change in Late Modern English.
408 pages. 2024. 978-3-0343-4642-9

Vol. 309 Cristina Petras / Sonia Berbinski / Daciana Vlad / Raluca Balaţchi (eds.)
Marqueurs métalinguistiques : émergence, discours, variation /M etalinguistic Markers: Emergence, Discourse, Variation.
758 pages 2024. 978-3-0343-4908-6

Vol. 310 Micaela Rossi (éd.)
Néologie, terminologie et variation - Neología, terminología yvariación – Neologia, terminologia e variazione.
418 Pages. 2024. 978-3-0343-4696-2

Vol. 311 Sergio Maruenda-Bataller / Laura Mercé / Elena Castellano-Ortolà (eds.)
Discourse, gender, and violence: Insights from news and social media texts.
268 pages. 2024. 978-3-0343-4701-3

Vol. 312 Dario Del Fante
Migrating across times and cultures: Metaphorical images of migration in the U.S. and Italian newspaper discourse between the 20th and 21st centuries.
338 Pages. 2024. 978-3-0343-4659-7

Vol. 313 Francisco Jesús Alonso Almeida / Begoña Bellés Fortuño (eds.)
Corpus-based Studies in Specialized Discourses.
294 Pages. 2025. 978-3-0343-4261-2

Vol. 314 Elaine Millar
Multi-word verbs in English Language Teaching. Insights from research and practice
252 Pages. 2025. 978-3-0343-5441-7

Vol. 315 Irene Guzmán-Alcón / Richard Nightingale (eds.)
New Directions in Instructional Pragmatics Research.
424 Pages. 2025. 978-3-0343-5099-0

Vol. 316 Rosa Rabadán / Noelia Ramón (eds.)
Cross-linguistic Mediated Communication: Hybrid Text Production English-Spanish.
268 Pages. 2025. 978-3-0343-5100-3

Vol. 317 Alba E. Ruz
Directionality in English morphological conversion.
208 Pages. 2025. 978-3-0343-5788-3

www.ingramcontent.com/pod-product-compliance
Ingram Content Group UK Ltd.
Pitfield, Milton Keynes, MK11 3LW, UK
UKHW020841290926
15470UKWH00004B/1483

9 783034 35788